COCAÍNA

COCAÍNA

A BOOK ON THOSE WHO MAKE IT

MAGNUS LINTON

TRANSLATED BY JOHN EASON

SOFT SKULL PRESS
An imprint of COUNTERPOINT
BERKELEY

First published in Swedish by Atlas Bokförlag in 2010
First published in English by Scribe Australia 2013

Library of Congress Cataloging-in-Publication Data
Linton, Magnus, 1967–
[Cocaína. English]
Cocaina : a book on those who made it / Magnus Linton ; translated by John Eason.
pages cm
ISBN 978-1-61902-293-5
1. Cocaine industry—Columbia. 2. Drug traffic—Columbia. 3. Drug dealers—
Columbia. 4. Drug control—Columbia. 5. Drug control—United States. I. Title.
HV5840.C7L5613 2014
363.4509866—dc23
2013047448

Cover design by Quemadura

SOFT SKULL PRESS
An imprint of COUNTERPOINT
1919 Fifth Street
Berkeley, CA 94710
www.softskull.com
www.counterpointpress.com

Printed in the United States of America
Distributed by Publishers Group West

10 9 8 7 6 5 4 3 2 1

To Sid and Elina

CONTENTS

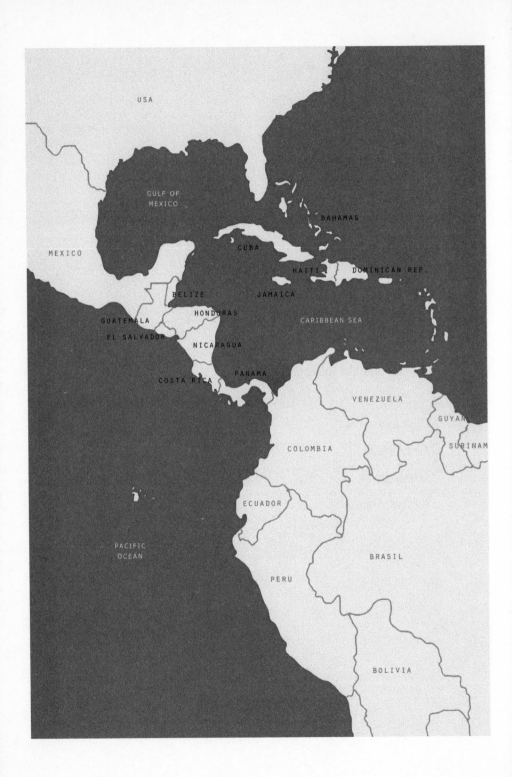

PREFACE

ON THE EVENING of 18 August 1989, I was in a taxi in Bogotá, on the way to meet a friend. The car was cruising down the colonial quarter, dodging potholes, but it was not until the headlights swept across the road as we crossed Avenida Jiménez that I was able to get a good look, and I realized the city center was dead. No one was hanging out by the statue in the park; no one but *los gamines*, street kids, sitting around like lifeless shadows with their noses stuck in bags, inhaling glue in an effort to numb their bodies against the impending cold of the night.

"*¡Mataron a Galán!* Galán's been murdered," said the driver.

Luis Carlos Galán was a liberal left-wing politician running for president in the upcoming 1990 election, and he had been the clear frontrunner. He had promised to reform Colombia's backward landownership structure, but first and foremost he had attacked the way the elite was protecting a man who would go down in history as one of the most bloodstained mobsters of all times: the "King of Cocaine," Pablo Escobar Gaviria.

We continued across the city. I wanted to keep talking about the murder, but the driver just shrugged his shoulders and dropped his head in what I would later recognize as a very common Colombian gesture. At the same time he uttered two words, a phrase that I would one day come to understand as a verbal accompaniment to the gesture. When poor Colombians say *lo mataron*—literally "they murdered him," but meant more in the sense of "he was murdered" so as to avoid the agent—they make a dismissive gesture in which the neck muscles relax, causing the head to drop. The motion signifies that the topic is closed for discussion; that you have touched on an issue foreigners seem unable to understand: the fact that almost everyone in Colombia has a friend or relative who has been murdered. A child. A parent. A friend. A sibling. It is a collective experience.

But in this case, the comment was not made in relation to a family member but about a presumptive president. Consequently, in this context the words and the gesture took on a less personal, more public meaning. It quite simply established the fact that what had happened was not at all unexpected, as in this country most big conflicts end in not just one murder but several.

When I continued to question the driver about what he thought had happened, he only ever answered me with those same two words, and at my destination I silently handed him a roll of pesos and got out of the car. He drove off, but his stiff answer had left me hanging with all my naïve questions about the elusive agents of Colombia. "*Lo mataron.*"

ONE DAY IN the 1990s, I went along with a Colombian friend, Alfonso, to buy a gram of *perico*—cocaine—in western Bogotá. It was a typical middle-class neighborhood, where families in some of the two-story houses had *tiendas*: little kiosk-like shops in a front room on the ground floor, where they sold cigarettes and staple foods. We entered one of them, and Alfonso asked the young man sorting through packets of gum behind the counter if the "philosopher" was home.

The guy nodded in the affirmative. "*Sí*. In the bedroom upstairs."

The question was superfluous, as Alfonso well knew, since the philosopher was paraplegic and could not leave the house. But Colombians are the politest people in the world, and an aspect of their good behavior is to never take anything for granted.

As we entered the living quarters I winced when I saw who was sitting there, but Alfonso quietly assured me that everything was okay. Four policemen were chatting around the dinner table, feasting on a chicken, and the philosopher's wife was joking with the uniformed men in a familiar way while she assisted the maid to serve them.

"Good evening; good evening." We greeted everyone as we circumnavigated the party and scuttled up a flight of stairs.

The bedridden philosopher, whose lifeless limbs were covered by a heavy layer of blankets, was flipping through the afternoon-television soap operas. He was somewhere between 60 and 70. Alfonso asked him how he was doing, and he responded with a wisecrack before asking, "How many?"

Alfonso held up his index finger.

The philosopher pulled a white envelope out from behind a burgundy silk pillow, placed it on the blanket before him, and accepted the cash.

We went downstairs and made another lap around the officers, wishing them *bon appétit*. "*Gracias*," they said in unison.

IN SPRING 2007 I had a temporary job with a Swedish aid organization in Bogotá. We had arranged, along with other non-government organizations, a lobbying meeting with one of the most powerful diplomats in the country: Adrianus Koetsenruijter, the head of the European Commission delegation to Colombia.

The purpose of the meeting was to find out the European Union's opinion on the human-rights situation in the country. New statistics indicated that the number of displaced people in "the world's longest ongoing armed conflict" was rapidly approaching four million, and everyone was aware that the cocaine industry had become the primary driving force behind the war. Broadly speaking, the guerrillas controlled the coca-growing peasants, the paramilitary groups controlled the higher levels of cocaine production, and the government waged war on the guerrillas (with support from the US military) under the banner of "the war on drugs." It was a strange triangle of combat, in which all the weapons were financed by some facet of cocaine production.

Koetsenruijter was in high spirits. He was about to resign and was pleased to be doing so, as a new job awaited him in another part of the world. We happened to catch him during some downtime, when he felt he could relax and speak off the record. He said it would be refreshing not to have to put on diplomatic airs anymore. But to be on the safe side, he requested that our conversation go no further, and we nodded in agreement.

He spoke from the heart. In his opinion, the sitting right-wing government had been good for Colombian society in many ways: cities were safer, people were more inclined to report attacks by armed groups, and there was even a left-wing party in Congress whose representatives could speak out without fear of being murdered. Yet when asked the key question—whether this progress was sustainable— he gave a deep sigh. "No."

And then he said something I have often heard from people in Colombia, but never from a top-ranking EU official. "Legalization. There's no other option. I don't know a single person in any high-ranking political post any longer who isn't in favor of legalizing drugs. But that, of course, is politically impossible."

WHAT THESE ANECDOTES illustrate is that every story about Colombia— and especially about cocaine—is complex or multifaceted. Just when you think an issue has been resolved, a more sophisticated layer emerges. And this continues until everything is so vague and all those involved seem so evasive that the only clear fact is that nothing is as it seems to be.

More than two decades have passed since that cold evening of Galán's assassination, and it is with mixed emotions I now present a book that's a bit of a failure. Over a decade ago I promised myself I'd one day write a book on Colombia in which the words "cocaine" and "violence" would be absent. This truly unique place is not just one of the most notorious countries in the world; it is also one of the most beautiful. My love of Colombians and the country's stunning cultural richness has grown every year since my first trip in 1989, and this passion made me want to write a book about the *other* Colombia. I felt the country deserved it. Of course, it would not be a superficial work that avoided the social and political problems, but rather one that focused on tales other than the same old stories of Colombia as a place of drugs and violence, and nothing more.

In February 2007 I received a grant that made it possible for me to move to Bogotá and start this project. I began to compile amazing stories of Colombian adventures: such as the story of revolutionary newborn Julio, adopted by a Swedish couple, who searched high and low for his family roots on the outskirts of Cali; the tale of the historic city of Cartagena, and its metamorphosis from a dreary port to a hotspot perfectly designed to cater for all of the new global elite's preferences; the account of young pregnant guerrilla fighter Andrea, and her desperate attempts to keep her baby despite the guerrillas' instructions to abort it; and the story of beauty queen Ximena and her unsuccessful attempts to become the first Miss Colombia not to have had plastic surgery.

The problem with this project, though, was that while the stories were certainly fascinating, it seemed that no matter where I turned, what I did, or which story I stumbled upon, everything always seemed to lead back to one thing. There was no way of getting around it: the presence of cocaine in modern Colombia was simply far too pervasive to be ignored, at least by a journalist whose main interest is politics. Histories and accounts of Cali, Cartagena, the guerrillas, and the beauty industry, like most issues in the nation, were too interwoven with the cocaine industry and its influence on all aspects of Colombian society to dismiss. Cocaine takes precedence over everything. And it links most things together.

So I soon realized it was essential to revise the project. I decided that the work, contrary to my original intention, must center on cocaine, its history, and its consequences. I abandoned my first idea and have consequently written a book exclusively about Colombia and cocaine. In many ways it is a tragic turn of events—though I think an inevitable one.

THE PURPOSE OF this work is not, as some might expect, to offer a solution to the problems surrounding the cocaine industry, but instead to describe these problems. Rather than providing answers as to how all drug-related misery could be eliminated—if such a thing were even possible—my goal is to expose a highly complex global problem at the ground level: to offer detailed accounts, in-depth experiences, and rarely heard opinions from the country that has suffered more than any other as a result of the worldwide cocaine boom and the related war on drugs.

Personally, I wouldn't want to see cocaine for sale at local supermarkets, but I wouldn't want to live in a completely drug-free society either. It is my hope that this book will interest as well as provoke those who love drugs, those who hate them, and all in between.

The question that occurred to me in the taxi on that cold night of Galán's murder—What is Colombia?—would compel me to live a quarter of my adult life in Bogotá. But it was only later I realized that being in Bogotá on that fateful evening meant I had ended up in the center of a worldwide political drama; that cocaine was the very essence of a number of contemporary global conflicts and debates, a sort of surface-level descriptor of serious problems that would characterize the relationship between rich and poor continents in the years to come: the marginalization of third-world farmers by free-market economics, the United States' need to find a new menace in the post-Soviet era, the resurgence of populism in Latin America, postmodern society's desperate effort to fill the existential gap left by the death of God, and so on.

This book is an attempt to get to the bottom of exactly what happened in the span of those 20 years, between 1989 and 2009. Using Colombia's troubling experience as a prism, but hopefully without further victimizing the country or its inhabitants, I have tried to point out some truly global stories about power and poverty in today's world. I hope, of course, that the reader will find food for thought in them.

COCATURISMO

Medellín as Heaven

'I don't take insults from anyone.
Everyone who has called me gay is dead, except my mother.'
— ALONSO, HIT MAN

AMONG A SEA of dancers Håkan, a young Swedish guy, towers over everyone else. After sticking his key in the three-gram bag he is holding and digging around a bit, he pulls up a small mound of snow-white powder that he holds up to his girlfriend, who snorts it with a quick *nschh*.

"Clubbing here is just a *liiiiiiittle* bit better than at home." He licks off the powder that is stuck in the steel grooves of the key, paying no mind to the policemen, who have taken bribes in exchange for turning a blind eye to the goings-on inside the club. It is 4.00 a.m., and before the cocaine has even had time to kick in Håkan places a pill on his middle finger and shoves it into his girlfriend's mouth, his arm outstretched. She swallows it with a gulp, licking his hand playfully in the process.

"I love Colombian women. They're real women. So fucking female."

She is barely half his height and tries clinging to his neck, but he keeps pushing her off; he isn't in the mood to make out. Eventually he grabs her behind, lifts her up off the floor, and sticks his tongue in her ear.

The club is in a hexagonal building in an industrial district. The pounding bass fills the room, where hundreds of dancers wearing sunglasses stomp away in the dark. "Alexi Delano deejayed here a while ago," Håkan says. "It was the best party I've been to. It was absolutely incredible. He's Swedish, too."

Swedish. He could just as well have been German, American, British, or Spanish. In fact, he could have been from almost any wealthy Western nation, for Håkan is just one of thousands in the latest crop of young globetrotters making their way to Medellín, the new mecca of drug tourism. The city that in the 1990s was known as "the murder capital of the world" has since been transformed into an urban paradise where the sky's the limit—at least, for those who have the money.

In El Poblado, an area of Medellín filled with tranquil shopping malls, sushi bars, and internet cafes, a new hostel has opened every other month for the last year. Economic globalization has transformed the traditional backpacker into the flashpacker: a well-to-do traveler seeking a combination of comfort and adventure, reflecting the trend in tourism whereby travelers are more interested in themselves than in tourist attractions. For today's young travelers, *seeing* the Amazon or Patagonia is nowhere near as thrilling as *doing* Buenos Aires, Rio de Janeiro, or Medellín. Publishing powerhouses such as Lonely Planet now have more city guides than travel guides, as most traditional destinations have become so mainstream and consumerized that the so-called undiscovered places have to be sold in order to keep the money carousel going. Hanging out in, as opposed to visiting, the Third World is the new thing to do.

All this factors into the appeal and sudden success of Medellín. The city not only has superficial attributes and attractions—a perfect climate, good shopping, wild clubs, and hip people, all conveniently kept separate from violent gangs—but what makes Medellín truly special, and so attractive to the new traveling avant-garde, is something best described as an electrical charge in the air. A myth. In contrast to the tired old nostalgic stories of tango in Buenos Aires, of beaches in Rio de Janeiro, or of the revolution in Havana, Medellín has a more titillating product that, carefully packaged, can be sold with a great deal of success: cocaine. But cocaine packaged in such a way that the actual powder is just one aspect of the experience.

Today, "flashpacker" is an established term within the travel industry and an important demographic for hostel operators in many of the world's poorest nations. Those who run the hostels are often former backpackers themselves, mainly from the United States or Europe, and they know perfectly well that what today's travelers are seeking is not just high-caliber drugs at bargain prices, but also something that can add a bit of cultural cred to the experience. Consequently, experiences such as the Pablo Escobar tour—a guided excursion offering travelers a peek into the life of "the world's greatest outlaw"—have become successful, and it is easy to see why: the violent story of the rise and fall of the Medellín Cartel is indeed an incredible and, of course, highly marketable chronicle.

Close to Medellín are the remains of Hacienda Nápoles, Escobar's 3000-hectare ranch, complete with an airstrip, a bullring, and a private zoo. In its heyday in the 1980s, four planes a day took off from the property, bound for Miami and loaded with cocaine, and returned just as full with money. In Medellín there is also Barrio Pablo Escobar, a neighborhood of 400 houses that Escobar had built and donated to homeless families in the city. There are also the remains of La Catedral, the legendary prison Escobar designed himself and from which he fled effortlessly in 1992—an incident that brought shame to the White House and the Colombian government as the entire world watched. In another part of the city people can visit the roof where the man known as El Patrón, who in 1989 made *Forbes'* list of the top-ten richest men in the world, finally met his death in 1993. The killing of Escobar was the result of a controversial joint effort in which the US Central Intelligence Agency, the National Police of Colombia, and the United States Drug Enforcement Administration (the DEA) conspired with hired assassins and the drug mafia—a cooperative operation that caused great political rifts and had an impact on both nations for many years to come.

But Medellín's attraction as a destination for cutting-edge travelers also reflects an ever-increasing interest in visiting, albeit at a safe distance, the site from which one of the biggest criminal complexes in the world originates. The illegal drug trade today generates an estimated 300 billion USD globally—far more than the gross domestic product of most countries—and the world's two main hard drugs, heroin and cocaine, are linked to two nations: Afghanistan, where 90 per cent of the world's heroin is produced; and this country, Colombia, where 60 per cent of the cocaine consumed globally comes from.

If heroin breeds misery, cocaine has successfully held on to its image as the narcotic for those wishing to disassociate themselves from junkies. It is the undisputed drug of choice for the wealthy in the world's richest nations, and it has been growing in popularity, with no sign of slowing, since German chemists first isolated the alkaloid in 1860. Cocaine continues to find its way into new parts of the world—Eastern Europe and certain parts of Asia are booming markets—and, perhaps to an even greater extent, into social milieus previously untouched by the white powder. While the trend for "clean living" is growing within the elite classes of the United States and Europe, environments often socially safeguarded from drug abuse, cocaine use among middle- and working-class Americans and Europeans is on the rise.

Håkan pushes his girlfriend away and vanishes into a swarm of dancers. He has stains from a red lollipop around his mouth, visible as he approaches another blond young man, who has a plastic bottle in his back pocket.

"Nice parties here, eh? Acid? Ecstasy? Cocaine?"

Their eyes meet and they exchange the goods.

Suddenly an army of smiling former fashion models bursts onto the scene, dispersing over the dance floor, moving like green projectiles into the crowd. They're promoting a new brand of cigarettes and are all wearing identical form-fitting tops that coordinate with the colors on the cigarette packets. They scurry about, handing out free smokes to anyone who wants one. And everyone does. Håkan and his new friend are in paradise; they throw their arms in the air, flapping their hands around in a way that's reminiscent of the 1990s rave scene.

Globalization and increased travel have brought together all sorts of subcultures, which have gelled in a relatively short period of time. Behavior that is banned or discouraged in one country may not only be possible but encouraged in another, and many of the poor nations in the Southern Hemisphere have developed into recreational regions for an entire gamut of activities stigmatized and criminalized elsewhere in the world. These safe havens are not so much a consequence of different laws in these countries but of mass corruption, and specifically the fact that the poorer members of the police force can be bought easily. This club is called Carnival, a name that unintentionally, yet amicably enough, finds itself at the intersection of Catholicism, hedonism, and commercialism, all three of which manifest here on a nightly basis: in a nation where corrupt policemen can obtain instant absolution, young Europeans can obtain immediate sensual gratification—and both can come together in a diabolical dancing circus where cash is the indisputable king.

The cigarette girls exit the area together. The names of upcoming deejays are projected on the walls in futuristic fonts as the place becomes even more packed with people. The odor, a mix of sweat and smoke, fills the air, while clubbers use their fingernails and the corners of credit cards to transport little mounds of white powder to their noses. Håkan's own baggie of cocaine was bought in a poor neighborhood he calls "the shopping center." "It's fucking awesome. It only cost 7000 pesos a gram. Four US dollars."

AT THE PIT STOP HOSTEL it is 7.00 p.m. on a Friday evening, and Greg, Lucy, Brent, and Ana are all sitting around a large table, talking loudly over each other, recounting their travel adventures. "Wow! That's wild," says one.

Thongs are slapping against the concrete around the pool, and an askew ping-pong table sits off to the side. Two guys covered in tattoos circle around a pool table, while three blonde girls are busy updating their Facebook status on the public computers in the lobby. Greg, 23, from Canada, takes center stage: "I was just 13 when a girl at my school tricked me into doing acid. Later on, when I went out to look for a restroom, I saw a man on a bicycle with no arms or legs. The pedals were spinning and the bike was riding by itself. He just sat there like a bump on a log as it coasted along. Then, after that, I started to take a leak and suddenly felt that if I continued, I would eventually pee out my entire body. It was like my whole body was coming out of my cock. Even so, I just couldn't stop. I was completely terrified." He laughs.

Luz, a cleaner and the only Colombian present, understands nothing of the story but tries to join in the laughter at all the right places. She asks a guy with a fauxhawk how much he paid for his mobile phone, but no one hears her.

Brent, another guy in his twenties, launches into his story: "One time I was absolutely certain that my entire body was made of vomit and that my insides were pouring out of every orifice; it was as if my skin was so thin I would explode at any moment. I did everything I could to hold it in: I squeezed my eyes shut, pinched my butt cheeks together, held my nose. After a while we went out for a walk and I started tripping again, uncontrollably. All of a sudden I was too scared to move my legs, afraid that a blood clot would burst in my ass or in one of my eyes and that everything would go gushing out. I was riveted to the spot and completely paralyzed. Ha ha ha."

Then Lucy, 24, from Ireland, takes her turn: "I met a girl in Vancouver who was absolutely determined to go hang-gliding while tripping on acid. She walked out along the crest of the mountain holding the wing, but then suddenly jumped off the cliff before she'd had a chance to make the adjustments to her equipment. She ended up breaking her back in two places, but survived."

Two hammocks dangle between four trees. Around the corner, a number of people laze about with their eyes shut while Eurosport plays on a large screen. There are around 40 people present, most of whom are backpackers in their twenties. English is the dominant language here, with a host of dialects from around the world represented: Irish, American, Australian, British, and a number of versions of broken English. Though from many different backgrounds, everyone's topic of conversation is the same: the night's cocaine party. It's the same as yesterday. And the day before that. Everyone knows that after 12 straight hours of clubbing, the only excitement to be had after the sun comes up is the endless conversation at the hostel—and telling stories is more fun if they involve absurd and twisted experiences. LSD stories attract more interest than tales of cocaine and are usually more fun and entertaining, since cocaine is not a "trip drug," but a "talk drug."

Most hostels in Medellín today are designed to handle the growing demand for cocaine among travelers. At Pit Stop, the owner has created a concrete bunker that is completely detached from the rooms and dormitories so that the post-clubbing, early morning chatter won't disturb the guests trying to sleep. Each hostel has a network of dealers who ensure that the patrons' needs and desires are satisfied. On every door there is a sign stating "No Drugs—Please!!!" to appease the authorities in the event of an unexpected raid.

When the "world's first cocaine bar" opened in Bolivia in 2009, it was a telling sign of a seemingly inevitable development. At hostels in Medellín today, as elsewhere, backpacking isn't primarily about seeing something new but about meeting like-minded people with similar interests and stories. Rehashing tales of one's travel experiences, whether they're based in reality or hallucination, has become an important component of the modern hostel experience. If backpackers in Latin America in the 1990s were mostly interested in seeing sights and attractions—the untouched beaches of Brazil or the secret paths to Machu Picchu—accounts from the first decade of the 21st century revolved around individual experiences and adventures of a more physical nature, such as hang-gliding in Venezuela, mountain-biking in Bolivia, or white-water rafting in Ecuador. Backpacker stories in the 2010s have reflected yet another change of focus, as the emphasis on cutting-edge experience has shifted from body to mind: it's now about *yajé* ceremonies with South American Indian tribes, LSD-fueled snorkeling trips in the Pacific, nights on methamphetamines in clubs in São Paulo, or entire days of snorting coke in the hometown of Pablo Escobar.

From this perspective, it makes sense that cocaine tourism has become a booming commercial aspect of the Andes, and that the white powder has become the playmate of choice in the isolated backpacking culture of Latin America. There is also the fact that as the desire for individualized, unique experiences has increased, it's become more important to share those experiences. Cocaine is the perfect spice for such narrative rituals. So few destinations are better suited than Medellín to satisfy the increasingly sophisticated consumer preferences of American and European middle-class tourists.

"Yes, we sure do a lot of talking here." Lucy has retired to a chair by a plastic table harboring the remains of a fast-food meal, along with cigarette butts and trimmed fingernail particles. Locks of red hair cascade down her cheeks like fine copper wires. She says that Colombia was not on her original itinerary, least of all the notorious city of Medellín, but when she landed in southern South America everyone she met told her the most amazing stories about the country. These stories were not just about cocaine, but also about what an incredibly beautiful place it was and how wonderful the people were. "Everyone said, 'You have to go.' So I went."

Since her arrival a week ago, though, she hasn't seen any of the country or gotten to know any of its people. She's just been clubbing. "I haven't done anything else." She laughs. "Haven't seen a thing. Just been partying so far. But I only do coke. You can find everything else here as well, and it's everywhere. For me it's just coke though. That's it. You can get it here at the hostel. Everybody has it. Somebody just buys it and then we all split the cost."

The combination of low prices and high quality make people go crazy, she says. Especially Australians and New Zealanders, who come from countries far removed from the big markets, where drug prices are sky-high.

Lucy had never done cocaine prior to coming to the Andes. The first time she used it was in Bolivia. Then Peru. Now Colombia. "The quality improves and the price goes down the further north you go. Everybody you meet says, 'Oh, it's so cheap!' I think that's why everybody does it."

Greg arrives. He has a ruddy complexion and broad shoulders, and he's wearing white sunglasses. His journey to Medellín was like Lucy's and almost everyone else's: he arrived in Latin America with no intention of going to Colombia, but decided to visit after reading glowing blog and Facebook recommendations, which described nightlife in Medellín as among the best in the world. "At home you never heard anything good about Colombia. But when you come to South America and start talking to folks, everybody says the complete opposite. People who travel a lot say it's one of the most beautiful countries in the world, and so far they haven't been wrong. I've had a fantastic experience."

But as in Lucy's case, Greg's experience so far has only consisted of one thing. "The first people I met offered me coke. Not selling it to me, you know, but just offering me some. To be friendly. They were Colombian. I'd never experienced anything like it—giving away coke for free! It happened as soon as I crossed over the border. Our passports hadn't even been stamped."

THE TALE OF how cocaine conquered Colombia can be said to have begun at many different points in the last millennium. When Spanish conquistador Francisco Pizarro arrived in the New World in 1502, the people in the eastern Andes had already been chewing coca leaves for millennia—since at least 3000 BC. The leaf has always been, and still is, an important symbolic and religious object in many indigenous cultures. On its own the coca leaf is harmless, even beneficial, and is to cocaine more or less what the grape is to wine; you can chew as much as you like without getting a stronger buzz than you would from a cup of coffee. The architects and laborers who built Machu Picchu chewed coca, as did the Aymara people, who constructed the Kalasasaya Temple thousands of years ago in what is today Bolivia, and many other Andean indigenous groups.

Coca was among the first plants to be cultivated in the Western Hemisphere, and when the 16th-century Spaniards had to choose between banning or accepting the indigenous custom of chewing it, the colonizers' material interests steered their decision; because the leaves and their mild psychoactive effect kept the slaves in the silver mines going, they decided to let the local people use it. The few times the Spaniards chose to pay their serfs, they did so in coca. Moreover, when the men running the mines discovered just what effect the leaves had on their workers' performance, they began to establish a more commercial coca market. Tom Feiling writes in *The Candy Machine: how cocaine took over the world* that by the 1600s the sacred plant of the indigenous people had, ironically, been turned into a tool for exploiting them, and it could thus be said that the Catholic envoy of the Spanish Crown became the first drug dealers of the Americas.

In Europe the plant went unnoticed for hundreds of years, as the few coca shipments that did make it to the Old World were often so poorly packaged that the contents had rotted during the sea journey. It was not until 1860 that German chemist Albert Niemann managed to explain the process of extracting cocaine from the leaves—a simple method known today to every farmer in Bolivia and Peru, not to mention in Colombia. A few decades after Niemann's death, a

Corsican pharmacist obtained a patent for a cocaine-laced Bordeaux wine, Vin Mariani, that by the end of the 19th century was known around the world as a refreshing drink. It quickly became popular with intellectuals and members of the cultural elite; Mark Twain, Jules Verne, Abraham Lincoln, Thomas Edison, Emile Zola, Tsar Alexander III, and Pope Leo XIII were just a few of the many who praised the coca wine for its curative effects.

David T. Courtwright, in *Forces of Habit: drugs and the making of the modern world*, states that Vin Mariani became an unintentional predecessor to one of the world's most profitable trademarks of all time: Coca-Cola. It was the establishment of The Coca-Cola Company in 1892 that ushered in the first *fin-de-siècle* wave of coca mania on a global scale. The drink, initially but briefly sold as Peruvian Wine Cola, became an immediate hit around the world, and for the next 22 years cocaine extract was a key ingredient in Coca-Cola's legendary secret recipe. Yet when the US Congress passed the Harrison Narcotics Tax Act in 1914, Coca-Cola had to eliminate cocaine extract from its formula. Today, the red and white colors of the Peruvian flag are, as Tom Feiling concludes, "the only reminder of Coca-Cola's Andean origins."

The history of cocaine as a recreational drug is similar. In his legendary 1884 essay "Über Coca," Sigmund Freud enthusiastically systematized the beneficial effects of the drug—at that stage classified as a medicine—praising its ability to counteract indigestion, alcoholism, and impotence. Soon after that, cocaine made its real breakthrough in Europe, as an effective local anesthetic. Problems in shipment were resolved once large pharmaceutical companies such as Merck began producing raw cocaine in the Andes before the transatlantic journey, rather than after. With industrialization, and with cocaine being widely distributed among doctors and at hospitals, large quantities of the drug went astray—as would later be the case with so many other drugs. By the early 20th century, the habit of sniffing and injecting the powder had spread to various underground scenes throughout

Europe and the United States. The world—or at least the wealthier nations in it—entered into its first cocaine epidemic.

However, as early as the end of World War I this first cocaine boom was on the decline. It was not until the 1970s that any major confiscations of the drug were reported. Yet during the 1960s and 1970s, as the world was about to enter into its second major cocaine epidemic, the colonial roots of the problem became visible, and the seed of what would eventually blossom into the Andean neo-revolutionary ethnopolitics of the new millennium was planted. The United Nations' desire to prohibit all forms of coca failed to take into account the integral role the plant played in indigenous culture and belief, and this resulted in the decision in 1961 to put the entire coca plant, including the harmless leaves, on the world list of banned drugs. (This then paved the way for the implementation of widespread herbicide spraying, a practice that to this day continues to force Colombian farmers to seek out guerrilla protection.)

Cocaine had begun to make its comeback on the global scene in 1969 with the film *Easy Rider,* in which Dennis Hopper and Peter Fonda are seen stuffing the powder into the gas tanks of their motorcycles. It was the final year of the revolutionary 1960s—a decade dominated by marijuana and LSD—and cocaine was still a drug about which the general public knew very little. This played into the screenwriter's decision to choose it; cannabis was too run-of-the-mill and heroin too dangerous. Cocaine, however, had all the right connotations: it was new, exotic, and fun.

But cocaine had yet another quality that paved the way for its eventual impact on Western cultures. While loss of control and wild hallucinations were the goals of drug users in bohemian, avant-garde circles, cocaine offered the complete opposite; it sharpened the mind, and thus came to appeal to an entirely different class of people. In an article featured in *Time*, cocaine was called "the drug of choice for perhaps millions of solid, conventional, and often upwardly mobile citizens." Unlike marijuana or LSD, cocaine wasn't linked to any sort of rebellious political movement or associated with bloody syringes, and the fact that it was too expensive for the average person contributed to its high-class status. Cocaine was the perfect drug for people who hated junkies, as Tom Feiling and several historians have noted, and as late as 1975 cocaine addiction was not widely recognized.

Yet by the 1970s cocaine was becoming a pervasive plague on contemporary society, which would not only reconfigure popular culture and generate millions of addicts, but would also—and above all else—destroy democracy in a number of already impoverished countries. Three distinct patterns, which to this day continue to characterize the world's escalating and increasingly bloody cocaine war, were by this time already on their way to becoming firmly established: demand would not subside; the United States' war on drugs would expand, eventually alongside the war on terror; and both the production of cocaine and the fight against it would be concentrated in one place: Colombia.

ONE OF THE most beautiful natural wonders in the Andes is a snow-clad pyramid right in the Caribbean. The Sierra Nevada de Santa Marta range is home to the world's highest coastal mountain, and the massif's peaks stretch 5800 meters into the sky a mere 45 kilometers away from the coconut palms on the sun-drenched Caribbean beaches. If you had the ability to travel back in time and climbed the massif with a pair of long-range binoculars, you would find yourself geographically situated in the middle of the most tragic, 30-year-long cocaine drama—with an incredible view.

Directly north and not too far away is Miami: where a war broke out between Cuban and Colombian gangsters in the late 1970s for control over the main entryway to the once booming US cocaine market, as immortalized in the Brian De Palma film *Scarface.*

In the west, much closer, is Panama City: bombed by US president George Bush senior in 1989 after the country's leader, CIA agent and

cocaine trafficker Manuel Noriega, went from being an asset to a
burden with respect to US interests in Panama.

A little north of the Panama Canal, near the Colombian drug-
smuggling island of San Andrés, is Nicaragua: the center of the 1986
Iran–Contra affair, during which the United States paid 48 million
USD to the Contras, a terrorist organization whose war against the
left-wing Sandinistas was financed—along with support from the
United States—by cocaine trafficking.

Further north is Mexico: a nation currently on the verge of
collapse, with over 22,000 drug-related murders reported between
2007 and 2010, as a result of the mafia gaining control over the
drug routes between Colombia and the United States following the
dismantling of the Medellín and Cali Cartels.

In the east, at the foot of the Sierra Nevada de Santa Marta, is
the beginning of the 2200-kilometer jungle border with Venezuela:
the socialist nation that, in the space of just a few years, has become
one of the world's most important routes for cocaine trafficking.
According to the United Nations, 40 per cent of all cocaine smuggled
from the northern Andes to Europe today passes through Venezuela.

South of the snow-capped peaks is the hub itself: Colombia,
the heart of the global cocaine market, the source of the millions of
packages of powder shipped out on a daily basis to all corners of the
globe. This is the chaotic country where the assassination of Pablo
Escobar in 1993 gave rise to even worse monsters —paramilitary
right-wing terrorists who, backed by drug money, were able to
interfere with a third of the seats in the nation's congress during the
2000s.

But the most interesting thing about the Sierra Nevada de
Santa Marta is that this is where the story began. In recent decades
Colombia has produced the lion's share of all the cocaine consumed
in the world, and the mystery is how this came to be. Technically
speaking, cocaine can be grown and processed in some 30 countries
around the world; over time, however, the vast majority of cultivation

and production came to be concentrated in this nation. Today Colombia is the only nation where all three of the most sought-after recreational drugs—cocaine, heroin, and marijuana—are produced in large quantities, and in no other country has illegal drug production had such dramatic consequences. Being the world's largest supplier of cocaine has significantly altered the nation in many ways: from transforming legal institutions, to sparking major changes in the value system of the inhabitants, to dictating the financial terms of the country, and to making armed conflict a permanent fixture of society. Not least, drugs have come to play an increasingly pivotal role in Colombian politics.

Most climates are represented in Sierra Nevada de Santa Marta, from icy glaciers to sunny beaches, and the lower regions are covered by thick rainforest and arid deserts inhabited by ancient indigenous tribes. The place has always been an isolated entity—culturally and geologically an island of sorts, albeit on solid ground—which, like many other parts of Colombia, has over the years been difficult to access for authorities and invaders alike.

In the northwestern-most corners of South America, there was—unlike in the places today known as Peru, Bolivia, or Mexico—no dominant Inca or Aztec empire whose leaders and structures of power could be conquered and used by the Spanish. Rather, in Colombia there were hundreds of small, separate indigenous tribes, each with their own culture, language, economy, and history. The Spaniards found a solution to their frustration over their inability to dominate the disparate tribes by importing slaves from Africa. However, given the rough terrain of Colombia, which consists of three mountain ranges and long coasts on both oceans—not to mention that half the country is covered in jungle—many slaves were able to escape, hide, and ultimately establish their own small, autonomous communities far from any central governing body.

The drug industry has undoubtedly been able to benefit from the persistent social and cultural aspects of this isolation, which has carried over to modern times. To this day decentralization and diversification, for better or worse, are two of the nation's most distinctive qualities, and they've shown to be sadly integral to the creation of settings ideal for a wide range of criminal activity.

Illegal drug production and trafficking began in earnest in Colombia in the mid-1960s, and the Sierra Nevada de Santa Marta was its first foothold. Yet it did not start with cocaine but with marijuana, which was not only the favorite drug of Colombians but also the preferred drug of Pablo Escobar. And then, as now, the driving force behind the rapid development of drug-producing structures was the never-ending demand for drugs in the United States.

During the 1960s, the explosion in demand for cannabis in the United States prompted a vast increase in the number of large marijuana plantations in Mexico and Jamaica. However, by the end of the decade the White House had implemented a sweeping anti-drug campaign; poisonous herbicides were sprayed over marijuana fields in Mexico, resulting in an urgent need for new growing regions—a void that Colombian farmers were more than happy to fill. Owing to its isolation, favorable climate, and relative proximity to the American market, the Sierra Nevada de Santa Marta provided a number of good reasons for US cannabis entrepreneurs to relocate their business. By the time herbicide spraying in Mexico was drawing to a close, 75 per cent of all the grass smoked in the United States was being cultivated along the Caribbean coast of Colombia.

In the early stages of this relocation, the American cannabis pioneers who visited the mountains assisted the poor farmers by providing them with seeds and other resources necessary for the initial cultivation. Yet after just a few years, Colombian upstarts were able to take control over the plantations and edge out the Americans in production and export. But *los gringos*, the Yanks, maintained control of the main market, the United States. In 1972 in Santa Marta, the city by the foot of the mountains, newspaper articles began circulating about strange men who had been boasting openly about the money they were earning from illegal marijuana sales. News of the lucrative green crop quickly spread, and by the end of the 1970s large marijuana fields had popped up all over the country. In whichever region this took place, two common features were present, and they would be crucial to the success of the next drug boom in Colombia: these regions were recently settled and they were out of the reach of governmental authorities.

The export organizations at the time, the precursors to the Medellín and Cali Cartels, were relatively simple in terms of composition. They consisted mainly of farmers—indigenous people, the descendents of slaves, or *mestizo* settlers in search of land—who tilled the soil for a local exporter, who often owned a few runways or a small port and had made an agreement with an importer on the other side of the Caribbean. Most growers around the Sierra Nevada de Santa Marta already had roots in this area, and many opted to stop cultivating cannabis after a few lucrative harvests made it financially possible for them to return to legal agriculture without compromising their comfortable lifestyles. The marijuana rush, *la bonanza marimbera*, is today romanticized in Colombian folklore as a wild and carefree era—probably more because it stands in stark contrast to the violence that was to follow than because it was a particularly glorious period in itself.

The green boom differed from the white boom that was to come in one important cultural respect, which was integral to the fact that Colombia would become one of the most violent places in the world in the 1980s, and also probably contributed to the era's rose-tinted reputation: it was aristocratic. The rural parts of Colombia, such as those along the Caribbean coast, have always been essentially feudal, where landowners with deep pockets and cultural capital maintain a peaceful reign over the politicians and the economy, and control the peasants and the infrastructure. If these landowners were not mayors, governors, presidents, or any other sort of elected officials, they were the neighbors, cousins, business partners, or friends of those in *la clase política*, the political class, which has ruled the Colombian countryside with strategic violence for centuries. Soon after the profits from the cannabis boom started rolling in, the local ruling elite consolidated their control over drug activity, and the gap widened between the poor mountain farmers and those working in transport, trade, and export (*los marimberos*). In this environment, it stood to reason that influential landowning families—and often the young males, in this patriarchal hierarchy—gained control over the commerce. This dynamic, between an isolated and illiterate agrarian population and an elite class who had easy access to the coast and its infrastructure, either by owning it themselves or because they were able to bribe those who administrated it, was fundamental to the export success.

Initially, trafficking only involved small cargo boats and light aircrafts departing from docks and landing strips located on private estates. But as global demand increased, the need for new and more efficient departure routes arose. The cannabis lords invested in larger aircraft, DC-3s in particular, and made nightly departures from the commercial airport in Santa Marta. Air-traffic controllers, guards, and the management of the Colombian Civil Aviation Authority (CCAA) were bribed to ensure that the airport's identity remained secret, instigating intentional "blackouts" whenever planes carrying cannabis took off.

Ever since then, the position of director of the CCAA—a role that would prove even more crucial during the next boom period—has played a pivotal role in the nation's drug trade; but it has often carried fatal consequences for the incumbent. The CCAA and its management have been a buzzing epicenter surrounded by murder and political scandals, and it is still the center of attention for those attempting to shed light on the role that present-day politicians played in the drug trafficking of the past. Álvaro Uribe, the revered right-wing president of Colombia from 2002 to 2010, was director of the CCAA from 1980 to 1982, and, according to César Gaviria, president from 1990 to 1994, Uribe was forced to step down for having turned a blind eye to the actions of his closest subordinate: a politician and civil servant by the name of César Villegas, who had collaborated with the mafia for many years, making airports available to emerging cocaine cartels. It is Uribe's word against others about his role in past narcotics transactions, but regardless of the truth in his particular case, the drug lords' way of dealing with the Civil Aviation Authority speaks volumes about how the *marimba* bonanza was the launching pad for a corrupt political culture that would soon become permanent reality—a milieu of nepotism and a system in which landowners, politicians, director-generals, and drug dealers spun an increasingly large, entangled, and bloodstained web.

The fact that the *marimba* boom had its origins in the aristocracy made it, in some absurd way, the "nice guys" bonanza—as opposed to the coca boom, run by Pablo Escobar's Medellín Cartel, with its roots in a much rougher, urban middle class. *Los marimberos* already had the power Escobar and his men had to gain by murdering those in their way, and today Colombian literature and folk music is replete with depictions, often satirical, of the cultural contrasts between *marimberos* and *coqueros*. One of the nation's most famous television celebrities, who had connections to both worlds, wrote about this contrast when she recounted meeting the Dávilas—one of the largest landowning families on the coast, who had control during the cannabis boom and were also, incidentally, close friends with Colombia's beloved president Alfonso López Michelsen. She wrote:

> Unlike the coca guys, who are, with few exceptions, like the Ochoas, poor or lower middle class, the Dávila family is an integral part of the coastal aristocracy. *Los coqueros* are short and ugly, whereas the cannabis kings are tall and handsome. A number of women from the Dávila family have married powerful men, such as President López Pumarejo; President Turbay's son; and Julio Mario Santo Domingo, the wealthiest man in Colombia.

Another aristocratic element inherent in the green bonanza was impunity. Colombia was and is a place where anything can be bought, and as long as you have the right name, the right skin color, and a solid bank account, there is little to fear—at least from the authorities. With their strong ties in patriarchal and feudal tradition, and a cultural perception that they were out of reach of the law, the regions involved in the *marimba* boom did at times foster extreme, sometimes reckless, arrogance in young white men from wealthy families. Among *los marimberos*, this reckless abandon—combined with the intoxicating feeling of riding the wave of the boom—became a sort of brazen disregard, which at times even extended across national boundaries. Juan Miguel Retal, a young man from Santa Marta's upper class, flew his DC-6 loaded with marijuana to Jetmore, Kansas, where he landed on a five-kilometer stretch after his partner blocked off road traffic by staging fake truck accidents at both ends. Retal was arrested and his bail set at one million US dollars, but he just paid up and flew home to Santa Marta, laughing all the way.

As early as 1978, however, the *marimba* bonanza was beginning to subside, once again along the lines of what would later become a pattern. The United States had discovered connections between marijuana smugglers and Julio César Turbay, López Michelsen's successor as Colombian president, and in an effort to redeem the Colombian government's credibility after the White House started questioning its anti-drug ambitions, Turbay stepped up military efforts significantly. He launched a drug-eradication campaign, and marijuana crops were destroyed, processing plants bombed, and export boats and aircraft seized. Meanwhile, US domestic cultivation was quickly gaining momentum, as new and more resistant strains of cannabis were being developed. A variety called sinsemilla spread quickly in the United States, since it could be grown just about anywhere, including in small spaces such as balconies, and cultivation manuals soon became widely available. With the coinciding of these events, the Colombian marijuana business lost profits.

But by now, canny drug entrepreneurs were already aware of the fatal side of Colombia. The *marimba* bonanza had uncovered a complete and, for their purposes, very expedient system: a finely woven fabric of poverty, racism, impunity, corruption, and petty drug lords that, when combined with the strategic geographical location, was perfect for the production of illegal goods. Colombia, it transpired, was skillful at adapting quietly to whatever whimsical impulse came from the apparently insatiable drug markets up north. During the *marimba* rush, smugglers had begun weighing, rather than counting, the dollars. Moreover, the emergence of a new army of vigilant drug pioneers, all with noses for profit, coincided with an equally new drug that was just starting to become fashionable in wealthy living rooms around the world. It was the 1980s, a decade characterized by prosperity and yuppiedom, and in the coming years, one product, one city, and one man would come into global focus, and the nation of Colombia—and the rest of the world—would never be the same again.

THE CITY OF Medellín stretches across a green valley, from the point where the western and central mountain ranges converge into a massive arrow pointing toward the Caribbean. A ring of mountains encircles the city's downtown skyscrapers, and in the north and the west shantytowns dot the hillsides like scattered shards of broken tiles. The metropolitan area of El Poblado, one of the districts in the south, has a great deal in common with the nicer parts of Los Angeles: SUVs cruise down city blocks lined with lustrous buildings, culminating in a commercial maze of banks, boutiques, and restaurants. Streams of water ripple through the neighborhood, and here and there coconut trees provide passers-by with just the right amount of shade from the eternally beating sun. Paul Thoreson, a 33-year-old American of Norwegian decent from Seattle, came here by sheer coincidence six years ago and thought he had encountered a sort of heaven: "The ideal climate, hot girls, and a fantastic nightlife. I love it."

The lower part of El Poblado is covered with Blockbusters and McDonald's, whereas the streets a bit further up the hill offer a more refined European selection of wine shops, coffee bars, and Italian bakeries. At the end of one of these streets, embedded in the aroma of roasted coffee and freshly baked muffins, is Paul Thoreson's Casa Kiwi, the first hostel opened in El Poblado.

While brushing his ponytail to the side, Paul explains that he no longer accepts guests who do cocaine in front of the cleaning staff: "Everything got out of hand very quickly. We had to kick out a bunch of people after I found out what they were doing. Guests were starting to deal drugs and a lot of them stayed for several months." People simply liked the city too much and started looking for a way to make money, but they didn't want to teach English. A deal was made with some Colombian guy who sold cheap coke, says Thoreson, and these long-term guests would buy a large amount and divvy it up. "They'd sell it to people staying at the hostel and make a killing. It was totally crazy. Cocaine is just so unbelievably cheap here. But now I've woken up to it."

Casa Kiwi opened five years ago, and with all the chatter about Medellín on blogs and Facebook, things have grown by leaps and bounds. Thoreson has already built a number of extensions onto Casa Kiwi, and today, in this part of the city, it is just one of many hostels acting as a budget mini-oasis in this sea of green opulence. The investment climate is "fantastic," and Casa Kiwi found itself with no vacancies after it had been in operation a mere six weeks. And so it continued; the money just kept rolling in. Today, Thoreson is a millionaire. "I can't complain."

One of the hostel employees comes upstairs and asks "Don Paul" if he can take a call, which he declines. From the small terrace he glances over his creation. Below, a thin guy in a Che Guevara sweatshirt is updating a website with photos from this morning's party, while some men with waxed surfboards wander in, and fliers advertising the night's attractions are scattered everywhere.

To Thoreson, the trick to sustaining his thriving business is to make sure that drug use at the hostel does not get out of control. At Casa Kiwi there is no concrete bunker and no open dealing, and there are explicit warnings on the hostel's website under the heading "Thinking of Using Cocaine in Colombia?" Everything is aimed at encouraging visitors "to behave"—to indulge in whatever pleasures they like but without overdoing it and, above all, not openly. Acting responsibly is what it's all about.

"A lot of the younger guys are just out for drugs. That's all, really. They think it's cool to come and do coke in the city of Pablo Escobar, and there was certainly a lot of this going on when we first opened and were known for our parties. But this sort of behavior makes for a bad atmosphere and fills the place with negative energy. When a lot of people are doing drugs, you can cut the tension with a knife. It's incredibly intense. In the early days, I thought parties were good for business, which of course is true to a certain extent: when people are enjoying themselves and having a good time, they spend money. So I was really open-minded in the beginning, but in the grand scheme of things it just means trouble. It becomes a downward spiral."

The maturing process that Casa Kiwi has undergone shows in microcosm what the entire city of Medellín has experienced, going back to when it was notorious as "the murder capital of the world." Drug dealing is no less common today than it ever was. Crime networks are just as strong in the present as in the past, and Medellín's role as the hub of global drug traffic is no less pronounced now than in the days of the Cartel. The difference today is that nothing is done out in the open. All that has been taken care of. Escobar's successors are smarter, shrewder businessmen who realize that there is nothing worse for business, and in particular for illegal business, than violence, war, fighting, and media attention. In the 1990s cocaine production doubled in Colombia, but after this Medellín scored praise in headlines around the world for having transformed itself from the "city of murder" to the "city of the future."

And it wasn't a lie. In 1991, when it was at its worst, Medellín had a rate of 381 murders per 100,000 inhabitants, a figure that by 2007 had decreased to 26—comparable to the rates in Washington, D.C., and Los Angeles. *The Washington Post* called it "The Medellín Miracle," while *The New York Times* ran the headline "A Drug-Runners' Stronghold Finds a New Life," and *Newsweek* reported "Good Times in Medellín."

Medellín's new and improved reputation as a safe, secure city continued to dominate in the media until one of the biggest political scandals in Latin American history broke: the revelation that the principles upon which this newfound virtue were based were not those of basic peace and safety, as widely reported, but rather were firmly rooted in drug money and terror, as in the days of Pablo Escobar. Or, as academic Forrest Hylton later wrote in his essay "Extreme Makeover—Medellín in the New Millennium," "Terror was the core of 'pacification' after 2000, effecting reforms needed for Medellín's makeover into a paradise for tourists and investors. This is civilization as barbarism. As the exhumation of mass graves attests, even the dead are not safe."

This is a long, violent, and complicated story. The truth was kept under wraps for many years, until in 2009 undercurrents of the drug industry, which were still very much intact, rose to the surface again. Poverty and violence were reunited—as they had been so many times before in Colombian history—and the result was bloodshed. But all this happened in an underworld conveniently removed from the happy minds of the young people at Pit Stop, Casa Kiwi, or any of the other oases in Medellín.

THE SHOTS CAME moments after Diego left the house. There were seven. Lina ran into the street in nothing but a towel and a chemise, only to discover the body of the man with whom she had spent her 26 years on earth. He was lying in a pool of blood outside the door. She fainted. He had been shot four times in the head and three in the stomach. Little plastic-like clumps of brain matter were stuck in his hair.

"This was five months and nine days ago." Lina Cuevas sits beside a decorated Christmas tree in Comuna 13, one of the most notorious parts of Medellín. She has been counting the days since the incident. Although Lina is 26 she does not look a day over 18, and while she recaps her story she twists her hair into a ponytail behind a round but thin face. She is in control of her emotions, and not the least bit surprised about what happened: "They're fighting over how to divide up Medellín between them."

Diego was Lina's brother and just one of many young men who had lost their lives in recent fighting over hubs of drug activity. Medellín, Cali, and Bogotá are not just financial metropolises and indispensable centers of money laundering, arms trading, and everything else to do with the global export of cocaine; they are also growing markets in their own right. While the powder much coveted in the United States and Europe has never been especially popular in Colombia, this is fast changing. With tourism on the rise, the foreign-aid sector growing, an increasing number of business investments from abroad, and the growth of language schools, awareness of American and European tastes in recreational drugs has also expanded. Domestic demand has begun to boom.

Diego worked for an organization that controlled drug trading in a neighborhood of Medellín, and was just one of the many to fall prey, according to a pattern of violence that has become a nationwide trend. When one armed group reigns over a territory everything is calm, and people for the most part are happy and content. It does not usually matter, at least to the poor, whether the guerrillas, a paramilitary group, or the government is in control, as long as there is peace and stability. The real chaos begins when fighting breaks out over territories, and killing ensues on a large scale.

It is the same with drugs. Routes, labs, growing regions, and shops are all relatively calm, and usually completely undetectable, as long as one drug lord and his military apparatus have control. But as soon as he is caught or killed, all hell breaks loose, as previously peaceful areas are quickly transformed into the worst war zones imaginable. Poverty is so widespread throughout the entire cocaine region, from Bolivia to Peru, Colombia, Central America, Mexico, and Venezuela, that when any link in the chain is broken there are always thousands of candidates ready to replace it. Some of the violence generated by the cocaine industry has to do with the murdering of police, prosecutors, politicians, journalists, and others who stand in the way of the mafia and their financial interests, but the vast majority of those dying in drug-related violence are poor young men battling over rank within their own criminal hierarchies.

Since the death of Escobar, Medellín's criminal elements had been kept in check by Diego Murillo, aka Don Berna, El Patrón's one-time partner who then allied himself with the Colombian military and the United States in the war against the Medellín Cartel. As long as he ruled the city's criminal network with an iron fist, everything was calm. Berna's philosophy was quite simple: don't rock the boat. The criminal world soon became the lubricant for the law-abiding one, and because it strengthened the already existing power structures, it was allowed to carry on without obstruction. Between 1998 and 2002, with the help of the military, Don Berna succeeded in purging Medellín of all guerrilla groups, a process that resulted in a temporary spike in the murder rate—in 2001 the city once again reported unparalleled statistics, with 220 murders per 100,000 inhabitants. However, when the last urban strongholds of the Fuerzas Armadas Revolucionarias de Colombia (the FARC) were dealt the final deathblow, peace prevailed. Shortly thereafter Don Berna consolidated his rule over the 200 crime gangs in town, totaling 8000 young people. Homicide rates dropped dramatically. As long as law enforcement kept out of drug matters— along with any number of other, more sophisticated illegal activities associated with his criminal syndicate—Berna was more than willing to cooperate with the government in its efforts to combat common revolutionaries, as well as street crime such as robbery, car theft, rape, riots, and other atrocities committed against the general public.

It looked as though Medellín was finally entering a golden age. The price tag, however, was not just the death of the guerrillas, but also of thousands of innocent people. Human-rights organizations reported finding large numbers of bodies in the shantytowns, and Don Berna would later explain that this was the unfortunate price of having to re-create the "necessary climate [for] investment returns, particularly foreign, which is fundamental if we do not want to be left behind by the engine of globalization."

Diego Cuevas' downfall was that Don Berna's reign, like Escobar's before it, came to an end. In an effort to demobilize the Colombian paramilitary groups, the government ran a demobilization program in the 2000s. Berna, along with a number of other drug terrorists, decided to turn himself in, in exchange for a greatly reduced prison sentence for the mass murders he had committed. Most of the prisoners, including Berna, were able to continue their illegal business activities from prison—as Escobar had once done—so in May 2008 the government extradited 13 paramilitary leaders to the United States. One year later, a US court condemned Don Berna, the anti-communist who had brought peace to Medellín, to 31 years in prison, on a conviction for major drug offenses.

When Don Berna was sentenced in the United States, his mafia network, La Oficina de Envigado, began to crack. Mass confusion ensued, and new positions soon became available. No one was sure from whom to take orders, so paranoia and murder spread throughout the ranks of the drug industry. It became clear that one of the most lucrative cocaine infrastructures in the world, the portal to the Caribbean, was no longer the tight operation it had once been. No one was at the helm; everything was free for the taking. War became a fact, gang fights broke out, murder rates soared, and it was soon obvious that the ultimate guarantor of Medellín's newfound security had not been the police or the military, but Don Berna himself. In

2009 alone there were a total of 2185 murders in Medellín, more than twice as many as in 2008, and in just about every case the killing could be traced back to drugs.

Lina's brother Diego was far down the ladder in terms of rank and suffered a fate similar to that of many others. His job, which he did on motorcycle, had simply been to collect the daily take at various sales points and deliver it to a certain man at a certain time—a task completely cut and dried. But when the gang's leader was killed, fighting broke out among the middle ranks and the group Diego was working for split up, causing chaos. Which gang, which leader, was strongest? Who would come out on top? These are the issues most in the bottom ranks have to address; they have to quickly choose a new leader to support and work for, and then pray that they have made the right decision and that the group they abandoned does not have time to seek revenge before the new organization has assured them of protection. And it was in this respect that Diego made a fatal error.

Lina looks down. Her brother was not the only one she knew to pay with his life; two of her closest friends were also recently shot and killed. Though these two deaths were unrelated, both occurred on the same day. And six months earlier, just before her brother was killed, her boyfriend had been murdered. Before that, it was her uncle. "This sort of violence is completely new. I'd never been afraid prior to this. My daughter is seven years old, and in the days before all this happened I used to let her play outside. I would never let her do that today. Mama hasn't left the house since Diego was killed. We'll have to move. The fact that he was murdered right outside our front door isn't just something you can shake off. You're never able to forget what happened. As soon as you open the door, there it is again."

IN THE PLACE HÅKAN calls "the shopping center"—Barrio Antioquia, Medellín's premier drug district—some 50,000-peso bills change eager hands in what looks like an ordinary office supplies store while people enjoy themselves outside. The area is aflutter with all sorts of activity.

A happy mother stumbles while pushing her prattling daughter along in a pram. An old man cruises down the street on a bicycle, a box of popcorn balanced precariously on the handlebars. Small glasses of brandy pass from hand to hand between men sitting in plastic chairs that flank the sidewalk. Salsa music blasts from loudspeakers, and the smell of marijuana fills the air. It is Friday. People are laughing and having a good time. The most recent body has been removed and the sidewalk has been cleaned.

Alonso, Javier, and Deyner have been saving up their money for a Llama Martial .38 Special revolver, though it is still unclear what the weapon will be used for. Perhaps for exacting revenge on the person who killed Javier's brother here exactly six months ago. Maybe it will be used to carry out Alonso's next murder assignment. Or perhaps Deyner will use it in his newly formed vigilante group, which tries to rid his neighborhood of crime. Or maybe for all these things.

Alonso, a hit man who is busy cleaning his glasses, steps off to the side a bit before he begins philosophizing about his particular areas of expertise: murder and drugs. Mostly the former, through what is almost always a consequence of the latter. "Here the power isn't to the people, but to the drugs. They are what steer all decision-making, and ultimately reign supreme. All the wars and fighting between gangs, leaders, children, mafias, cities, neighborhoods—everything is attributable to drugs. Cocaine is the main culprit, but marijuana also plays a role. Actually, it's pretty much 50-50. The reason there's so much violence at Barrio Antioquia is because historically it's the part of the city with the most drug activity. Drugs are sold on absolutely every street corner. Literally in every nook and cranny."

Christmas decorations twinkle from a balcony across the street while scooters, taxis, and SUVs cruise by. Occasionally someone makes a mad dash between a car window and the front door of a building, but overall the drug activity is inconspicuous, lost in the pleasant, everyday bustle of the neighborhood. Eighty per cent of the residents here make their living on drugs, and the remaining 20 per cent get by on *remesas*, remittances—money sent to them by family in the United States or Europe. Pharmacies, stationery shops, kiosks, and bars serve as facades for dealing, and the vast majority of those who purchase their drugs here know exactly which dealer they are looking for and what the going rate is at any given moment. All business is carried out in silence.

Suddenly, two police motorcycles appear on the scene and park in the middle of the intersection. Alonso sniggers. "It's a little lockdown, but it won't last long."

Routine police checks in Barrio Antioquia are merely a way for the officers to play up to the crowd. These two men in shiny reflector vests, Alonso explains, have taken up a place in the middle of the street because they are disgruntled over their poor earnings. Normally they just pass through to collect their bribes, which are more like salaries, lying in wait for them in one of the shops. But tonight something has gone awry: they didn't get as much as they usually do and are irate. The motorcycles serve as a blockade, and the policemen are fully aware that as long as their vehicles remain parked in the middle of the intersection like luminous protest placards, all drug trading will cease. The customers will not recommence with their activities until the officers are gone. The standstill will only come to an end once the dealers have had a chance to quickly scrape together enough bribe money to appease the officers.

The policemen know exactly what they are doing. Ten minutes later they are gone.

"*Listo*. There we go," says Javier.

Alonso spent 13 years in prison, convicted for nine counts of murder, but was released two years ago. Since then, he has continued to work in a violent profession that in other countries would have made him a rare breed, but in Colombia during the cocaine boom of the 1980s became an accepted way of getting by: he is one of *los sicarios*, hit men, men who murder for pay.

Alonso never takes less than "*cinco*"—five million pesos, or 2500

USD. Often much more, in fact. It depends on who will be killed, but never why. "Motives are no concern of mine. The customer simply says what he wants and I do as he says. I don't ask questions. Price, place, person; that's all. It's no more complicated than ordering at a restaurant. I'm like the waiter: tell me what dish you want and how you want it, but I'll never ask you *why* you want it. The victims are like the courses—they can vary greatly in price. Foreigners are expensive. My latest victim was an American, and for him I charged 70 million pesos."

The murder of the American is a telling anecdote of how labyrinths of violence are constructed and dissipated in a society in which lies, poverty, drugs, informing, murder, and fast cash have all become so woven into the social fabric of life that almost everything revolves around them in some way. After an affair the American and his Colombian mistress decided to do away with the mistress's husband, a Colombian. Alonso charged 12 million pesos for the hit and carried out the deed. But the American was away in the States when the murder took place, and when his mistress asked him to send the money to pay Alonso she told him that it had cost 40 million. When the money arrived, she pocketed the extra 28 million pesos. The American immediately smelled a rat when he returned to Medellín, and soon worked out that he had been conned. A huge fight ensued. The woman phoned Alonso. "For me it was just good business. I not only got the 12 million, but an additional 70 million pesos in hand. Even considering that I had a ten-man team working for me on both hits, when all the expenses were accounted for and everyone was paid, I had made a grand total of 25 million. Two months transpired between these jobs. I usually never do more than one hit in any three-month period."

Alonso has lived nearly his entire life among Medellín's criminal elements. During the brutal Pablo Escobar years he was just a teenager, but in the mid-1990s he became involved in the violent battle against Las Milicias Populares, an urban guerrilla network that was gaining control of the city's favelas. Gang crime had existed in Medellín since the 1960s, but before Escobar it had never posed any significant threat to the inhabitants of the favelas. This all changed in the 1980s, when gang activity became a serious plague, threatening poor communities and the inhabitants' efforts to organize infrastructure such as housing, water, healthcare, schools, and law enforcement in the urban slopes neglected by the state. At the national level, negotiations continued with several guerrilla groups; a new, progressive constitution was drafted; a few new left-leaning parties were established; and a major issue was whether or not the new urban masses would play an active role in decisions about the nation's future, or if the impoverished parts of the city would be overtaken by gangsterism.

In view of the clear threat of such a takeover, and in the absence of governmental involvement, young men and women began to organize local armed militias to combat the degeneration of their neighborhoods. The militias took an active interest in matters of safety, dispute resolution, and self-determination—at least in theory. They patrolled the alleys at night, kept the sidewalks clean, and organized daytime sporting events. During the first phase, up until 1991, these militias were mostly independent, had a great deal of popular support, and grew rapidly, as they successfully kept petty and gang-related criminal activity away. But it was not long before the rural guerrillas—the National Liberation Army in the northern shantytowns and the FARC in the western ones—took control, and the Medellín suburbs soon fell victim to one of the most pervasive democratic problems in Colombia; large political movements have tended, for complex historical reasons, to become increasingly dependent on arms, after which they lose popular support and end up more along the lines of armed sects than popular movements.

Alonso, who was at the time a teenager heavily into marijuana, says that during this period the militias were extremely dangerous for those who refused to comply with their social and political regulations. "They killed people for just smoking dope or for hanging out on street corners in the evening. I killed three *milicianos*, and it wasn't because I wanted to but because if I hadn't, they would've killed me. We started robbing so that we could afford weapons, and after that established a vigilante group to drive the guerrillas out of the neighborhood. People were incredibly grateful to us."

What had begun as a movement to improve society ended in complete degeneration, as the militias became increasingly bogged down in precisely the same kind of criminality they had been established to combat. In 1993 Alonso ended up behind bars, while his comrades in the local armed group started to cooperate more and more with the police force and the military in order to run the guerrillas out of Medellín. The process ended with Don Berna taking complete control of the city. Weapons and drugs were now established as constituent parts of society, and from corporate and law-enforcement angles, all aspects of community organization were, from this point on, synonymous with guerrilla activity.

This tendency toward violence goes back to the civil war of the 1950s and is deeply intertwined with religious dogma, in a way that has resulted in a completely warped sense of values among sections of Colombian youth. There are such quick changes in who is regarded as "the law"—guerrillas, the state, the paramilitaries, the Church—that many young people have never had the chance to develop a sense of ethics. What is a life worth? Whose life? And how should respect for life be interpreted when those in power place little, if any, value on it themselves, as demonstrated by the murders they commit in public?

Sicarios always make the sign of the cross before they kill as a way of assuring themselves that they are on the correct side of the powers that be. In particular, if what they are doing is in the interest of their biological family, other reflections and sentiments become superfluous. When asked what's most "difficult" about killing another human being, Alonso's response has nothing to do with a moral dilemma but with what techniques will work best. "Dismembering. Stabbing," he says. "That's the most difficult. Anyone can murder, but not just anyone can do it right, leaving no clues or footprints or incriminating evidence. Everything must be pristine afterwards. Knifing someone without leaving a trace of blood is an art form. It's very difficult. I'm a much better hit man than a thief. Stealing makes me nervous because it's more difficult cleaning up afterwards, and is just overall a lot riskier. The victim is still alive. Can report the crime. May have seen what you look like. Taken in your scent. Maybe even heard your voice."

On the sidewalk outside, a couple of slot machines ring. The overall atmosphere in the street is reminiscent of an amusement park in the summertime: the scent of roasted nuts in the air, music blaring from competing loudspeakers, sweaty bodies, jolly people of all ages, and infectious laughter. Not a trace of violence.

"He really knows how to run a barrio." The man Alonso refers to as "he" is the paramilitary who governs the district. The ruptured system Don Berna left behind did not harm all districts equally, and Barrio Antioquia has managed quite well comparatively, even though Javier's brother and others have lost their lives. Violence in Colombia over the past few years has been refined, or "professionalized," as Alonso says; massacres and street fighting have all but vanished. It's getting "cleaner." The latest stats on violence look bad on paper, but the bloodshed is almost entirely concentrated in Comuna 13 and a few other poor areas. The rest of the city is flourishing under the "new climate."

"The mafia strictly prohibits robbery," says Alonso. "Anyone who commits theft is killed. They're hard as nails about that. Every barrio has someone who rules over it, and the man who rules over this one does a really good job. It's all about keeping everything running smoothly. Whoever wants to do or deal drugs should be able to do so, but not at the expense of others. Exposing children to drugs, robbing from the elderly, and raping women isn't tolerated."

Alonso rests his left elbow on his knee, letting his chin sink down into his palm, contemplative. His somewhat geeky outward appearance reflects, in a strange way, his double nature. While his clothes make him look like a gangster, his haircut and glasses give him an academic air. His fingernails are well manicured, and his nail polish glistens in the fluorescent shop lighting. The drawn-out silence and fixated expression give the impression of a man deep in thought, perhaps thinking about the strange society he's just described, or of his life, his two children. Or of what the future has in store for someone like him.

But all of a sudden he snaps out of his pensive trance and reaches for his mobile phone. He punches numbers into it frantically, and it soon becomes clear that he was not at all lost in existential thought, but just in a panic over whether the money for the Llama Martial had been divided up correctly. The figures on the screen put his mind at ease.

"*El futuro?*" he says with surprise, looking up at the question. "I've never thought about the future."

IT IS ALMOST 6.00 A.M. outside Carnival, and the morning sun in Medellín has all the intensity of car headlights set suddenly on high beam. The club has no windows in order to ensure that those wanting to party into the wee hours can enjoy their inebriated state to the fullest, without the intrusion of sunlight. As the new day approaches the building continues to pulsate to techno music, to the delight of the clientele, which at this hour consists primarily of gringos, *prepagos*, and *traquetos*—three social groups that play a key role in modern Medellín.

"Mother's Day! Fuck, it's Mother's Day today. I have to call Mom."

Håkan exits the club. His t-shirt is stretched and sweat-stained from a night of dancing, and flaps around like a skirt over his jeans. Neither he nor his girlfriend is ready to call it a night. Street vendors from the shantytowns have descended from the hills and stand around outside the club, holding small wooden boxes at stomach level to entice coming and going clubbers with a range of goodies, from chewing gum, cigarettes, candy, and nuts to small, hidden pouches of psychoactive drugs. Every once in a while a voice coming from what sounds like a megaphone scares the humble vendors off with a warning that they are in the way; honking SUVs roll into the parking lot and the usual array of high-spirited *prepagos* and *traquetos* climb out. The *prepagos* are female escorts, a large and growing industry in Colombia since the nation became a fast-cash society; *traquetos* are the young sons of poor families who have made sudden fortunes from one or several missions in the cocaine industry.

Everywhere today—in remote villages as well as urban favelas—young men donning white Nikes, oiled Diesel jeans, glittering Dolce & Gabbana shirts, and heavy gold chains present a sharp contrast to the sort of drabness and poverty associated with their origins. The *traqueto*'s physical appearance is a direct reflection of financial success, and to those from well-to-do families his two most defining features are bad taste and frivolous spending. Though the tackily clad *traqueto*'s over-the-top and shortsighted behavior may come across as irrational, it actually makes sense: he was poor yesterday, is rich today, and very well may be dead tomorrow, so his "live to the fullest today because tomorrow may never come" philosophy is understandable. And one important aspect of living fully in today's world is having sex: not with the impoverished, chubby girls he grew up with in the village, but with the kind of women he sees on television—tall, thin, and blonde—and can conquer with frivolous purchases and shows of wealth.

The term *traqueto* refers to a culture as much as to a certain type of person, and as dawn draws closer the more *traqueto* the atmosphere becomes, as silicone and gold pour out of stretched limos to mingle with the flashpackers. Most of the ordinary Colombians, who like their pot but are bored with coke, have left the scene, knowing that the early-morning hours are devoted to this strange ménage à trios: dressed-down travelers, dressed-up *traquetos*, and minimally dressed *prepagos*—a disparate combination to the eye, but all three happily united around the club's white gold and its ability to provide total, instant gratification.

All of a sudden a police van rolls into the parking lot. Two officers step out. They just happen to stop in the middle of a line of people entering the club, right in front of a girl wearing high heels and a tight dress. The officers walk two laps around their vehicle, one stopping for a few seconds to rub his neck as he surveys the scene, pondering over his and his colleague's institutionalized degradation. Once they are done, they climb back into their van and head off against the light.

Håkan is now rummaging through one of the vendor's boxes, but does not find what he wants. Suddenly he remembers something and happily blurts out, "Right!" He maneuvers the battery out of his mobile phone. Voila! Enclosed between the interworks, like a pressed white flower, is an ecstasy tablet. After a night of incessant cocaine use, his teeth rattle like a child in the morning cold as he sticks the pill in his mouth and mutters, "Mother's Day, Mother's Day … Haaave to call." He snaps the battery back in. Switches the phone on. Finds his mother's number and hits "call."

Standing straight, his eyes fixated on the club entrance, where a stream of high-spirited *traquetos* and drab gringos enter and exit, Håkan rings his mother's phone, on the other side of the world. He waits.

From the air, Medellín resembles a vulva: a river runs from north to south like a slit cutting the oval city into two halves. Over the past 50 years, this place has been the site of a vast number of recurrent cycles of violence, at the root of which lies all sorts of patriarchal desires, especially the desire for control. The ultimate guarantor of this has always been physical strength, and weapons in particular. And the vicious cycles seem ongoing. Given the subtle symbiotic relationship between the mafia and both the upper and lower stratas of society, it stands to reason that the city has not only become more attractive and a safer bet for a wide range of investors, but also a highlight on "the cocaine trail." It is incredibly well suited to the avant-garde of postmodern backpacking; a thrilling but safe stop for gringos, in a setting surrounded by gangsters, whores, and cocaine—sometimes with Mom only a phone call away.

But not now. Håkan lowers the phone. "Damn it. She's not answering."

GREEN GOLD
The Carousel of War

'Just eight years ago there wasn't a coca plant in the region.
Today there's nothing else.'
— Graciano, coca grower

SEVEN SMALL CANOES dance around in the water like pieces of flotsam. The arrival of the morning sun does nothing to alter the appearance of the jungle, beach, town, cliffs, sky, or people, all of which remain dark. Coal-gray clouds block out the day and, as usual, a light rain falls over those living by the Pacific. But suddenly a beam of light breaks through the gray and meets Leo's glance.

"*Vamos!*" he says.

Each fisherman has his own canoe, and Leo's, a hollowed-out tree stump like all the others, has a number of deep gashes in its sides where fishing lines can be fastened permanently. The lines are used to exhaust the beasts, which are as big as men, by dragging them through the water so they can more easily be knocked out and pulled into the boat.

The canoes are now about a kilometer from shore, and the seven men have finally caught enough sardines to use for bait later that day. With their buckets full, they drift across the long groundswells, in the hopes of returning in a few hours with one of two things, preferably both. They paddle in a long, chain-like row, 20 meters between each of them. Leo stands up. The others sit. His canoe is a bit larger, allowing room for three fish rather than two, if luck prevails. "It's also good to have a little extra space, just in case we get the 'miracle catch'."

Leo is 33 and one of the best fishermen in the village, but despite the fact that he grew up during the cocaine boom, he has never had his big break. His matchstick legs disappear into rubber boots, and the imitation Tommy Hilfiger label on his threadbare shorts flaps in the wind under his oversized football jersey. "It's my turn now," he says. "Many people in the village have already gotten one, but not me."

Pozón is just one of hundreds of fishing villages that have been turned upside-down since *el Pacífico*, the Colombian Pacific coast, became the highway for 90 per cent of all cocaine trafficking to the United States. As the Caribbean has become intensely guarded, and the Mexican cartels inherited control over the US market—once held by the Medellín and Cali Cartels—at the turn of the millennium, the poor provinces along Colombia's west coast have become the hub of modern cocaine production. Today, two key things characterize the jungle regions of Nariño, Cauca, Valle del Cauca, and Chocó: cocaine and fish. The former is increasingly more important than the latter.

Besides two simple roads linking seaports Buenaventura and Tumaco to the inland, the 1300-kilometer coast consists exclusively of dense rainforest inhabited by the descendants of slaves and isolated American Indian tribes. The multitude of rivers—the sophisticated nervous system of the cocaine trade—flow from the western mountain range, down through the jungle, and then out to sea. At the far end, closest to the mountains, are the fields and the paste labs. Further out, usually just a few kilometers from the coast, are the refining laboratories: *las cocinas*, or "the kitchens." In many of the thousands of estuaries, well-packed boats—simply called "go-fast boats" by the Coast Guard and the US drug squad, the DEA—are hidden, ready for departure to Panama, El Salvador, Costa Rica, and Mexico.

Every year around 200 tonnes of cocaine passes through the water outside Pozón, and since the Coast Guard acquired more helicopters, a better radar system, and a faster armada, more and more overloaded boats have been caught as they make their dangerous, high-speed journey to the north. As soon as they are discovered but before the police catch up to them, the smugglers throw their cargo overboard. Once caught, they attempt to convince the officers that they have "just been out fishing," but since these boats are always equipped with four 250-horsepower motors, these kinds of excuses tend to fall on deaf ears. The young men end up in prison; but as the Colombian Pacific coast is one of the poorest regions in Latin America, there is never a shortage of new recruits ready to step in and replace them. They have nothing to lose, and the mafia has jobs for everyone.

"The drums that come floating in are of two varieties," Leo says. "Either 20 or 60 kilograms. Sometimes they break, and then the kilo packets drift around freely."

In the rest of the country "miracle catch" is a slang term for the guerrilla kidnappings of wealthy people, but here it refers to the attractive stuff that may be found in the water. Lucho, a young man from the area, has found goods on a number of occasions and now owns a large plastic boat equipped with two Yamaha motors. Today, all he ever does is surf and look for coca. For him, fishing is a thing of the past.

Leo's wet arms glisten as he gazes out to sea longingly. For the last 20 years he has been taking his canoe out at 5.00 a.m. six days a week, in the hopes of catching one, two, or three marlin, the mighty swordfish of the Pacific Ocean, and selling them in town for 20,000 pesos, 11 USD, each. But for a while now he has been crossing his fingers every morning, hoping that he will soon be able to leave this profession behind and spend his time drinking beer and watching television, activities he would like to indulge in once he has met with the same good fortune as the many other villagers whose prayers have been answered.

As the rain subsides, the men reach the area where marlin always congregate in abundance. This place is the primary source of income for the village, a small circle in the green sea where the loyal fish come every morning just to be caught. And so it has been from year's end to year's end. Their well of food is a blessing, but the problem here is that the quiet lifestyle, filled with repetition, gets boring. Nothing ever changes. Yesterday and tomorrow are always the same as today, while the people in Pozón dream about doing the things they see others do on television: driving around in cars, going to the movies, shopping, studying.

Shadows from a flock of pelicans overhead pass over the water like a rolling chain just above the surface. Yet again, Leo searches the approaching waves. Up to now he has always come back empty-handed, apart from fish. "All the same, I feel good. Maybe it'll be my turn today."

POZÓN IS JUST one of the many villages in Colombia where every absurd facet of the modern cocaine complex is represented. The town's fate was determined by its location on the largest smuggling route in the world, and whether they like it or not, the inhabitants have been subjected to the consequences of drug trafficking, thanks to all the valuable cargo that floats ashore and somehow has to be dealt with.

The first time cargo drifted ashore was more than two decades ago, when the villagers still hadn't developed the more modern sense of commerce that would later refine their way of handling it. Pozón is located in Chocó, the poorest region in Colombia, and is just as cut off from the rest of the country socially and culturally as it is geographically. More than 70 per cent of *los chocoanos* are illiterate— three times the national average—and since 1819, when the Republic of Colombia was established, the central government has ignored the region in every respect, with the exception of the military. But gold prospectors, gem hunters, and loggers have occasionally, with the blessing of the state, come out every now and then from the white interior with their private mini-armies, and, convinced of being on a holy crusade, executed the few savages who have dared to stand in their way. This is how it still works today, though now cocaine is the cause of bloodshed and the guerrillas have become yet another stakeholder. Wise from experience and naturally skeptical of the state, many *chocoanos* have difficulty in identifying as Colombians, and whether they are the descendants of slaves or indigenous people, cooperation and collectivism have, for better or worse, been their only means of survival.

When the inhabitants of Pozón gradually became aware of what the strange goods bobbing up from the sea were, they sold it all to Leopoldo—the only man in the village who expressed an interest— for a song. It still seemed quite a sizeable amount to the fishermen, who were not used to handling large sums of money, and after sharing the cash, weeklong parties broke out in the village. No one went fishing again until a food shortage caused the women and children of the town to revolt. Once the money gave out, it was a return to the toils of everyday life.

Today the village still consists of little more than a muddy collection of shacks. The place is surrounded by tropical rainforest, with an incredible range of plant and animal species; a huge lagoon, which is home to mating whales every September; and long black-sand beaches with occasional odd-looking limestone pillars sticking up. It rains here almost constantly. Only a spot in Hawaii, atop a volcano, has more annual precipitation than Chocó, and when the sun does manage to break out following a thunderstorm, both the rainforest and the largest ocean in the world are cast in a dramatic and beautiful light.

Yet as more fishermen returned home with a plastic-wrapped white catch instead of fish, the sense of community began to deteriorate, and new forces started to steer the village in a different direction. The increased presence of policemen, and the villagers' growing knowledge of what cocaine is actually worth, made for more discreet business dealings, and the fishermen began to divide their fortune between as few, instead of as many, as possible. But here everyone knows everyone else's business.

Leopoldo is still the most talked-about person in town and, according to the village gossips, he is still the one who purchases the found cargo, though he has gradually had to pay more for it. The prerequisites for managing the logistics of getting the illegal cargo into another boat heading north—especially dealing with the essential police and mafia contacts—include both money and personal connections, qualifications that only Leopoldo has.

Another person who has made a great deal of money and is the object of Leo's envy is Lucho, who distinguishes himself from everyone else by his expensive shorts and surfboard, and by taking frequent trips out to sea on his new boat, equipped with large motors. When asked how his life circumstances changed overnight, Lucho just smiles and says "no comment," though a number of men in the village confirm Leo's version of the story: Lucho found two undamaged 64-kilogram drums five years ago and sold them right away for what was becoming a standard price—2.7 million pesos, or 1500 USD, per kilo—and with his newfound fortune purchased a fast boat. This made it possible for him to find floating cargo much more easily than all the slow-canoe fishermen; over time, the inhabitants of Pozón have learned how to assess the ocean currents and have realized that drums dumped far out at sea tend to be drawn toward a particular bay located several nautical miles southward, and the only way to get there is by motorboat. By now Lucho and some other men have somewhat of a monopoly on the business, and they search this treasure chest of nature regularly. The relationship between these men with motorboats and the police and guerrillas grew, leaving the poor fishermen, with their patched-up canoes, more and more often without their share of this modern maritime bounty.

Iván, a fisherman with leathery skin, is one of the many village elders to have found large quantities of cocaine, although the only place it took him was down a slippery slope. While chronic alcoholism is common in the village, when Iván pulled up no one knows how many kilos, he took a mental vacation by another means: pot. Using cocaine goes against Chocó's cultural norms, and considering how quickly it can be turned into cash, it rarely occurs to the villagers to use it themselves; cannabis, on the other hand, is a well-established drug. Iván's children watched their father's status as the most prosperous fisherman in the village decline, and today he compensates for his glorious past with overblown mythomania.

ONE DAY A man named John Wayne comes walking into town. His arrival follows yet another tropical rainstorm, and all the dirt roads in the village are flooded. He pronounces his name "John Veiner," and explains that his mother idolizes a film star he does not really know much about, except for his name.

"I got here yesterday," he says. "Things were getting too intense down there."

There is a rhinestone stud in his left ear, and it is readily apparent that he is not a local. It is not so much his clothes or features that give him away as an outsider as his anxious expression, nervous body language, and obvious desire to participate in whatever is going on, to get involved. He is looking to make new friends. Someone with a *lancha*—a motorboat. He has heard of Lucho.

John Wayne is from Buenaventura, a city inhabited primarily by mothers who have lost sons and daughters to drug-related warfare. One of these women, Fabiola Rodriquez, had a son named Jeffrey, who was shot by a paramilitary. Shortly after the murder, two men came to her home and warned her that if she reported the incident to the police, they would kill the rest of her family. But soon after that, the murderer was killed. Luz-Dary Santiesteban, a mother from the Buenaventura district of La Gloria, was recently informed that the six neighborhood boys who had left a few weeks prior to "work in Chocó" were all dead. Melba Canga, who lives in the Punta del Este district, found her son Pepe's body one day in a pile of 12 massacred youths. The murderers—five policemen were involved, according to Melba—had poked out the boys' eyes, doused the bodies with acid, and flayed them. The process is referred to as "rendering unidentifiable." But they had neglected to burn the clothes, so Melba and the other mothers—fathers are usually missing—could identify whose son was whom based on their jeans, shoes, and body parts.

"My mom told me to leave," says John Wayne. "It didn't matter where. Just to get away."

The cocaine industry—in the modern guise of decentralized "mini-cartels," which often work in cooperation with the police or the guerrillas—has been the largest employer in Buenaventura for a very long time, and the range of available jobs is endless: hiding weapons, moving packages, fetching boats, packing, purchasing fuel, killing snitchers, recruiting workers, collecting money, bribing authorities, conveying threats, diverting guards, and so on. But it was not until a new role started to generate a large number of jobs that rumors began to make even those at the bottom of the ranks uncomfortable. As the drug squad gained more resources and a better intelligence system, drug syndicates suddenly needed young people who could act as decoys and create confusion. Successfully launching a boat with, for example, 500 kilos on board will often require dispatching several other boats with smaller amounts to distract the law-enforcement officers so that the big loads can make it out while those on guard are busy elsewhere. The people running the decoy boats are either captured and end up in prison, or are lost at sea once their fuel runs out, while the people running the big loads stand to make 25,000 USD. The problem is that the young people doing the running never know what sort of trip awaits them: death or dollar. But Rodrigo, one of the teenagers in the town, claims that half of his classmates from high school are now working in drug trafficking, and thinks that the prospective payoff is worth the risk of getting caught: "All the young people in Buenaventura dream of being approached by someone asking them if they'd like to take a boat to Panama for 50 million pesos [25,000 USD] for eight days' work. Who would say no to that? Who?"

At first John Wayne is not completely sure why he has ended up in Pozón, of all places, a little hole in the ground in a dense rainforest landscape several days' travel from his hometown. A huge rainbow behind him forms what looks like an enormous halo around his weather-beaten face, a rainbow that ends in what could be Panama, the place where most of the drugs are reloaded and the desperate adventurers get paid. With his back to the colorful arch and the scent of wet forest surrounding him, John Wayne says that, judging by his own family's track record, the odds are stacked against many of these types of trips going well. He is willing to take risks to make money, but not any risk. His father is in prison in Panama, having been caught on arrival; his brother is also in jail for the same offense, as is his godfather. But this notwithstanding, the cocaine coast is still a more attractive destination than that forced upon so many other internally displaced people, who end up having to relocate to Bogotá or Medellín for a life in the slums. Being on the lookout for abandoned cargo is relatively easy, and it isn't really considered illegal: it's considered a passive crime to find and retrieve a drifting load, not something one does with malice aforethought. And not even the authorities consider it feasible to demand that poor people turn in any cocaine they find.

But to succeed in this harmless yet occasionally very lucrative activity, John Wayne needs a boat, preferably a motorboat, plus someone to work either for or with. He looks up. "Where does Lucho live?"

WHEN VIEWED FROM out at sea, the coast looks like a giant oil spill has just washed up over the beaches, cliffs, and jungle. All is black and white. When the sun is behind the clouds and the rain pours down, the forest is black and the sea gray. But as soon as the sun comes out, color returns and the sea becomes a beautiful emerald green again. The water is soft and warm, and the scent of the sea permeates the air. Life.

Leo bites down hard on a thick fishing line, more like a rope, and proceeds to measure out how many arms' lengths from the plastic can, a sort of float, he will attach the hook, which has a freshly caught sardine on it as bait. His friends do the same, and soon the little waves are capped with homemade fishing floats in a vast array of colors. It should not be too long before something big happens.

But when it does, it is not what they have been hoping for.

Leo sits, sets his paddle down like a spatula against the edge of the boat, and begins bailing out water with a decapitated plastic bottle. But he only manages three scoops before a huge steel-blue body shoots up out of the sea like a rocket.

"*Hijoepucchhha!* Oh my God!"

The fish shoots up toward the sky, taking the hook, line, and sinker with it, only to plummet down helplessly with a giant splash some ten meters from the canoe. The little boat rocks from the backwash, and the other guys give congratulatory whistles. But they do not have the chance to watch how things develop, as several hooks suddenly get bites. In the middle of a circle formed by the seven canoes—each about a hundred meters from the next—blue bodies shoot up out of the water all around, like miniature explosions. Each fisherman has three buoys, and the one that Leo has a bite on spins like a bobbin, causing water to squirt up as he sits back and calmly begins to bail water again. "Wait," he says. "Now you just have to wait. The dog will soon be tired."

When a marlin—they call them *perros*, dogs—bites down on a hook, it jumps up like a dolphin. Then it disappears beneath the surface until the water suddenly becomes ablaze with silver and black, five meters down in the bathtub-green sea. Leo watches contentedly, explaining that he usually lets it jump three or four times before hauling it in because otherwise it's impossible to handle.

In a few minutes the calm water is disturbed again. Soon the marlin starts flapping around in the open air before collapsing on its fin, rather than diving down with its sword in front, like a dolphin unable to complete its loop in the air.

"Now it's time," Leo says.

He drifts over to the buoy and begins to haul in the line. Calmly, with his left hand, he pulls the line toward him meter by meter until the fish appears. The marlin is tired now, but still occasionally spasms. Leo swings the canoe around, bringing it closer to the fish. Like a stern master holding a leashed dog, he grips the line. Just half a meter of it separates him from the fish. He fumbles for the paddle.

The long sword has lost all its firmness and droops to the left, like a large machete bouncing in and out of the water, while the marlin's mouth hangs open dejectedly. The fish is half the length of the canoe.

One of the other men pulls up. "*Mátalo*," he yells. "Kill it!"

Leo lifts up the paddle and stops for a moment like a matador just about to drive his sword through the head of an exhausted bull. He concentrates on getting his aim just right, and then strikes with full force, banging the skull right between the eyes. The fish gives a final jolt and lies there, like a log floating in the water. Leo kneels, shoving his entire arm down the throat and ripping out the heart. He throws the red lump at his friend as a joke. "*Listo*. Done," he says.

The canoe is floating in a pool of blood, but the fish still is not onboard. It starts to thunder. Nearby, all around the circle of canoes, other fish are being hauled in. The water turns red.

Leo pulls his "dog" up into the canoe little by little. First he pulls the sword over the edge, and along with it a third of the fish's body, and balances it on the rim before moving back a few meters in the canoe. He grabs hold of the fin with both arms and then rolls the whole fish onboard.

There are no sharp parts on the fish. The skin is smooth, and the sail-like fin is large and black but soft, like the bellows of an accordion. The body, although lifeless, is still warm. It takes up the entire floor of the canoe, but before Leo can even get it properly situated, another of his buoys starts to spin. Some water squirts up, a new missile is launched from the bottom, and the whole procedure is repeated.

Half an hour later, it is 9.00 p.m. The sky is dark. It is going to rain again. By now the canoe is so heavy and low in the water that only a mere decimeter keeps it from filling up and sinking. Leo says that he has to hurry, as there is a place in the village where people will buy the catch, but the later he gets there, the less he will be offered. "*Vamos.*"

He paddles away from his friends, but halfway back to shore a cargo ship full of felled rainforest crosses his path. No other boats are in sight. The high-grade timber is being dragged behind the boat like a bundle of gold ingots, making a long, yellow trail of woodchips in the water. Leo signals to the captain to slow down. The boat is headed for Buenaventura, and if he can sell his fish directly to the crew he will get an even better price than if he is the first one back to the village. Plus he will not have to carry it.

They agree to buy it. From the boat's gunwale, a seaman lowers a large meat hook three meters down to Leo's little dugout and picks up the marlin like they are a couple of slaughtered pigs. Once he has pulled them up, he lowers 40,000 pesos, 22 USD, in a plastic bag.

The boat chugs along on its way. Leo drops a gob of spit into the water and points with his thumb toward the boat and the glimmering timber. "Illegal," he says. "Everything's illegal around here."

In a way it sounds as though he's trying to comfort himself for not having received his "miracle catch" again today. It is as if he wants to say that at least his livelihood is honest, compared with all the other boats going up and down this coast. He goes on to tell other stories about cocaine and people in the village as if to prove that sudden wealth does not guarantee eternal happiness. Today Iván is a laughing-stock, Leopoldo is increasingly ostracized by people in town the more money he rakes in, and it is the same with the others. Except for Lucho. He is doing well.

The canoe is still half full of bloody sludge, and Leo sits and starts bailing again. His grumbling comes across a bit like sour grapes, but there is a very serious background to everything he says: Chocó has changed completely. Many people would go so far as to say it has been ruined, but it has nothing to do with the occasional white catch making the fishermen rich overnight or turning them into alcoholics. It is because of the arrival of production facilities here—both plantations and labs. That is entirely new. Trafficking by boat has been around since the days of Pablo Escobar, though on a smaller scale, but now the entire malignant social and political cancer that spread warfare to the poorest corners of Colombia has taken root here as well. Just eight years ago there were no plantations in Chocó at all. Today, they are everywhere.

Chocó is the latest chapter in the story of how most of the cocaine production in the world—from cultivation to processing and exportation—came to be concentrated in one specific nation, but it begins in the province that has played a greater role than any other in the production of and battle against cocaine: Putumayo. And the story has several layers: about how a war over drugs became a war financed by drugs, about how the cultivation of coca became the guerrillas' most effective weapon, about why the US war on drugs failed, and finally, about how the white powder fueled one of the worst refugee disasters of all time.

Leo lets the waves sweep the canoe to shore. It is 10.00 p.m., and he is back on land. His daily work is done, and now he will see what is on television. Have a beer and a chinwag. Not very different from what he would have been doing had he been a millionaire. And when he turns his dugout upside down and the last of the bloody water gushes out, he says two sentences, and it's not clear whether he is alluding to his catch that day or to his life in general, but either way they presuppose that he and his family can go on living here. Which applies to fewer and fewer people. Because the problem with the arrival of all facets of the drug complex is that the profits are now individualized while the costs are collective. What comes in the wake of this industry, people have learned, is always violence, war, guerrillas, corruption, massacres, and environmental degradation, and the price tag ends up pretty much even for the Leos and Luchos of society—even though these days it is mostly the Luchos, the guys with the motorboats, who stand to reap the benefits of the floating drums in the sea. The long collective tradition in Chocó has been cut short, and today the only thing that is divvied out in equal amounts is misery.

What Leo says is that until he gets his miracle catch, he will just try to "stand aside." To think of his family's interests, not those of society. "I'm doing alright. As long as I can fish."

THREE MONKEYS ARE playing in the mango trees when Edgar starts the lawn trimmer, which causes a steel-blue smoke cloud to shoot out of the engine. His son quickly puts away his toy cars and his daughter hides behind an oil drum. Dad is off to work.

"I have nine bags today. That'll make 300 grams."

He straddles the mound of coca leaves as he runs his trimmer in them. The machine causes the leaves to spin as it chops them to tiny shreds, and in just a quarter of an hour the pile has shrunk to less than half its size. You don't have to shred the leaves, but shredding saves space as it cuts down on the amount of air in the raw material.

The lab is just a stone's throw away from the shack Edgar and his family live in, and consists of a simple wooden floor, seven by seven meters, built on stakes and covered with a thin tin roof to keep out the tropical rain. In addition, there are four rusty oil drums, six cans of fuel, three plastic barrels, two bags of cement, a small bag of fertilizer, and some buckets with all the other necessities: sulfuric acid, sodium hydroxide, and potassium permanganate. On one side is the corrugated-iron chute, the most defining feature of a lab.

There is now a 111-kilogram pile of raw material on the floor, like a heap of freshly cut grass, waiting to be processed and become the most sought-after powder in the world.

"That'll do it," Edgar says. "Now it will all go into one barrel instead of three. That means less fuel, less cement, and fewer chemicals. Two-thirds less. That saves money."

It is 7.00 a.m., and Edgar is just one of the hundreds of thousands of coca farmers on the slopes of the Andes who has started up his shearing machine. In the Colombian southern provinces this morning, like all mornings, small motors buzz in the hands of illiterate family men and women who wear themselves ragged in an effort to respond to an ever-growing global need. Demand in the United States has stabilized or even decreased in recent years, while the opposite is occurring in Europe, Australia, parts of Asia, Africa, and, not least, in the most well-developed Latin American countries—Chile, Argentina, Brazil, Peru, Mexico, and Colombia—where demand has been rapidly increasing over the last decade.

Edgar picks up a leaf missed by the shearer and holds it reverently, like a priceless stamp, between his thumb and forefinger before slowly folding it and snapping it in two. "This is a good leaf, ripe. It should feel like paper. If it's soft like cloth it's been harvested too early, and the paste won't harden as it should. No one buys a bad product. One time I couldn't get it to harden and had to throw all of it out. It was a financial disaster for my family, because I still had to pay all the farmers I'd bought the leaves from, and then I'd also spent a lot of money on chemicals and fuel. But if you just have ripe leaves from the beginning, you can hardly mess it up. It's a simple process."

Edgar turns the mythical leaves of the coca bush into coca paste: the first and most labor-intensive, but least profitable, link in the cocaine chain. He sells the paste to local buyers, who are under the wing of either the guerrillas or paramilitary groups, and who in turn take it to the more sophisticated labs—*cocinas*, usually strategically located adjacent to the points of exit—where the final stage of production takes place. After that, the cartels take over transporting *la mercancía*, "the goods"—the only term used here—to modern-day mafias, who distribute it to old and new markets.

Since the war on drugs has escalated and large plantations are no longer possible in the region, the entire hierarchy is based on this network, which consists of thousands of small contributors. But even though Edgar and his colleagues' grunt-work is absolutely essential if everything is going to work, the financial allocation of the narcotics pyramid is brutal. Less than one per cent of the going street price ends up in the pockets of the coca farmers. Four per cent goes to the groups involved in the fine processing of the powder and 20 per cent goes to the smugglers, while those who benefit most are the people who control sales in the United States and European markets. This is also where most of the money laundering takes place: 75 per cent of the enormous earnings generated by cocaine trafficking remains in the country where the end product is sold.

It requires 1.2 grams of coca paste to produce one gram of pure cocaine and, according to current street rates in Europe and the United States, Edgar's little daily harvest is worth around 21,000 USD. His own earnings after two days' work—when leaves, fuel, and chemicals have been paid for—is 50,000 pesos (27 USD). About 1.50 USD per hour. But he is satisfied. "Yes, very. It's four times more than I get for other crops. No product brings in a profit like coca. Sometimes the authorities show up, gather us villagers around, and try to convince us that there are other crops that are more profitable, but it's not true. If I grow pineapples or yuccas there's never anyone who wants to buy them. Coca paste, on the other hand, I can get rid of in five minutes."

This is Putumayo, the epicenter of the shady side of contemporary cocaine history. The remote province was an almost entirely uninhabited jungle region until the 1980s, when it started to attract residents thanks to the coca boom, but two decades later it would become the foremost military target of the global war on drugs. In the years prior the new millennium, nearly half of all the coca plantations in the country were here, and the province was picked as the strategic target for the largest-ever coca-eradication campaign: Plan Colombia, a US-led attempt to eliminate all coca plantations in Putumayo within a five-year period through herbicide spraying."

BANANA LEAVES ARE brushing against the tin roof of the lab when Ester, a slight woman in large boots, comes up lugging a huge sack—

about 20 kilos, she guesses. She is the fifth person so far who has come to sell coca leaves to Edgar. He takes it, weighs it, and promises to pay her once he has sold the paste.

The green leaves rustle like dollars bills as he pours the contents of her sack out onto the wooden floor. Eight years ago, when the American and Colombian armies began herbicide spraying in Putumayo, he and the others signed a contract promising to give up growing coca. But contracts, agreements, forms, and signatures are every bit as watertight for the bureaucrats in the capital city as they are vague concepts for the illiterate farmers whose lives are caught up in an economy founded on nothing but loyalty to whoever happens to have the weapons at any given time. Edgar and his family—his wife Nelcy and their four children—sold a bull in 2007 so that they could invest in the DMG, a money-laundering pyramid scheme that was enormously popular at the time, causing quite a stir in the district for several years before collapsing. Everyone lost money. So now they consider it God's blessing that they can grow the only crop that can make up for the loss and turn a quick profit.

The physical consequences of the worldwide demand for cocaine are felt all the way down to the bottom of the cocaine hierarchy. There is barely enough time to produce a few kilos of cocaine paste before the global drug trade swoops down over the Andean countryside like an octopus, with its ominous, illegal tentacles sucking up the fruit of the farmers' labor in exchange for little but fast cash.

Edgar starts up his shearing machine again. "*Es lo mismo acá.* Coca is synonymous with money here."

His story, like the whole region's, is a circular chronicle reflecting both the successes and failures associated with the war on drugs, and it shows just how integrated cocaine production has become with other, more general problems plaguing Colombia today: rural poverty, armed conflict, absence of government, and most importantly, coca as an "economic mattress."

In the 1980s Colombia was where cocaine was refined from the coca paste imported from Bolivia and Peru. But by the 1990s, after eradication campaigns had taken effect in those countries, the number of plantations in Colombia increased rapidly. The "balloon effect"—as long as there is demand, you can put the squeeze on any region because there will always be new ones—gave birth to new cultivation regions, such as Putumayo, a jungle area where a waning oil boom had suddenly left workers unemployed and unable to provide for their families.

During the oil boom, foreign companies had made all the oil profits—with support from the Colombian government—and when it was over they pulled out without having made any lasting social investment. It was a well-known socioeconomic pattern: the resource was gone and the people living there were left destitute. The state, which had had very little legitimacy even before this happened, now had none at all, and the guerrillas had no trouble positioning themselves as a more credible authority in the region by offering protection for the desperate inhabitants in their newfound livelihood: coca farming.

A rumor, that there was white gold to be found along the banks of the rivers marking the border to Ecuador, spread like wildfire to the neighboring provinces, and in just 15 years the population of Putumayo tripled. Nelcy, Edgar's wife, originally hails from the neighboring province of Nariño, like most other inhabitants of the region. But there were no jobs at home, so in 1997 she and her oldest daughters became economic refugees in Putumayo, where they could *raspar*, pick coca leaves, to get by. Edgar is also from Nariño; he came here in 1996, with his brother and some friends. Before meeting Nelcy he also worked as a leaf-picker, but after the two joined forces they were able to purchase a couple hectares and start to cultivate for themselves. They soon had two children.

Ester's route to Putumayo was different, but no less typical. She and her six children immigrated from Huila, a province in the central mountain region, to southern Putumayo during the coca boom.

Like other settlers, the family made their home deep in the jungle; however, when the oldest son turned 18 he was drafted into the army, a process that dragged the family into one of most classic recurrent problems plaguing rural Colombia. In the late 1990s Putumayo was under the control of the FARC, which made every family that "cooperated" with the military a legitimate target for the guerrillas. Thousands of families in Colombia have seen loved ones punished, often murdered, by the rebels for this reason, and now it was Ester's family's turn. In what was almost a routine move for the guerrillas, the son who went off to serve in the armed forces was labeled a *sapo*—a snitch, an informant—and told that if he did not opt to return home immediately to join the guerrillas instead, his family would be murdered within 24 hours. Ester took the remaining children and they all managed to escape with the clothes on their backs, having to leave everything else behind: the house and land, animals, furniture, and toys. But she did not have the means to get very far; just to another corner of Putumayo, where they moved next door to Edgar and his family and were once again able to carry on doing the only thing they knew how: growing coca.

José, a man who has come to give Edgar a hand, arrived in 1981 and is now part of the whole mythical history surrounding Putumayo and the green gold. As early as 1952 author William S. Burroughs, then in Putumayo in search of *yajé*—one of the Beat generation's psychoactive favorites—pointed out the eternal curse of the region in a letter to Allen Ginsberg. "As a matter of fact," Burroughs wrote in an attempt to describe the situation of a few farmers, the land in the Putumayo region "is poor and there is no way to get produce out." José arrived here as a young settler, and says it was the very shortage of roads that determined how things turned out around here. When the farmers did successfully manage to produce a modest surplus of bananas, yuccas, corn, and other things, it just lay there and rotted, as there was no way for them to get the products out to customers. And since then, the combination of poor soil and lack of markets has come to characterize every geographical area of strategic interest to those in the cocaine industry.

In the late 1970s, just as the marijuana boom was winding down and coca was taking off, settlers from the north came and introduced the wondrous crop that solved all problems at once: coca grows well in poor soil, yields four harvests a year, and most importantly, has a market in which the dealers will come right to the door to collect the product. It was not even necessary for the farmers to purchase seeds; they were simply given to them by these passing benefactors. In the desperate years, it was as if God had answered their prayers.

Shortly thereafter, life in Putumayo was turned upside down. Money literally started pouring in. The enormous value placed on cocaine in recently globalized metropolitan areas had extreme consequences, of course, for the poor farmers' understanding of the raw material, the leaves they were wading around in. Money generated from coca farming opened the floodgates for capital and for consumer goods, the likes of which none of the destitute inhabitants in the district had ever seen before. According to Swedish anthropologist Oscar Jansson, author of *The Cursed Leaf*, for the farmers it was as if dollar bills—or clothes, watches, tools, motorcycles, beer, television sets, alcohol, parties, music, and sheer joy—were growing on the very branches of their coca bushes:

> It was as though nature itself had offered them a magical pimp between their desire and the very object of their desire. The leaf was *green gold*, and coca paste was *white gold*. To those poor tropical pioneers who had colonized Putumayo in search of a plot of land, it was a gift from heaven—they rejoiced in exploiting it.

But all good things come to an end. Putumayo had experienced what scholars call a "cosmetic modernization" under the thumb of international organized crime, and by the late 1980s the effects of the hangover were already being felt. It was not just that people became greedy and began to obtain firearms to protect their stashes of money, or that the habit of smoking coca paste, *basuco*, had spread to the farmers; it was mostly due to the inevitable arrival of violence. From 1987 on, Putumayo was the textbook example of the contemporary Colombian conflict, which later spread like a poisonous disease throughout the rest of the country. But now, unlike in the past, everything revolved around cocaine. The illegal nature of the narcotics industry makes it dependent on the backing of some kind of private violent instrument of enforcement. The forms of this arrangement may vary from country to country, but in Colombia the drug mafia was able to grow freely without obstruction. And soon they became the primary driving force behind the corruption of national institutions and political systems.

When police attacked the plantations belonging to the Medellín Cartel in the central Magdalena Valley in 1987, the group began setting up new regions for cultivation in remote Putumayo and they paid their leaf-pickers in coca paste. Not far from where Edgar lives today, the cartel built the notorious El Azul, a giant lab where paste from the district and that flown in from Peru and Bolivia was refined into a tonne of high-quality cocaine every week. However, it was only a matter of months before the FARC, who had territorial control, began placing demands on these activities, and after a while the cartel started to receive armed protection on the basis of conditions set by the guerrillas: that the drug lords respect the FARC's monopoly on the right to bear arms in the area, that they pay an agreed "tax" to the guerrillas, and that they not pay the lab workers in coca paste. The latter condition was greatly appreciated by the people of the region, as many families had seen their relatives fall prey to the paste.

The agreement was honored for a while, but soon the laws of capitalism trumped local arrangements. The men of the Medellín Cartel—Pablo Escobar, José Rodríguez Gacha, Fabio Ochoa, and Carlos Lehder—increasingly began to look upon the FARC as financial parasites; the guerrillas imposed "taxes" on exports, which quickly rose in proportion to revenues. Despite their already enormous earnings, the cartel felt that the amount of money going to the guerrillas was excessive, and the drug lords wanted to drive down the costs. Some of Gacha's paramilitary groups in Magdalena Medio were moved down to Putumayo, and it was here in 1988 that the Colombian mafia's long tradition of anti-guerrilla warfare began. Escobar's at that time well-known flirtations with the left, as well as with various guerrilla groups, were now definitely over. Los Masetos and Los Combos, the cartel's private armies, began killing off FARC men, and it was not long before Putumayo was an ever-expanding war zone.

While the FARC were a sort of leech, sucking money out of a lucrative but illegal financial endeavor, the private armies strictly protected the owners' profit interests. A classic Marxist conflict consequently took root in the narcotics-driven war in Colombia, and to this day it continues to play a crucial role in the understanding of what is happening and why it never ends. The guerrillas not only took payment in order to be able to buy arms, but also, more or less, raised costs by playing the roles of both the trade union, attempting to negotiate the workers' conditions, and of the state, investing in infrastructure, while the function of paramilitary groups was and continues to be the opposite: to eliminate everything that drives up production costs. This tension between labor and capital, going back to pioneer days in Putumayo, has intensified over the years and today continues to play a significant role in the dynamics of relations between the drug mafia, the paramilitaries, the guerrillas, and the coca farmers.

In the 1990s the FARC finally fought back with a vengeance when it instigated a violent attack against the Los Masetos camp in El Azul, leaving 77 paramilitaries dead. As a result the guerrillas regained control of the area, and yet another tragic tradition was spawned and later integrated into the dynamics of Colombian violence: the FARC's strategic games with the civilian population, often coca farmers, in the circles of war. From this point, one of the guerrillas' most common tactics became forcing the farmers, usually at gunpoint, to participate in various demonstrations against the central government—supposedly under the banner of "social justice," when it was actually about defending "the right to grow coca." The Medellín Cartel lost control over Putumayo, and the more coca was cultivated, the better it was for the FARC, for two reasons: first, the "taxes" they now charged the farmers helped to strengthen the movement monetarily and militarily; and second, expansion in coca cultivation showed that the government was losing control of the nation—which is what the guerrillas always have to demonstrate to reinforce their own legitimacy.

Both the guerrillas and paramilitaries in Colombia build their identity around a populist rhetoric about "victims." Although they often employ the same methods and their warriors come from similar social backgrounds, they represent completely different interests and worldviews. The FARC sees itself as representing an excluded, marginalized peasant farming population, stripped of their economic and civil rights by capitalism, and thus believe it is "protecting" the right of the oppressed to grow coca, owing to the absence of other means of livelihood. The paramilitaries also offer protection, but based on a completely different logic: their "victims" are ambitious entrepreneurs whose financially rewarding business ventures are sabotaged by guerrilla kidnappings, extortion, murders, and "taxes." What the two groups have in common is their conviction that the government is incapable of protecting its citizens or their property; this is, in their view, what legitimizes armed groups, and they see their violent methods as not only justifiable but also completely necessary.

Between 1993 and 1996 the FARC grew at a record pace, and it did not take long before southern Putumayo found itself entirely under guerrilla control. Police officers, mayors, and farmers weren't able to take on any initiative without consulting the rebels—who not only gradually permitted the farmers to grow as much coca as they could but demanded they do so, and because coca cultivation was an effective instrument in their revolutionary project, this practice was repeated all over rural Colombia. According to their Leninist logic that there is no position between pro and contra, anyone who refused to grow coca was seen as acting in opposition to the FARC. This "law" was one families in guerrilla-dominated territories had to abide by, unless they wanted to run the risk of being killed. Consequently, the number of cultivated hectares increased dramatically. Entire villages and small towns developed with coca as their only means of sustenance, and by 2000 green gold was being cultivated on 66,000 hectares in Putumayo, representing 40 per cent of all the coca grown in Colombia that year. This fact flew in the face of the US and Colombian governments, who, after the 9/11 attack in 2001, launched a historic retaliation in the form of Plan Colombia, the strategic military effort that would not only change Putumayo and Colombia, but also all of Latin America.

EDGAR PULLS ON his galoshes and splashes some water, cement, and fertilizer over the heap before wading back and forth in the green mound to mix everything together until it becomes a thick, leafy pulp. The sludge is then dumped into oil barrels, which are filled with fuel. The stench of ammonia fills the air once the chemicals start to react, and four-year-old Luis holds his nose as his dad picks him up and moves him away from the fuel can.

"I've only been found out once," Edgar says. "The military was passing through, but I just gave them a bag of fish. They thanked me and left. They're poor guys like us. The police are worse, but I've never seen any of them here."

Nelcy comes to tell him that lunch is ready. The family bands together, along with José, and crosses the creek, which glistens rainbow from a can of used fuel Edgar has dumped in the water. They walk about 200 meters through the mud, passing a brown fishpond before reaching the stairs of their home. A wall calendar showing a bikini-clad girl is the only colorful object in an otherwise completely gray wooden house. The dwelling is built on stakes, and under the floor fuel cans and hoses are packed in, together with broken toys. Two agitated tethered cocks flap their wings wildly in anticipation of the weekend's cockfight, a sport as important to the lives of Colombian coca farmers as soccer is to the European working classes.

Nelcy puts out a couple glasses of fresh milk and some fried fish from their farm and apologizes for their small size. Once the family could afford to wait until the fish were big enough to have some meat on their bones, but not anymore. She serves her children and then tells the story about "the airplanes." "We were crying. They sprayed everywhere: the water, animals, crops. We had dug a well and it was ruined. It was terrible to see the coca die—because, of course, that's our livelihood. We tried to wash the plants, but it didn't work. Everything died. Even the monkeys died because there was nothing left on the trees for them to eat."

When the White House under Richard Nixon, the man who coined the term "the war on drugs," shifted focus from demand to supply, a theory was born that would steer the approach of every future Washington administration to the global cocaine problem. It was thought that spraying coca fields with herbicides, destroying laboratories, confiscating shipments, and arresting smugglers would reduce the amount of cocaine reaching US and European markets, whereupon the quality would drop and prices would soar—and eventually the curves would intersect, causing the entire industry to implode, since it would no longer be profitable to produce and transport an increasingly diluted drug to the wealthy markets of the world. Since then the graphs have, in reality, been pointing in very different directions, and since Obama was elected the theory has been called into question, but in the second decade of the 21st century it is still the logic that's dictating the war on drugs.

What was new about Plan Colombia, instigated by Bill Clinton in 1999, was that it was to implement herbicide spraying on a massive scale. A package, which would grow to five billion dollars, was given to the Colombian government—70 per cent of it earmarked for the military—to cut the number of coca fields in the country by half within a five-year period by employing a systematic herbicide-spraying campaign. Like Nelcy and Edgar, an average farmer owns four hectares of land, lives in a hovel without running water, and is lucky to get a couple of hours of electricity a day from a fuel-driven generator. Farmers earn less than any other group working in the lucrative cocaine chain, and are not only oppressed by poverty but also terrorized by all parties involved in the Colombian conflict. In Putumayo the short coca boom may have created a state of consumer hysteria for a few years, but it did nothing for prosperity, or to change the fact that 85 per cent of the rural population lives in poverty.

It was these socially crippled farmers who, at the turn of the new millennium, found themselves the target of the US-led war on drugs, and plenty of environmental, human-rights, and indigenous community organizations were infuriated. Putumayo—the greenhouse for nearly half of all the cocaine consumed in the world—became the central warzone. When herbicide spraying began, the goal was to eradicate all the coca growing there within five years; after two years over 104,000 hectares in the region had been sprayed, almost twice the area that had ever been cultivated. Even the legal crops the farmers were growing were destroyed, and they protested, with the assistance of environmental organizations and international NGOs, while the government highlighted the results: by 2004, 66,000 hectares of coca fields in Putumayo had been reduced to 4400.

"It was a terrible time," says Nelcy. "All the yucca and banana trees died. We had to go and beg from the people living in areas that had escaped the spraying. Then we planted again, but the planes returned. After the second time we didn't plant any more—but they came back and sprayed anyway."

By 2006 almost 900,000 hectares in Colombia had been sprayed, most of which were in Putumayo. It resulted in an actual reduction of 85,000 hectares of coca fields, meaning that more than ten hectares had to be sprayed to eliminate just one. Herbicide spraying seemed extremely ineffective as a method to eradicate coca crops, and the environmental repercussions were enormous; but what was worse, in the long run, was the social cost.

Nelcy wipes the milk from Luis' mouth. "It's as if they're all against us: the police and the military. It's like we are their enemies. It feels as if they don't care about our situation. If we grow a little coca, we end up in prison. If someone here is murdered, nothing happens. You can't help but wonder why it's like that."

For the people of Putumayo, the concept of "government" does not exist—only *la ley*, the law. Edgar says that there are many laws here, but for him and his neighbors "the law" does not mean a set of rules but whoever represents the prevailing rules at the time. He talks about the law like it's a living being. The law is in the woods. The law moves. The law is alive. If you do this or that, he says, "the law gets mad" and "the law is armed." It's a bit like he's talking about a hibernating bear that can't be woken under any circumstances, and this is because here "the law" is just the term for whichever armed group is in charge. First the guerrillas were the law, and then Los Masetos, and then it was the guerrillas again—and then in December 2000 all the planes loaded with poisonous herbicides arrived, flanked by several Black Hawk helicopters, and no one had any idea who had sent them. Los Masetos? The military? The government? The United States? Somebody else? Regardless of where they came from, it was obvious that they were now the law. Eventually the farmers were told that the planes came from something called "the state," and that they had no reason for fear as long as they cooperated.

It was hard for the farmers to figure it out. "The law" meant too many different things by now—and if you made one law mad, another one came and killed you. The year before the state sprayed herbicides over the farms, one of the laws—one that was a blend of new and old, *los paras*, the paramilitaries—re-established itself in the region in a strange way that was also difficult to understand.

In 1997 Carlos Castaño, an anti-guerrilla warrior who would later unite paramilitaries across the country in the illegal anti-communist organization Autodefensas Unidas de Colombia (the AUC), had let it be known that he intended to send some of his troops to Putumayo to eradicate the rebels in "their own jungle" and to kill all the mayors, who were "guerrilla soldiers in civilian clothing."

The following year the AUC arrived, and human-rights organizations sounded the alarm when eight massacres—most of which took place within the densest coca-producing districts—resulted in 96 victims. One year later, 13 massacres were reported, with a total of 77 deaths. Many of these murders happened during the course of a single sanguinary night: on 9 January 1999, 150 men from the AUC received assistance from the 24th brigade of the national army to obstruct the road to the little village of El Tigre, and after dark they began calling names from a list. In a pattern that was being repeated all over the country at this time, people who were considered to be cooperating or sympathizing with the guerrillas were killed off, one by one. Terror-stricken villagers were forced to stand by and watch, the pedagogical purpose being to demonstrate what would happen the next time anyone offered a guerrilla soldier some food or a glass of water. According to the reports that followed, the military and police—both practically and ideologically allied with the AUC, which was to be labeled a terrorist organization by the United States in 2001—had no objections. This is the way it happened in many isolated regions where the state had taken territorial control back from the guerrillas: the AUC carried out a number of pedagogical massacres; then came the army. And Putumayo was just another example. A year after the massacre in El Tigre, airplanes loaded with herbicides arrived—Plan Colombia—and the military, police, and paramilitaries have been in control ever since. The guerrillas were forced over the border into Ecuador, or deeper into the Amazonian rainforests.

"It's no longer possible to move around at will," says Edgar. "When they take you in they ask if you know people in the village, and if you can't immediately track down people who can vouch for who you are and confirm that you live here, they simply assume that you're with the guerrillas and cart you off. This is how so many people have been murdered. The village was full of paramilitaries for a while. There was always someone being taken away. Of course I live here, so I could always just say I know this or that person. But everybody who couldn't was killed."

As a result of the clashes between the guerrillas and the AUC, an informants' culture—a legacy from the civil war in the 1950s—also resurfaced. The bloodshed that has characterized the country for so long is not just the result of a political conflict between more or less rational, albeit perverted, interests, but is also sometimes of a more personal nature. In the swarm of armed stakeholders and in the absence of the rule of law, people have learned over time to take advantage of these purges, which sweep back and forth across the country seasonally, and more than ever in the wake of drug trafficking. Regardless of whether the problem is a dispute with one's neighbor, a crime of jealousy, over the settlement of a debt, or a disagreement about inheritance, the easiest way to take revenge on someone is to single them out as a collaborator with this or that group. Death will quickly result, although it may have absolutely nothing to do with the truth. It is a commonly used method that breeds lies, which in turn feeds the paranoia that breeds new lies, eventually causing violence to spread.

José looks up from his plate. His best friend was killed yesterday. Shot in the eye. Buried this morning. Who did it? Why was it done? No one knows. No one wants to know. "It's incredibly easy to have someone killed here," he says. "All you have to do is go to *los paras* and say that this or that person is a *guerillero*. Or you go to the guerrillas and say that this or that person is a *paraco*."

Edgar finishes his lunch, licks off his milk mustache, and says that it's time to get back to work. The first "washing" of the leaves is done. Now they have to be soaked in fuel three times, for at least 40 minutes each time, so that "the product" is released from the leaf pulp. But before standing, he gives Luis a kiss and reflects for a moment on how he defines *la ley*. For him, the law is in a constant state of flux—in the sense that what it decrees is constantly changing, as well as its being in the hands of different groups at different times—but in any case it always refers to whoever is strongest militarily at the moment.

"The law is whoever gives the orders," he says.

DOGS AND CHICKENS scatter around the drums and barrels, while eight-year-old Diana clings to her father's leg. By now the leaves have been completely voided of all the desirable alkaloids, and soon the raw cocaine will be separated from the fuel, water, and chemicals before it is finally "broken," which results in a white, cheese-like substance: the paste itself. "Tomorrow I'll sell it in the village," Edgar says. "There're plenty of guys there who'll buy it. One of them will then take it somewhere else, where the product will be turned into pure cocaine; but as to where they go exactly, hardly anyone knows. Someplace deep in the jungle. But it's extremely dangerous to know the exact location."

The "guys" Edgar is talking about are those who, in terms of rank, are just above the cultivator in the cocaine-production hierarchy. The hierarchy has four levels, roughly speaking, wherein the farmer with his simple paste lab is at the bottom. Ranked above the farmer is the itinerant middleman, who purchases the paste from the cultivators and sells it to the refining laboratories, and this is the task that generates so much of the violence associated with cocaine production. The exchange between the farmers and the refining laboratories is always under the supervision of an armed group, the guerrillas or one of the paramilitary groups, and this organization either manages all of the dealing itself—usually in those areas under FARC control—or the transaction is overseen by individuals who have been given the organization's consent to conduct such business. Since the FARC was forced out of the villages of Putumayo around the turn of the millennium all of this is now handled by the paramilitaries, and there is no longer a *cocina* in the neighboring area, which means that purchasers must now work in alliance with the police and military to make it past the roadblocks lining the only road out. This also means that the price the farmers get for their paste drops; the further from a *cocina* the paste is sold, the lower the rate is, since a number of costly fees—bribes being the greatest expense—are added to the business transaction. According to today's market value in Putumayo, one kilo of paste is worth the equivalent of 700 USD. That same kilo in Buenaventura or by the Venezuelan border, where there are hundreds of labs, goes for 1000 USD.

"It's always good to have a *cocina* nearby," says José. "The rate goes up immediately."

Together Edgar and José empty the barrels of fuel, and José says he believes some of the *cocinas* that have disappeared from Putumayo will eventually be built again. Following the massive efforts of Plan Colombia, the government, police, and the DEA—the body that, in effect, controls the drug war—now all declare that they have the situation under control and, according to official statistics, cultivation in the province has almost been completely eradicated. But any newcomer to the area will see farmers busy at work in minutes. Plenty of coca remains, but not like in the old days, when it was on large plantations, easily detectable by aircraft and satellite surveillance. Rather, coca bushes today are dispersed among other crops. Camouflaged.

José thinks that criminal groups are not only trying to evade the police and the DEA when they decide on a location for a lab; they're also on the lookout for a particular culture. "Things are pretty calm here today, and there aren't any big fields, so the police don't interfere much. It would be easy for the mafioso to build a *cocina* here now. They always want to be where the inhabitants have a tradition of cultivating and selling paste because then everything runs so smoothly. They know people aren't going to talk here. That we keep quiet. Just work. Everybody knows this is best for everyone."

The middlemen who buy and sell the paste, most often young men, make much larger profits than the farmers because the sale price greatly exceeds the purchase price. But fights and uncertainties can arise over who controls an area, and these territorial disputes often result in the death of the middleman if he makes a false move: buys or sells without the consent of "the law," sells to an agent not affiliated with the organization in charge, or is careless with what could be deadly knowledge—the location of the lab.

The third level of the hierarchy consists of those responsible for the refining process; that is, for turning the paste into pure cocaine. It is here that the criminal structure dissipates into a social and economic haze; everything is top-secret, the labs are carefully hidden, and the bosses work under assumed names. This is also where the really big profits start to be made. One kilo of paste is purchased for about 700 USD, while that very same kilo, after being refined into pure cocaine and reaching its final market, will have a street value of around 27,000 USD. (Yet before it goes out onto the market it will be chopped into gram-sized packages, to be sold by whichever group happens to be in charge of the retail end. At this point it will go for about 100 USD per gram, resulting in a gross profit of around 100,000 USD per kilo. But in order to increase profits, during the final stage of production the cocaine will be "cut" with various powdery fillers to increase its weight. The adding of what, on average, will end up being one-third cornstarch or talcum powder to pure cocaine could raise the street value to just over 130,000 USD per kilo. The enormous profits that will be generated in the destination markets will remain in those markets—in Swiss, American, or offshore banks all over the world, part of the global financial network from which Colombia and other producing nations, and particularly the most isolated areas within those countries, are cut off.)

This third level is the lowest in the hierarchy of refined cocaine, but even these traders become millionaires after just one month of production. Their strategic role is to offer the necessary low-level infrastructure, and to manage all necessary contacts—mainly handling bribes to the police, the military, and the politicians—to ensure that exporting cocaine out of the country goes on unhindered.

The highest level of the hierarchy that can be physically traced to Colombia consists of the so-called drug lords, *los traficantes*, who "own" the routes, and have all the manpower and capital necessary to ensure that shipments make it to their final destinations. In the days of the Medellín and Cali Cartels the Colombian mafia also controlled the retail end, but during the first decade of the new millennium the US market passed into the hands of organized crime in both Mexico and North America. But no cocaine trade in the world can happen at all without contacts in the country of origin, and large parts of the European market are still governed by the Colombian mafia in sophisticated collaboration with Old World underworld organizations, particularly Italian ones.

Of course, these emperors of powder never turn up in the muddy recesses of Putumayo. Since the fall of Escobar a large number of his successors have been arrested or killed in Colombia and Mexico, but there are always new ones waiting in the wings. When Arturo Beltrán Leyva, head of one of the largest cartels in Mexico, was killed on 11 December 2009, the killing was carried out in the midst of vast opulence: world-famous musicians and 20 high-class prostitutes were entertaining drug lords at a Christmas party, in a house with 280,000 USD in pin money on the premises. What was most interesting about this, though, was what the authorities did the day after. Beltrán Leyva's blood had barely had time to dry before the police had completely shifted their attention to the individual who would emerge as his successor; no one—least of all the DEA—expected the drug lord's death to have even the slightest effect on narcotics trafficking. In Mexico alone, the drug war had resulted in 22,000 victims in the past three years—low figures when compared with those of Colombia, but serious nonetheless, since the number of murders has increased every year—while drug trafficking just carried on.

Edgar empties a drum of a urine-colored liquid through a hose and admits that he does think sometimes about the fact that what he is making generates misery, and that when all is said and done this work does factor into an illegal activity that leads to violence and death, not just in Colombia but all over the world. Yet such considerations are only transient. He has never seen pure cocaine, does not even really know what the continent of South America is and, since coming here 14 years ago, has never traveled further than the 70 kilometers to where his mother lives. José is more experienced in the ways of the world, and has not only cultivated and processed paste but has also been a cocaine courier, transporting the finished product over the mountains and into Ecuador. Once. When the *cocinas* were still local, he and a friend left around lunchtime on a Saturday, each with 12 kilos, arriving in Ecuador on Monday morning. There they found two older men sitting at a restaurant, waiting to give them 300 USD. José and his friend had never earned such a large sum of money, even after several months of work. Now they had made it in just 48 hours. "For us, coca has always been a way to resolve economic hardships," he says. "We don't think about the fact that what we do leads to some mafioso getting rich, buying weapons, and killing people. People here don't think about things like that. Everybody grows coca so they can keep on living here, so they won't have to move. There's no feeling here that coca is implicitly evil. Of course we know that this or that drug lord does terrible things, but that's their problem."

WHEN PLAN COLOMBIA was introduced, its primary objective was to reduce the number of cultivated coca hectares in Colombia by half within five years. Between 2000 and 2006, 857,000 hectares in different parts of the country were sprayed with the herbicide glyphosate, resulting in the de facto eradication of 85,000 hectares. In 2004, 136,000 hectares were sprayed, resulting in the eradication of just 6000 hectares, and in 2005 the situation was even worse: after the dosage of herbicides was raised—and 139,000 hectares were sprayed—the number of fields cultivated that same year actually *increased* by 6000 hectares. Toward the end of the decade a million hectares had been sprayed, but cultivation and production continued. The balloon effect was at work: following recurrent herbicide spraying efforts in Putumayo in 2004 the number of fields indeed shrank to 4400 hectares, but as soon as the focus shifted away from the region and the military began spraying elsewhere, the coca cultivators resumed planting. The following year, Putumayo was the province that experienced the greatest increase in the number of coca fields, a trend that remained unchanged until the planes returned again.

And so it continued. But these drastic statistical ups and downs pertaining to Edgar's home turf were far from the only consequences of Plan Colombia. What upset its harshest critics most of all was that herbicide spraying seemed to be driving the coca cultivators away, scattering them all around the country like rats that had been disturbed in their nest; when satellite imagery was studied to determine the pattern of spreading coca fields during the first decade of the new millennium, it looked as though someone had sneezed in an ashtray. Having been concentrated to six provinces at the beginning of the implementation of Plan Colombia, by now the fields and the dynamics of violence had spread all over the country, and today, cultivation can be found in 24 of 32 of the nation's provinces. In a veritable exodus, coca cultivators in Putumayo fled to the even poorer neighboring province of Nariño, the place from which most of them had originated. And when the planes followed in pursuit, the fields were relocated up along the ecologically vulnerable Pacific coast. Today, large parts of the country continue to be sprayed with poisonous herbicides.

Environmental and human-rights organizations have since sounded the alarm, claiming that an *ecocidio*, ecocide against the entire nation, is underway. In terms of biodiversity, Colombia has more species of flora and fauna than any other country in the world but Brazil: there are 1800 native bird species—20 per cent of all the bird species in the world—3300 animal species, and more than 55,000 plant species. Colombia is home to 90 indigenous peoples, living on 638 reservations in a vast range of climates, from icy glaciers to vast deserts. Over 40 per cent of the country is located in the delicate Amazon rainforest, and the greatest diversity of species is found within a range of 600 to 1200 meters above sea level—the very level where virtually all coca cultivation occurs.

At first the nature reserves in the country were protected by law, but over time the Colombian government was forced to give in to the second Bush administration's demands that these areas also be sprayed, and after six years of meager results, the efforts to eradicate coca fields were expanded; in 2006 key national parks and indigenous people's reservations in Colombia were sprayed for the first time. The Washington Office on Latin America, WOLA, is just one of a number of organizations to have delivered harsh criticism of Plan Colombia in general, and ecological criticism in particular. In a report entitled *A Failed Strategy*, WOLA states: "The majority of all coca fields sprayed with hazardous herbicides today is carried out in those areas which house the greatest biodiversity and which are ecologically irreplaceable."

But not everyone agreed that no results had been achieved. According to the United Nations Office on Drugs and Crime (UNODC), which regularly examines cultivation patterns in Colombia via satellite imagery, in 2006 the number of cultivated hectares had dropped to 80,000, half the 160,000 that had been cultivated in 2000. The problem is that these statistics, which are published every year to a great deal of media fanfare, lost their credibility ages ago, since critics claim that it is impossible to differentiate, with aerial surveillance, between new, small, and hidden fields, as when seen from the air coca plants are virtually indistinguishable from other types of shrubs. That same year the other well-funded organization monitoring anti-drug progress in Colombia—the White House's Office of National Drug Control Policy—published a report claiming that in 2006 there were

160,000 hectares of coca in the country, an increase on the previous year of 13,000 hectares—and 160,000 hectares is the same number of cultivated hectares when the spraying began in 2000. There was thus a discrepancy of 80,000 between the hectarage found by the two organizations. This was a joke and, as WOLA summed it up after it attempted to set the record straight, no one has any idea as to how much coca there is in Colombia today—just that it is an incredible amount.

The loss of credibility generated by this numerical exercise, combined with political populism, culminated with the publishing of UNODC reports from 2007 and 2008. In light of the growing criticism of Plan Colombia it became increasingly important to present clear findings, and several UN statisticians resigned after the political pressure to lie about the statistics became too great. When the figures for the Colombian coca fields in 2007 were presented—showing a dramatic 27-per cent increase from the year before—the then president, Álvaro Uribe, shot back with indignation that this was impossible as the efforts to eradicate drug fields had been intensified that very year, and the Colombian government declared the organization incompetent. But in 2008, the UNODC, using the same survey methods, reported an equally dramatic *reduction* in the number of cultivated hectares, after which the government built a large media campaign around the statistics from the recently debunked organization, claiming that the war on drugs was nearly won. According to Francisco Thoumi, an economics professor appointed by the United Nations to coordinate the UNODC *World Drug Report* and based in Vienna from 1999 to 2001, the entire system—in both Colombia and at the UN level—has been corrupted by political interests. After it was proven that their research had been manipulated time and time again, he resigned in protest, stating: "The statistics the UN produces today with regard to drugs and drug production are purely political. Data and statistics are systematically falsified to serve various purposes. It's all just very tragic."

But even if the Colombian government's logic had been right—that the statistics for 2007 were completely wrong, while those for 2008, based on the same methodology, were correct—their successes would still only have been successes from a national perspective, not a global one. According to calculations by the UNOCD for the same year, the amount of cultivated hectarage gained in Bolivia and Peru was now proportionate to what had been lost in Colombia, and thus just as much coca was being cultivated in the Andes by the end of the first decade of the new millennium as at the beginning. And the same applied to cocaine production: in 2002, 730 tonnes were produced in the Andes, while in 2008 it was 820 tonnes, more than half of which was produced in Colombia. After ten years, 6.8 billion US dollars, and a million sprayed hectares in Colombia, nothing like a reduction in cultivation or production had occurred in the Andes.

Regardless of whether the statistics were true or false, when it came to combating the actual problem the priorities of Plan Colombia were difficult to fathom. Manual elimination—the process by which soldiers go out into the fields and uproot plants by hand in an effort to keep fields free from coca—had long proven to be both a superior strategy and a cheaper one, costing a mere quarter of the price of herbicide spraying: it costs 750 USD to spray just one hectare by plane, whereas the cost to eliminate the same area by hand, without any of the environmental consequences, is a mere 180 USD. Despite this, however, both the US and Colombian governments chose to continue mostly with the former method. Critics argued that the difference in expenditure would make it possible to unlock the social potential of Plan Colombia to a much greater extent, and consequently would allow for funds to be invested in schools, health care, infrastructure, and micro loans to impoverished peasants, as well as alternative-livelihood programs for farmers in the affected parts of the country. This notwithstanding, herbicide spraying became a permanent fixture.

By evening the monkeys are back and Nelcy has come to assist

Edgar. Next to the lab a mound of leaf residue accumulates under a cloud of fuel vapors, which rises up into the trees, where the primates revel in the stink. Edgar and Nelcy treat the water with chemicals one last time, turning it a milky color and causing it to curdle. After wrapping the separated mass in a towel, they begin wringing it out together until every last drop of liquid has been squeezed out, and the lump inside is packed solidly, as big as a bowling ball.

"Phew. One more round."

"OK, phew, ha ha."

They stand face to face, with eyes locked as if in an arm-wrestling match, while José sweeps up scattered bits of leaves and Luis makes *vroom-vroom* sounds with a plastic toy car between the oil drums. It is almost 6.00 p.m., and a familiar sound of muffled motors is heard coming from the mountains, a noise that has become somewhat of a soundtrack to life for indigenous peoples, Afro-Colombians, and recently settled farmers since the beginning of the new millennium: military helicopters.

No sight in the air space above southern Colombia today is more common than that of the arrival of the Black Hawks, which appear in the sky like ships in formation, all on different assignments in conjunction with the DEA-led war on drugs. Control, presence, and power: that is the message. It is a symbolic language directed at the guerrillas and at individuals suspected of sympathizing with them, and even if the spraying is ineffective and perhaps even counterproductive as a means to fight drugs, such activity in the sky plays an integral role in anti-guerrilla warfare. Ecological destruction, financial depletion, and failed results with regard to coca is a price the US and Colombian governments are willing to pay to keep the FARC in check and to create the feeling that, despite everything, the state is in control.

THE FOLLOWING MORNING, rain patters down over the house. Edgar melts the white paste in a saucepan over a fire before allowing the creamy white substance to harden on the bottom. Now it is ready.

"It's no good if it doesn't harden. You can't sell a soft product."

It should have the consistency of taffy but the color of meringue. He stirs it with a ladle, mixing it until it has achieved just the right texture. After a little while it dries as it should and can be broken into pieces like hardened chocolate. He looks pleased. Nevertheless, a sense of sadness hovers over the entire process, the activity to which Edgar has devoted himself for the past two days. Nothing is as it used to be. While the green leaf was once regarded as a sign of prosperity, today it is associated with an entirely new set of connotations and no one has pleasure any more from the mere sight of a coca plant or a kilo of paste.

"We don't make our living from coca any longer," Edgar says. "We do it to bring in pesos. It's money you just can't get any other way. The food we eat doesn't come from coca, but rather from other things we have here: fish farming, chickens, potatoes, yuccas, corn. A little of everything. And then we also have two cows."

For the farmers of Putumayo, just as in most other parts of the country, coca cultivation has always been viewed as a legitimate activity, not only because coca is always in demand but also because they see themselves as *exploited*, something the guerrillas never tire in pointing out. But 15 years after the boom, the concept of what has always been known as green gold is a double-edged sword; the leaf that distinguished itself as sacred in the past is now somewhat of a curse. Those wild heydays that characterized Putumayo long before the region became the bloody battlefield did not exactly make for a paradise, either. Edgar maintains that he does not yearn for the past and the exorbitant spending, but rather looks to the future. The people living in the villages and cities born out of the coca boom in the 1980s and 1990s were suspicious and jealous of each other, and the streets were lined with whorehouses and populated with people recovering from excessive liquor consumption and partying. Today, people are well aware that much of the misery that followed has to do with coca in one way or another. That there will always be a hangover.

For Edgar, Nelcy, Ester, José, and the vast majority of other farmers living in the province, *la coquita*, coca, is an extra income, not a primary one. There was more to Plan Colombia than just chemical aerial bombs; one-fifth of the resources were dedicated to social funding, aimed at eliminating the incentive to cultivate coca— at combating poverty, in other words. While most of the money was lost to corruption and bureaucracy, a small amount did manage to trickle down to the farmers, and Edgar's fish farm is the result of such assistance. It will never measure up to coca in terms of proceeds, but in the long run it could prove very profitable for, just like coca, fish also has an immediate market.

But the lesson the farmers of Putumayo, the region where coca has been cultivated the longest, have learned from their financially treacherous dealings with the cocaine industry have not really spread to other parts of Colombia. The promise of fast cash sweeps across the country like a giant windstorm, shaking up everything in its path, and out of all the socially vulnerable regions presently on the verge of being sucked into the carousel, none is as typical as the coastal jungles where Leo and his fishermen hunt for the miracle catch: Chocó.

After scraping his finger over the product, Luis licks the white film from his fingertips. He giggles when his tongue goes numb. Dad does the same and nods approvingly. The quality is good. Nelcy says that there is less than she had been hoping for. Diana teases one of the fighting cocks. Maria, the eldest daughter, comes home in her school uniform and passes by her parents with a resounding "God bless you," to which Edgar and Nelcy respond by shifting attention from the raw cocaine to their daughter, answering back in unison: "God bless you."

THE CANOE ROCKS slightly in the turns as Graciano steers his dugout deeper, into the heart of the business. Vines, branches, brushwood, trees, and leaves as large as bedsheets hang over the water as he carefully guides the canoe through the foliage and its dark, cave-like passages, like a tiny strand of thread through the eye of a needle.

"Almost there."

The sun flashes sporadically through the thick jungle coverage, and the quick shift from total darkness to intense sunlight gives the setting the appearance of a fast-winding newsreel in sepia tones. The dense river water is mustard-colored, and here and there dragonflies stop in midflight, hovering like helicopters.

Graciano suddenly whistles and points to the right. "There," he says.

Three men, standing in a glade in black bathing suits and pouring water over each other, look up when Graciano arches the canoe around them, greeting him with a familiar hello. The guerrilla soldiers are taking a swim, their guns having been left on the riverbank. A bit further up are the remains of a house where some armed silhouettes are seen moving about. This is the checkpoint—the border, defense, security. It is what the farmers are paying for; no military, no police, and no paramilitaries pass by here. On the other side of this point, everything is safe. Graciano's little outboard motor–driven canoe sails on for two more kilometers toward the mountains before he switches it off by a mud bank and glides in among five other canoes all pointing in the direction of a tree, like fish surrounding a food source.

"This is where it begins. All of this is new. Eight years ago there wasn't a single coca plant here. No one even knew what coca was. Now there's nothing else. And nobody talks about anything else. Many of these fields are no more than a couple years old. Everybody here knows that it's a golden opportunity—but that its time is nearly up and it won't be coming back."

This is the inland of Chocó, the last of the new frontiers of the cocaine industry. The province, wedged between the Pacific Ocean and the western mountain range, consists of impenetrable rainforests crisscrossed by thousands of rivers, comprising one of the largest water systems in the world. The Atrato River flows north into the Caribbean and is the economic artery of Chocó, while the San Juan, the second-largest river in the region, runs south into the Pacific. If these two waterways could be connected, Colombia would have a navigable channel between the waters of the Atlantic and the Pacific that could compete with the Panama Canal; it's been a moneymaking dream of many past governments. But there is a long way to go. So far Chocó only has one main road, hardly drivable, and is inhabited exclusively by waterborne people no one has ever cared about. Living here far below the poverty line are the descendants of slaves, indigenous peoples, and settlers, whose slow-paced lives, centerd on fishing and small-scale farming, are only interrupted by occasional short-lived economic booms based on sudden and whimsical demands and desires from the outside world—gold, wood, silver, coca.

"*Buenos días*. Done already?" He laughs.

A group of *raspachines*—leaf pickers—have finished for the day and are now heading back home to the village. Graciano exchanges pleasantries with them, asking about their day, before climbing up a steep slope and making his way down into a valley of glistening coca fields. Hectare upon hectare has been thoroughly cleared, and newly planted coca bushes shine like emeralds in a black landscape of burned logs. And then suddenly a familiar sound is heard, followed by another. Adjacent to each plot is a lab, and in the clearing far below the afternoon sun beats down on a tarp, stretched across a simple wood construction that protects Solin, César, and Andrea from the sun. The process is now in full swing, and the shearing machine's motor roars, causing leaves to whirl and insects to scatter. Andrea is cooking, César is cutting the leaves, and Solin is mixing chemicals. And soon the lab is full of the pungent vapors of ammonia and fuel.

"You get a bit groggy," Solin says. "But we're used to it. We've been here for eight days straight."

They are a team of three, each of whom have a different role, but all work together to deal with the harvest from César's plot. Today the pickers have gathered 12 *arrobas*, which will now be turned into paste, and when that is done—the harvest will generate 3.5 kilograms of paste—it will be sold to local buyers, the sale authorized by the guerrillas, for a total of 8.4 million pesos, or 5320 USD. One *arroba*, equivalent to 12 kilos, is the base unit of the coca economy. *Los raspachínes*, who are the bottom level of the cocaine hierarchy, earn 6000 pesos per *arroba*, which means an average daily pay of about 15,000 pesos, or 11 USD. But they also get three meals, which Andrea is responsible for providing. One hectare yields about 150 *arrobas* per harvest, and there are four harvests a year. The smallholders usually own between two and five hectares each.

"But after I've paid all the workers, including those who've delivered the chemicals, there's only 1.5 million pesos left over for me," César says. "It's not great business. Just a little better than others."

Like Graciano, César is one of the thousands of new coca cultivators along the San Juan River, a growing agrarian proletariat who, on the one hand, are simply happy that some money has finally come to the region, but on the other are also very much aware that the prosperity will be short-lived, and that the military aircraft can come at any time and chemical-bomb everything, just like in Putumayo. This is what makes it a rush. In fact, the whole idea of striking while the iron is hot has, along with cocaine's grip on Colombia, become one of the most distinctive cultural hallmarks of the nation. Some would call it a national disease: *el cortoplazismo*, shortsightedness.

Andrea peels a banana while Solin and César kick about in the green mound in an effort to mix all the leaves together before the pulpy mass can be dumped into the oil drum filled with fuel. Andrea is 24 years old and César's live-in partner, and she hopes to become pregnant soon. For her, the rush was a godsend because, as she says, it rescued her "from slavery." "I'm free now. I can do what I want."

Although slavery was abolished in Colombia in 1851, a deep-seated historical racism continues to characterize both city and country life alike, and it is quite common to see young, white couples driving through remote villages in search of girls "to take care of"—that is, offering them lifelong servitude in exchange for room and board and Saturday nights off. Destitute families have received verification via television that life in the city is better than in the country, and because this analysis is often correct, daughter and parents alike often consent to such arrangements when they are offered. The white couple feels as if it has done a good deed, and the African or indigenous family is happy to have one less mouth to feed. The demand for boys is also great—most often for custodial work—but not at all to the same extent as for girls, which is why thousands of young men are sent to join the guerrillas or a paramilitary group, either of which the family often regards as a better option than life at home.

Problems arise for the girls when they become pregnant, which often occurs around the same time that the woman of the host family also finds herself expecting. Usually, the servant is around 15 years old and the lady of the house 25. Since the intention is that the domestic help, that is, the person of color, is to take care of the white couple's child, one of the newborns has to be given up, and often the solution is adoption. An excursion to an orphanage is arranged, where the servant, assisted by the lady of the house, hands over the child and verifies in writing that everything has been done of her own volition. A visit to the church follows, where the priest offers forgiveness and the matter is closed once and for all, after which the young woman of color is expected to project her motherly instincts onto the white child.

Andrea began working as a domestic servant in Cali at the age of 12. Her only exposure to the big city and its enticements was through the bus window, for when she did have a Saturday night off she was always either broke or on call, and thus was never able to enjoy it. After a number of years of this, she sensed that her life was becoming increasingly meaningless. Then she started longing to have her own children. And as soon as she realized what sort of life a black maid without money had in store, she contacted people from her hometown, who told her that coca had come to the village and that there was now, finally, money to be made.

"I just left. Escaped. We don't have much here either, but at least

I'm not locked up. Today we own this plot of land and can make our own decisions. I also sell candy in the streets. I purchase it in a town upriver and sell it in the village."

The village is El Caraño, a small riverside community consisting of a hundred simple wooden houses, where everyone who owns coca fields on the surrounding hills lives. Graciano has lived in El Caraño his entire life, whereas César and Solin wandered around the country for many years searching for money, but like Andrea, were enticed back by coca. Solin is not a landowner, but because he is the chemist he is the team's most important member, without whose itinerant skills the industry could not function. In historically experienced parts of the country such as Putumayo, just about any farmer can handle the proportions, the chemicals, and the simple process coca demands, but in more recently converted areas the chemists play a crucial role.

"It's not difficult, but no one can afford to make a mistake."

Solin's dirty cap teeters slightly atop his curly head. He is one of a few Caucasians living among the thousands of Afro-Colombians in El Caraño. With a calm voice and a steady hand, he leads the work for which César pays him 60,000 pesos, or 30 USD, a day. During the harvest they live in the lab day and night, and when all the work is done they travel the five kilometers home to the village by canoe, where they sell the paste and rest for a few days.

Solin is originally from Meta, a region in the east where coca quickly emerged after Putumayo was sprayed, but the area was also eventually visited by the planes. "I had a small farm there with coca, yucca, bananas, and other things. They sprayed everywhere, so leaving was the only option. The chickens died—everything. It's extremely poisonous. The first time it happens you just start over, you replant everything. But after they come back and spray again and again, it begins to take its toll. I knew a guy who lived here and said it was peaceful and quiet. So I came here."

His wife lives with their three daughters in Armenia, a city in the coffee region. He sends them money, but as long as there is work to be done here, he only sees them once every other month. "This is a temporary situation. If I got a job in the city I would leave. But the pay's no good. I worked at a cardboard recycling plant in Villavicencio and earned 15,000 pesos a day, and while that bought food for the children and my wife, there was never anything left over for me. You just get fed up. It doesn't work. There are people claiming they can live just fine on 15,000 pesos a day, but those making such claims are also involved in some sort of illegal activity on the side. Everybody knows this is how it works. One hand is legal, the other one isn't."

He organizes the rest of the chemicals and declares that he just cannot understand how there can be such high demand for what he produces. "No one here uses cocaine. Those of us who work with the stuff are all too aware of just how deadly the chemicals are that go into making the powder. We're already suffering the extreme physical effects from having to stand in these vapors every day, and then to go home at the end of the day and inhale it in a concentrated form would be unthinkable. This is dangerous stuff. You can get totally hooked. If I see a child using drugs I say something, but not if I see an adult. That's their responsibility. As for me, I've never tried it. I would never do it. I know what it consists of. Dangerous, dangerous, dangerous."

César stirs the pot of leaves with a big branch and begins to tell his own story. He came here in search of gold at 13, from Pizarro, a village by the coast, after the death of his father. Like many others here, César's father's death was brought about by a *palo*, a tree trunk, which, word has it, fell on him while he was working out in the forest one day. But in Chocó, everyone knows that when someone is said to have died from a *palo* what they actually mean is that the person was murdered for a reason too dangerous to inquire about. Consequently, it is easiest for everyone to agree that the death was an unfortunate accident caused by a falling tree and not question the matter further. César, his mother, and his siblings all saw the body, which had been dragged up the stairs and left on their doorstep. He had a long machete wound from one of his ears all the way down to his Adam's apple, but no one dared to discuss why. There are nine siblings in the family, who today are scattered all over the country. César and Andrea take care of his sick mother, and the lion's share of the income they bring in goes toward the treatments she needs for her rheumatism.

"There's something really strange about all this," César suddenly blurts out. He is not talking about his parents any longer, but about the guerrilla-controlled cocaine economy in which he is involved. Although the United States is where most of the consumers are, he says, it never seems as though any of the people he refers to as "them" are punished. The punishment always seems to befall those he refers to as "us." "Almost everything we produce goes there, and that's where all the money ends up. But the gringos never get caught. Never. You see the stories on TV, and it's always a Mexican, Colombian, Brazilian, or Puerto Rican in the hands of the police. That strikes me as very odd. We all know the buyers are in the US. That's where the money is. The banks. Celebrities. Everything. I really just don't understand. Why is it like that?"

Andrea whistles to signal that the meal is ready. It is chicken and rice. Plastic bowls are passed around, and Solin dries his green-stained hands on his t-shirt and scoffs down his food, while the wind outside causes the tarp on the roof to rustle. César goes silent. They eat sitting on the ground. Solin has listened to César's speculations, but he claims that no one who lives along the river is afraid of going to prison for anything to do with coca; they worry instead about being subjected to something much worse. César nods slowly in agreement. The drumstick between his teeth moves back and forth as he chews. Andrea pours brown juice out of a bucket in a way that conveys the topic of conversation is not to her liking. But Solin carries on, and utters the two words of which all destitute Colombians are most afraid these days, whether they live in the countryside or in the urban favelas. Actually, it is not so much the words they fear, but rather what they are terrified of *becoming*.

"*Falsos positivos.*"

OF ALL THE scandals to have rocked Colombia over the years, nothing can compare to what is known as *falsos positivos*, false positives. The phenomenon is complicated and horrifying, and occupies what Colombian author Daniel Samper has called a unique place in the history of the nation: "In the specifically Colombian chamber of horrors—which expands daily, with new atrocities committed by the drug industry, the guerrillas, the paramilitaries, criminal gangs or our own military, the false positives are in a league of their own."

The story, which is far from over, is a gruesome response to how poverty and corruption feed into the demand for results, which became increasingly important in Colombia in the first decade of the new millennium. Measuring, calculating, keeping records, and publicizing successful military accomplishments in the fight against guerrillas and drugs became a central component of the war in itself, and it produced a completely new trend in violence, built on the fact that such a large percentage of the population consists of homeless people no one cares much about. Numbers that created an image of victory—weakened guerrillas, demobilized paramilitaries, and reduced coca fields—were transformed under Uribe's administration into strategic hard currency in the struggle for voter sympathies and increased financial support from the United States. Statistics, whether accurate or manipulated, became more important than truth, since a national sentiment of success and good results is crucial for each and every political scheme. The objective was to validate the government's promise to destroy guerrilla forces once and for all. Fatalities became the currency of war, and everyone from generals to corporals was forced to keep track of how many guerrilla corpses their troops were able to generate.

On 10 February 2004, a street vendor named Edwin Arias was reported missing in Sincelejo, a city near the Caribbean coast, along with three other young men: Luis Campo, José Peréz, and Alberto Arias. Two days later, on 12 February, all four were reported as having been killed in a conflict the military claimed had broken out between themselves and the guerrillas near the Panama border. However, as time went by a number of unanswered questions arose. Edwin Arias had already been reported dead once before, and then, just as now, as a guerrilla soldier who had lost his life in armed combat. Moreover, the helicopter that supposedly flew the four bodies back to the camp had been on another assignment that day.

Edwin Arias was just one of the first *falsos positivos* in what would later become a wave of mass killings, resulting in the execution of nearly 2000 boys—all civilians, most of them destitute and homeless—whose bodies were viewed as attractive merchandise in an increasingly gruesome business practice spreading throughout the nation, the sole purpose of which was to improve statistics. In Colombia, a country with an already long-standing tradition of creative criminality, taking dead bodies, dressing them up as guerrilla warriors, and registering them as slain rebels was a practice that soon gained a life of its own, since everyone working in the military stood to benefit from the operation: in exchange for guerrilla corpses, low-ranking soldiers were compensated with days off and other benefits, while middle-ranked officers in command were given promotions according to their results, and those highest in the hierarchy, the generals, could provide the national Congress, government, and the general public with an image of the war as being won.

But when ready cash began to be factored in, state terrorism exploded and the practice became more organized. In 2008, Soacha—a huge working-class suburb in southern Bogotá—became the scene of one of the most telling events of the entire scandal, after sergeant John Jairo Muñoz of the 15th brigade received repeated complaints from superiors that his platoon was underperforming.

Muñoz—as he later explained in court—asked another sergeant, Sandro Pérez, to help him improve his platoon's statistics, whereupon his colleague, who was working in military intelligence at the time, offered the following: "If you want, I can get you people you can report as having been killed in combat." Each person would come with a price tag of a million pesos, 500 USD, and, according to Muñoz, the brigade's colonel, Gabriel Rincón Amado, approved the deal. A network was established whereby a shopkeeper in Soacha was to be the main recruiter of young men. Through the shop, a rumor was circulated that jobs were available and that there was money to be made in Ocaña, a community located close to the border with Venezuela, and, after being offered free bus rides there, a number of unemployed young men living in Soacha, including Jonathan Orlando Soto, 17, and Julio César Meza, 24, took the bait.

On 25 January 2008 the two young men left Soacha and, two days later, the army's 15th brigade was able to report that two guerrilla warriors had been killed in combat. A sum of 2.2 million pesos was paid for Soto and Meza, plus expenditures for their bus tickets, and the evening on which they were killed and their bodies sold, the murderers toasted each other with glasses of rum at a bar in Ocaña. The money used in the transaction originated partially from the military budget, but also from individual soldiers and officers who took the initiative to pool their own pesos toward purchasing both the bodies and the weapons needed to pass the dead men off as fallen guerrilla soldiers. As the shopkeeper, Alexander Carretero, later explained in the investigation: "The troops took it as a duty to collect money for bodies. Officers and soldiers contributed out of their own pockets." After the men's deaths, Colonel Rincón Amado made another order from the shop-owner in Soacha.

In 2009, when Philip Alston, United Nations Special Rapporteur on extrajudicial executions, investigated the full extent of the scandal, he claimed to find no evidence that the government should have known anything about such a practice, but that the killings had been carried out in a "more or less systematic fashion" and that "significant elements within the military" were involved. He also said that he found the media-coined term "*falsos positivos*" misleading because the euphemism gave a false impression of a practice that could be better described as the "cold-blooded, premeditated murder of in-

nocent civilians for profit"; the victims the military had passed off as
"dangerous terrorists" included disabled teenagers. A vast number of
the bodies presented as killed in combat were photographed wearing
newly ironed uniforms and boots several sizes too large. Moreover, in
some pictures men known to have been left-handed were shown holding weapons that had been tucked into their right hands. Worse still,
according to Alston, was the fact that the survivors or relatives who
attempted to report the incidents and to testify were subjected to "systematic military persecution," and that the unraveling of the alliances
between the military and hit men in Soacha, which had become the
center of the scandal, were just "the tip of the iceberg." These structures could be found all over the country and, according to Alston,
one mother's testimony of what had happened was typical: after her
son had been killed, his brother, the second-eldest son, began inquir-
ing into what had happened, and a couple months later he was also
found dead. Soon after, the mother began to receive death threats.

In the wake of the scandal the government discharged 27
officers—including three generals and 11 colonels—and a number of
arrests were made. However, a year later the majority of the detainees
were released because no charges had yet been pressed. It was said
that there were "legal difficulties of a technical nature." By the early
2010s it looked as if yet another unresolved scandal would be added
to Colombia's already long history of military impunity for human-
rights violations. Under the headline "Legalized Barbarianism,"
Daniel Samper wrote in *El Tiempo*, the largest newspaper in the
country, that the worst part was not that cold-blooded murders were
being committed to improve statistics, but that this sort of crime was
on its way to becoming legalized:

> The accused didn't escape from prison or hide from the authorities—
> they were able to march right out through the main entrance, the
> door for legal disputes that have been resolved. It is the combination
> of this judicial ingenuity and its far-reaching consequences that

nurtures one of the most feared monsters in Colombia: state-sanctioned impunity.

IN EL CARAÑO, the village where Graciano and the others live, it is now Sunday evening, and both young and old alike are able to forget about the *falsos positivos* and the impending herbicide spraying. It is the weekend. Men toast to each other, while women pray. A girl plays with her laser pointer, aiming it at the anus of a stray dog, and laughs so loudly that she is heard inside the church just as the priest takes to the pulpit.

"Forgive us our sins."

The congregation consists almost exclusively of women and children, and along the main drag in the village—a kilometer-long mud bank—the thumping beat of Latino music blares from the open doors and windows of the wooden houses, while the brown water of the San Juan runs past tranquilly. The river gleams. Reflections from television sets and illuminated decorations give a new luster to the humble homes in the village. Many shacks have a satellite dish attached on the roof, stereos are booming everywhere, young men strut around in jeans with silver dragon ornaments, and every young girl has a beautiful beaded hairdo atop her head. Everything smells nice. Showered bodies. Catholic Sunday.

Tied and resting along the riverbed are the families' canoes, with recently installed motors; by the houses, fuel-operated generators give life to the sorts of things no one could have dreamed about before the arrival of coca: freezers, sound systems, karaoke machines. Everyone—children, parents, and senior citizens—is in a good mood, joking and dancing.

"But it will be over soon. People look happy now, but they actually live in fear of that moment. The end."

Mass is over now, and the priest sighs inside his little house, situated behind the simple concrete structure that is the church. Along the

San Juan and its tributaries hundreds of villages are populated with indigenous peoples or Afro-Colombians, and what the priest calls "the slavery of coca" is spreading like a capitalist cancer, with El Caraño just one of many examples. This is a boom, and everyone is making the most of the good days while they last. According to the priest, the very fact that Andrea maintains that coca has liberated her from slavery is reflective of the widespread tendency to be shortsighted.

"People here are obsessed with money now. It's toxic. They work round the clock up there and care about nothing else. The women are there because everybody needs to be fed: once harvesting begins, they sleep in the labs for weeks on end. And down here the children wander about totally unsupervised. The church has become the daycare center. The nuclear family is crumbling, and the men would rather drink and smoke than attend mass. Violence will break out soon, and then everybody will have to run away. Everybody here has their bags packed."

The history of El Caraño, and its current volatile state, is the same as that of the vast majority of other villages along Colombia's Pacific coast. Ten years ago farmers in the community staked everything on *borojó*, a fruit popular in Chocó but nowhere else, and of the 25 tonnes produced in the village weekly, only three would be sold. There was no market. The fruit rotted in mass amounts, while misery spread because there was no money being generated for the local economy. But one day a couple of foreign *señores*—who no one in El Caraño knew at all—paid a visit to the village and held a meeting with the inhabitants, offering them coca seeds free of charge. It was a scheme by which the foreigners would provide the seeds and the farmers would tend the crops; they would cooperate. Profits would be split 50-50. Disillusioned by the *borojó* failure, many seized the opportunity. Some farmers declined the offer, but then changed their minds once they saw their neighbors starting to renovate their houses and hang up their satellite dishes.

Yet it was not long before the all-too-familiar tendency toward violence resurfaced and left its unmistakable mark. One day, two new *señores* turned up and explained that the first men who had come were, in fact, *paracos*, paramilitaries, and the town was on the verge of entering into an alliance with guerrilla enemies. The farmers who feared the two FARC messengers stopped growing coca immediately, whereas others chose to carry on in the hope that everything would work out in the end. A few months later, however, the guerrillas arrived in earnest and explained that it was now time for the villagers to choose a side once and for all; all the *paracos* and farmers who chose to remain part of the alliance with rebel enemies were killed. Battles broke out in many of the villages along the river. The guerrillas gained control over the region and have kept it ever since.

"Now they rule everything."

Like everyone else in the village, the priest only ever refers to the guerrillas as "them." In the Colombian countryside, nothing can ever really be called by its exact name; in the same way that Edgar talks about "the law" in Putumayo, the inhabitants of El Caraño talk about "them," though all are alluding to the same thing: the armed group in power at the moment. The FARC have an agreement with everyone working in the chain: those selling fuel and chemicals, those purchasing the paste, those who own *las cocinas*—and, most importantly, the farmers. For the villagers, everything runs much more smoothly when one armed organization oversees all of it, in contrast to the sort of conflicts that precede any such takeover, which bring with them the worst sort of violence and human displacement. Afterwards everything is relatively calm; that is, until the day when the planes come. And it is because of this day that everyone has his or her bags packed.

"People have completely stopped cultivating other crops," the priest states. "In the past, every family set aside part of their plot for growing rice, corn, and other things for household use, but now it's just coca. And what are the farmers supposed to do once their fields get sprayed? After all, you can't eat coca."

Out on the river three canoes, filled to capacity with fuel drums and bags of cement, travel along upstream, while a much faster motorboat, part of international medical organization Doctors Without Borders, zigzags between them on its way south. Remote thunderstorms light up the jungle, and the tops of palm trees stiffen and become illuminated against the white explosions in the sky. In conjunction with the coca boom, chemical sheds turned up in all of the villages along the river, and these are the only places that are open on Sundays. They look like well-supplied hardware stores, shiny, bright, and always stocked with clean bags, cans, bottles, and tools, standing in sharp contrast to the otherwise disorderly villages.

The scent of rain fills the air. In a doorway, the silhouettes of two large sets of hips are swaying to the beat of salsa music, but the priest just looks on in misery. "What the state should be responsible for today has fallen into the hands of the guerrillas and charity organizations. There isn't a single Colombian nurse here, and hardly any doctors. Everything to do with civilian life is controlled by foreign NGOs: Lutheran Help, Doctors Without Borders, UNICEF. And guerrillas are in charge of coca production. It's all very sad."

RELYING ON HIS arms, both stretched straight out for balance, Graciano attempts to cross the terracotta-colored creek on a log that serves as a small bridge. All of a sudden he starts to lose his balance, but finally manages to jump the remaining meters, with only one foot slipping down to splash in the water.

It is Monday afternoon. Crescendos of birdsong stream out of the remains of a lush and vibrant rainforest like melodies from a music box, and everything is dry for a change. The sun beats down on a patchwork quilt of carved-out, clear-felled land, and standing on a slope in the middle of a coca field are the charred remains of a felled tree.

"These are almost ready to be harvested." He runs his hand through the ripened leaves in a few of the bushes. A couple of hundred meters separates them from Graciano's own field and lab.

In a month's time, the family will begin harvesting. Today he will just tend to his *viveros*, small flowerbeds from which the new seedlings will later be separated and planted out in the fields. His purple gabardine pants flap in the breeze and his straw hat sits on the back of his head as he takes the final steps up to his property.

"Look over there," he says pointing with his machete.

There are several cleared hectares on the other side of the valley, but the lime-green coca bushes that usually cover the clear-cut areas are missing. Everything is brown and gray. Burnt.

"That family cleared their land but couldn't afford to grow anything. It's very common here for people to run out of money halfway through the process. The land just lies there dead. It's a terrible shame."

For every gram of cocaine consumed four square meters of rainforest have to be cut down, and because the farmers are pushed deeper and deeper into the jungle, they have to make do with land that is increasingly less suited for coca, and thus end up using even more pesticides. About 550 kilos of weed-killer, fertilizer, fuel, ammonia, cement, and sulfuric acid go into transforming one hectare of coca into paste, and around 154,000 tonnes of chemical waste a year are dumped into some of the world's most diverse ecological systems, often in nature reserves and national parks.

In 2006 the Colombian government launched Shared Responsibility, a campaign designed to call attention to the global environmental damage being caused by the cocaine industry by appealing to the new wave of eco-activism in Europe and the United States. Since neither the violence nor the corruption associated with the cocaine trade had deterred Western consumers from using the drug, the government thought that the environmental perspective might make more of an impact.

However, the initiative was quickly met with thundering criticism, for as it turned out that the basis upon which the claim was made—that coca cultivation was "the major cause of pollution of the

Colombian rainforests"—was a lie. In comparison with the military's herbicide spraying, the farmers' contribution to the destruction of the environment was quite marginal, and nearly all of the hectares devastated during the first decade of the millennium were the result of the cultivators being forced to relocate to other parts of the country due to the lack of alternatives after their fields were sprayed with chemicals. And the industries the government had subsidized as alternatives to coca—cattle breeding and biofuel cultivation—were far more hazardous to the environment than coca cultivation. Colombia is about the same size as Spain and France combined, and today the main threat posed to Colombian ecosystems and food production is cattle raising, an industry whose expansion has driven away small farmers and caused large-scale deforestation. The same goes for biofuel. Palm oil—the main raw material for biodiesel, and one of the industries in which the government invested heavily as a part of its strategic plan to eradicate coca—not only causes serious environmental problems, but has also functioned as an economic base for paramilitary terrorist networks and money laundering by the drug mafia.

Graciano examines what resembles a dense patch of clover and says that his little crop is doing just fine. Every cultivator has these small light-green beds of new bushes here and there on his property, and in just a few months each of the plants will have grown into a bush and thus have made its own contribution to the global cocaine complex. "This little patch will result in some 300 bushes," says Graciano.

As one of the older men in the village born and raised in El Caraño, he has greater authority and a more thoughtful approach to what goes on than younger people. His comparative for how well or how badly people are doing in the village has to do with eating: "They eat more than us," 'He eats the most," "She eats the least," and his way of thinking about what coca has done to El Caraño extends far beyond how many home renovations people have accomplished with their earnings.

Graciano was one of the residents who were skeptical when coca first came. "But I didn't take a clear stance against it. Today, I agree with those who said coca was going to cause lots of problems. A lot of people have been killed in our village alone. Those who lost their lives were completely innocent guys, foolish enough to get involved in things they shouldn't have. When people get a lot of money, they act stupidly. Ask the wrong questions. Talk about the wrong things. Fight with the wrong people. It's most often little things, but here even the little things can get you killed."

The farmers in Chocó are in no-win situation, and the strange forces of the industry make it hard for even those who would like to quit growing to do so. Graciano is convinced that the state does not actually want to stamp out coca cultivation, because if the government and military really wanted to, he says, it would not be very hard. "What makes us so sure about this is how easy it is to get your hands on all the additives. To buy a bag of fertilizer just a few years ago, you had to go all the way to Quibdó. There was no place to get fertilizer anywhere along the San Juan. But when coca arrived, lots of shops opened all along the river. And those shops have to have a permit from the state. The owners come from inland. No one from here, not a single black man, has ever owned such a shop. We don't have access to that business. Cement, fertilizer, sulfuric acid, and anything else you'd ever need is there and in endless supply. It's always in stock. However much you want. If somebody really did want to put a stop to coca cultivation, all they'd have to do would be to cut off access to the additives. But no one is doing that."

Graciano sits with his back against one of the posts holding up his little lab. It has been 20 years since the coca boom shook up Putumayo and ten years since herbicide spraying caused coca cultivation to move out all over the country. As he gazes out over the cleared areas—some green, others dead—he maintains that everyone knows the priest is right: it will all come to an end. The farmers by the San Juan have cultivated way too much way too fast, and when military satellite images and computer screens detect that the size of the fields has exceeded a certain amount of hectarage, the planes will be dispatched. Since no one grows any food here today, there will be nothing they can do when the planes arrive, other than to grab their packed suitcases, get in their canoes, and head down the river—to Buenaventura, to join the rest of the four million displaced people in Colombia, who populate shantytowns all over the nation.

"Oooor," Graciano says, drawing the word out. Looking a bit uncertain, he strokes his well-trimmed mustache with his thumb and forefinger, while butterflies, soft as velvety pieces of cloth, circle around a banana tree. There is of course an alternative to running away, which is to take up arms and join the guerrillas. And the inhabitants of El Caraño will most likely be split 50-50 between these two options. Children, mothers, and the elderly will flee, and younger men will join the FARC. And so the gap between the state and its citizens will continue to widen, while the war will get renewed support.

Graciano rubs his hand through the bed of little green leaves and says, without specifying who he considers cocaine's primary victims— or whether he means that the guerrillas, the government, demand, the United States, prohibitions, abuse, global injustice, or the farmers' new materialistic desires are the root of the evil—that what he thinks about most today when he looks out over his glimmering crops is death.

"Death grows here. We're cultivating death."

PABLO'S PARTY
The State Gets Cancer

'There are types of military actions that others
have to carry out so that the State won't have to.'
— Carlos Castaño, founder of the AUC

VIRGINIA AND ANÍBAL were zooming along in a dune buggy, and as
the car picked up speed she understood, from the wild swill of the
glass of whisky in the driver's hand, that things were getting a bit
crazy. Virginia knew that Aníbal, the nephew of president Julio César
Turbay, was a typical Colombian madman—not afraid of anything—
but she liked thrills and long parties, and this weekend was certainly
starting to look promising.

On any other property of this size it would have been impossible
to drive at such high speed on such terrain; fences, barbed wire, gates,
walls, and other gloom and doom would be dividing up the property
to keep all the cows and bulls in place. But not here. Despite the fact
that the *hacienda* was just 100 kilometers from Medellín, it was as
if they were riding through the savannahs of Africa. The owner of
the estate, a local politician popular with the poor, was just about to
arrive, and as they drove around the 3000-hectare property, their tour
took them past elephants, giraffes, zebras, camels, hippopotamuses,
and other animals, none of which are indigenous to South America.
The property had its own helipads, a bullring, an airstrip, several
lakes, luxury villas, a dinosaur park, and a museum with some of the

most expensive vintage automobiles in the world.

She was impressed, overwhelmed. And that was the point. Virginia was the most famous television-news anchor in the country, known for her looks, and a media personality in great demand with every politician and businessman whose career was in need of positive exposure. They all wanted to be on her right side. She was from an intellectual family in Bogotá, and she already knew that Aníbal, her current boyfriend, was too fond of *perico* to be considered as a serious long-term partner, even though he was a member of the Turbay political clan. Grass could be smoked with style, but only gringos and men on the down-and-out snorted powder. Still, she was curious about and pleased by the invitation to spend a weekend at Hacienda Nápoles, a renowned place. Owned by a renowned man.

As they zigzagged between the hills, the heat from the afternoon sun only grew in intensity. The treetops aligning the rivers and brooks looked like tightly packed heads of broccoli, and each was home to a myriad of animals and fruits: sloths, monkeys, toucans; mangos, papayas, coconuts.

On a map Colombia resembles a slightly distorted star, and Virginia and Aníbal were now smack in the middle of this tropical wonderland, just north of the equator. They were in Magdalena Medio, a valley between the eastern and central *cordillera* whose communities, idyllic at first glance, would later become the settings of some of the most gruesome massacres in history, a replay of sorts of the violence characteristic of the 1950s. Rio Magdalena, a legendary mega-river in Colombia and the setting of much of the action in Gabriel García Márquez's novel *Love in the Time of Cholera*, is the dominant transport route in the area; it meanders through the entire country, from the convergence of two mountain chains in the south up to the warm Caribbean basin in the north.

A few hours on, as Virginia would later describe in her memoir, they crashed the car. But they must have had a guardian angel, for nothing serious happened. While they were getting their scrapes dressed at the estate's infirmary, a messenger came to announce that *el anfitrión*, the estate owner and their host for the weekend, had finally arrived. Not long after they had taken a seat in one of the larger formal living rooms, a short man with a broad smile and a well-kept mustache entered the room. He was only 170 centimeters, but carried himself in a way that suggested height had never been one of his problems. Virginia noticed immediately that his was the sort of body that could become quite fat over time; a prominent double chin hung over a strong yet abnormally short neck. Nevertheless, he exuded a youthful and appealing charm, along with what she perceived as an air of modest but natural authority.

"How wonderful to finally meet you!" he exclaimed. "How are your wounds? Not to worry. We'll compensate you. The important thing at Nápoles is that you're never bored. I'm terribly sorry I wasn't able to come sooner, but there were matters I had to attend to. Very pleased to meet you. I am Pablo Escobar."

IN THE EARLY 1980s, Hacienda Nápoles was the hub of Pablo Escobar's empire. In 1979 he and his cousin Gustavo Gaviria had purchased the land, a beautiful mix of dense jungle and wide-open spaces, for a reported sum of 63 million USD. They built, among other spectacular things, luxury homes, six swimming pools, several artificial lakes, and two airplane runways. The estate served as a comfortable retreat for business or pleasure, where Escobar could entertain anyone from international partners to beloved family members, close friends to acquaintances.

But the most amazing feature was the zoo, a completely illegal operation, but a venture that, interestingly, reflected the paradoxical sides of Escobar himself, specifically those vital to his career: an infallible talent for smuggling, ruthless cold-bloodedness, instinctual awareness, and an understanding of the common people, topped off by a monumental class complex.

How the vast array of exotic animals—including giraffes,

elephants, gazelles, buffalos, and lions from Africa and Asia—made it to Nápoles has been a topic of great speculation ever since the 1980s. Nonetheless, there they were. Escobar's zoo was open to the public, built with the intention of creating something special for the people whose votes he would need to make his dream come true: to obtain a seat in Congress, and perhaps even one day to become president. As he explained, "The Nápoles Zoo doesn't belong to us, but to the people of Colombia. We've built it for the enjoyment of all, young or old, rich or poor. Admission is free. Those who own the zoo shouldn't have to pay for what already belongs to them."

In September 1983, after the first congressional debate on the impact of drug money on Colombia, the exotic animals at the Nápoles Zoo were confiscated. Unfazed, Pablo happily paid the fine of 4500 USD, bought the animals back at auction, and took them home to Nápoles.

Around the same time, Escobar was also investing huge sums of money in regenerating the poorest neighborhoods of Medellín. He built about 100 soccer fields around the city, complete with lighting and other facilities so that people could make the most of their evenings. The same number of schools received a fresh coat of paint, and many churches in terrible disrepair were renovated. But his most important project politically was the one that would play the most defining role in his longevity as a hero of the working class: the building of Barrio Escobar, 400 single-family homes on the eastern slope of the city, for destitute families who were living on one of Medellín's landfills.

It was an ingenious project. Clientelism and populism are the most distinctive features of Colombian politics, but the difference between Escobar and the other politicians who bought public votes was that while the latter simply forgot about the people after gaining their support through false promises, Escobar did not. He kept his word. The day after campaigning for the proletariat vote, he was already working on fulfilling the promises he had made the day before. A few years later, delusions of grandeur would take over—like the time he would scatter dollar bills over the slums of Medellín from a plane—but in the early 1980s, his schemes were much more down-to-earth. The people adored him, and everywhere he went they chanted his name.

But greater than his philanthropic spirit was his ego. Everything he did had an ulterior motive. In 1981 an extradition treaty came into effect between the White House and the Colombian government, making drug trafficking a crime against the United States; from that point on, smugglers or suspected smugglers would be extradited and tried in the United States. Only members of Congress would be exempt. Escobar determined that if he could get into Congress, not only would he be able to escape a dreaded prison sentence in the United States, but he would also be in a better position to capitalize on his conviction that cocaine would one day be legalized and treated no differently from liquor and cigarettes. History, he felt, pointed in this direction. Or, as one of the men closest to him later said:

> Legalization was his dream. What Pablo wanted to do was to create an industrial product called "Escobar Cocaine." He used to ask me to cut out every article I could find in the American newspapers about the Hells Angels and to keep a list of various names. For, as he said, "When cocaine is legalized, those guys will be my distributors."

Yet a political career demanded that a wider audience know about his charitable contributions and good deeds. This was why media coverage, preferably television, was of the utmost importance. Escobar needed a journalist-cum-traveling-companion who could journey with him through the slums to document how he was actively working to improve the lives of the poor and acting as their savior. As he saw it, a beautiful woman was the fastest way to achieve the media attention he desired.

Two years earlier, around 1980, he had fallen in love—just like the rest of his countrymen—with a person he had seen in a television commercial for Ricchi pantyhose; as soon as he saw her he exclaimed, "I want her!" Moreover, she was also a smart and socially aware journalist hosting her own news program: Virginia Vallejo was on her way to becoming the country's most celebrated female media personality, just when he needed her. Using all his available resources, Escobar did everything within his power to make sure that she would accept his invitation to Nápoles, and after some time his men could deliver the message that she had finally taken him up on his offer. Señorita Vallejo was going to come.

IN 1982, LARGE parts of both urban and rural Colombia were under the control of various guerrilla movements battling two age-old problems: that Bogotá, the political center of the nation, was in the hands of a small, wealthy elite; and that 97 per cent of all the land and wealth was owned by just three per cent of the population. These rebel movements were made up of Marxists or Maoists of one kind or another, and they were devout admirers and supporters of the Cuban Revolution. Financially they relied on support from the Soviets, kidnappings, and stealing cattle from landed proprietors, but also on creative collaborations with small farmers located all over the nation and with the new, expanding urban proletariat.

Most loyal to Cuba was the National Liberation Army, Ejército de Liberación Nacional (ELN), a movement originating in the 1960s and based on the so-called liberation theology, an ideological cross between Marxism and Catholicism that was sweeping across Latin America during this time. The ELN's objective was, somewhat paradoxically, to solve Colombia's historical problems—poverty, corruption, concentration of landownership, and the political exclusion of the majority—through armed combat, in a way that was both Christian and communist.

Camilo Torres Restrepo, a radical and extremely popular priest known for his good looks, had joined the ELN in the 1960s but was killed early in the first battle. Nonetheless many men of the cloth, disillusioned by the landowning elite's determination to maintain injustice through violence, chose to follow in his footsteps, and for a long time the social arm of the movement was just as important as the military one. In the early 1970s the Colombian military nearly succeeded in finishing off the movement, but the ELN managed to recover after two new lucrative sources of income were discovered: kidnappings and extortion of foreign-oil companies. Its Christian roots did not prevent the movement from carrying out a vast number of fatal bombings, though its high moral standards did deter the ELN from becoming involved in the drug-production revolution, which, in the years to come, would characterize all the successful armed movements in Colombia. In terms of military strategy, this mistake would have fatal consequences; from 1990 on, the movement would begin to lose ground to other armed groups. Twenty years later, it would be a mere skeleton of its former self.

Around this time, the early 1980s, there was also the Popular Liberation Army, Ejército Popular de Liberación (EPL), originally a Maoist guerrilla group that was predominantly active in the banana-producing region of Urabá. This unusually fertile area east of the Panama border, better known as the Darién Gap, was a small yet strategically important strip of land linking North and South America.

Barely ten years later, in 1991, the EPL laid down its arms and formed a political party, the representatives of which were soon murdered in a series of historic massacres. They were attacked both by other guerrilla groups, accused of treason and of collaborating with opponents of the revolution, and by the military and its paramilitary groups, accused of still being engaged in guerrilla activities, albeit in civilian guise. In the 1990s, when Urabá became a popular route through which cocaine was smuggled out and North American arms in, locals began to find dismembered body parts in the ditches and rivers on a daily basis. In a paramilitary offensive known as Operation Genesis, designed to consolidate control over this drug corridor in the north, the area was cleansed of all guerrillas. Thousands of innocent people were murdered, and the landed proprietor, Carlos Castaño, commander of the attack, who allied himself with the generation of politicians who would rise to power in the 2000s, became to Colombia in the 1990s what Pablo Escobar was in the 1980s: the spin doctor of cocaine.

But there was one major difference: posterity held that the great Colombian cocaine boom was linked closely to the rise of the Medellín Cartel, but in truth both cultivation and production soared *after* Escobar was assassinated, when the increasingly sophisticated business was taken out of the hands of lower-class men from Medellín. In 1993, the year of Escobar's death, 40,000 hectares of coca were grown in Colombia—20 per cent of all the coca cultivated in the world—and that same year 90 tonnes of cocaine was produced in the country, or 13 per cent of the total amount produced globally. Seven years later coca was grown on 160,000 hectares in Colombia, constituting 73 per cent of all the coca cultivated in the world, and it made 640 tonnes of cocaine a year, or more than 80 per cent of the global total. This was a striking development, and a consequence of the modern drug industry's increasing reliance on the state and on status—a sordid story that Virginia Vallejo herself would later play a crucial role in unravelling.

Another actor in the revolution of the 1980s was an urban, intellectual, more liberally oriented movement called the M-19, a guerrilla group notorious for its spectacular actions. Formed on 19 April 1970, after one of the most fraudulent elections in history resulted in the conservatives coming to power once again, the M-19 was composed of academics, artists, blue-collar workers, feminists, radical members of the middle class, and Marxist military officers. By the early 1980s the group was one of the foremost guerrilla movements in Colombia. Unlike the other armed revolutionaries, who resided in the mountains and jungles, the M-19 was a distinctively urban organization that, owing to its largely unorthodox and off-the-wall tactics, attracted a great deal of media attention. On New Year's Eve

1979, in an effort to expose the military as ineffectual and at the same time show off its own strength, the M-19 set out to embarrass the military by digging a long tunnel to a secret depot and stealing 5000 weapons. Some time before this event they had made off with the sword of the country's historic liberator, Simón Bolívar, taken from a well-guarded museum to expose symbolically that the sitting government was illegitimate.

The M-19 identified with other urban guerrilla movements such as the Tupamaros in Uruguay or the Montoneros in Argentina, but the organization's image as largely harmless to democracy gradually began to crumble after a number of guerrilla cells within the group began to seek out funding by kidnapping certain individuals, including members of various mafia families. Most devastating was when they kidnapped Martha Nieves Ochoa, one of the sisters of the Ochoa mafia family—Escobar's most important ally—and demanded a ransom of more than ten million USD. Rather than give in to their demands, the drug lords formed a vigilante group called the MAS— Muerte a Secuestradores, Death to Kidnappers—which soon began decimating the M-19 by executing the rebels one by one in a series of ruthless murders. Ultimately, this unique guerrilla group was forced to sign a peace treaty with the mafia.

Not long after that, in 1985, the last remaining cells of the movement incited one of the most tragic incidents in Colombian history. In an act that shocked the nation, 35 members of the M-19 took more than 300 judges, lawyers, and jurists hostage inside the Colombian Palace of Justice, demanding that the Supreme Court justices bring incumbent president Belisario Betancur to trial for having committed what the rebels claimed was treason: acting against the people's desire for peace in a 20-year conflict. When the military found out what was going on, they descended upon the Palace of Justice and—against the hostages' explicit demands, as a compromize could have easily been reached—Betancur gave his generals the go-ahead to "handle the situation." The building, located in the heart of the capital, was stormed by tanks, artillery, and an elite force. Over 100 people were killed, including 11 Colombian Supreme Court justices; the Palace was completely destroyed; and only one of the 35 guerrilla soldiers managed to make it out alive. Moreover, a large amount of evidence and legal records were destroyed, and 11 people, who were arrested by the military after leaving the building, would later "disappear."

Since then a widely accepted theory has been that men from the Medellín Cartel, and Escobar in particular, paid the guerrillas two million USD to carry out the deed, the purpose being to destroy crucial evidence against the mafia. The movement's surviving representatives, several of whom are today successful politicians, have vehemently denied the accusation, and a great deal of controversy still lingers about whether it is true. Other facts and theories— many of which are presented in Ana Carrigan's book *El Palacio de Justicia*—suggest that several of the Supreme Court justices, some of whom were progressive human-rights advocates, were on the verge of revealing a number of incriminating cases that would prove once and for all that the military had made extensive use of torture and played a key role in several unexplained civilian massacres. These theories hold that the excessive use of violence at the Palace could only be explained by a military plan to do away with certain justices and destroy documentation housed in the Palace. Another similar theory suggests that the Betancur administration had, despite the rebels' perception, made considerable progress in peace negotiations with a number of guerrilla movements, and that a social and political settlement to this national conflict was well within reach—a compromize the oligarchy was determined to put a stop to at any cost.

An unresolved mystery to this day, the tragedy of the Palace of Justice goes down as one of the most violent episodes in Colombian history and remains a very sensitive topic. But whatever the truth is, two things are abundantly clear: first, that the building was not set on fire simply to get at the 35 guerrillas; and second, that Pablo Escobar stood to benefit greatly from the incident. Evidence against him was lost in the destruction, and the Colombian justice system, the cartel's enemy number one, was brought to its knees.

Before the Palace of Justice massacre, Escobar and his partners had initiated a campaign of intimidation and terror under the motto "better a tomb in Colombia than a prison in the United States," in order to prevent their extradition to the United States. Following the massacre, the Supreme Court justices—fearing for their lives right after being appointed to their posts—declared in a self-abasing decision that extradition was no longer an option. The official reason for their ruling was "legal technicalities." Escobar rejoiced. Many working-class individuals and leftist intellectuals supported his fight against extradition, since it fit in well with the anti-imperialist rhetoric about national sovereignty that had wide support at the time. The leading weekly, *Semana*, also lauded the decision, writing that extradition would be considered a "violation of Colombian dignity." Another newspaper called the ruling "a victory of the people." Escobar toasted to the decision and arranged a public fireworks display for the people of Medellín.

But during the 1980s, a decade replete with guerrilla movements, the ELN, EPL, and the M-19 were mere minor thorns in the government's side compared to the armed group that had actually been controlling much of the nation's territory (during some years, as much as half) since the 1960s: the Revolutionary Armed Forces of Colombia, Fuerzas Armadas Revolucionarias de Colombia (the FARC). Like other armed organizations, the FARC formally came into being in the 1960s, but has its roots in a historical time and place widely regarded as marking the birth of modern Colombia: Bogotá, 9 April 1948.

IN 1948 BOGOTÁ was one of Latin America's new intellectual metropolises, a place where people discussed literature and philosophy in the bookshops and cafés lining the beautiful city avenues. It was

a time of optimism, and the streets were aflutter with all sorts of
activity, from the universities and museums to the cathedrals and
the thriving downtown area, with its streetcars crisscrossing the city.
The increasingly politically aware population anticipated the coming
decade eagerly.

The Cuban Revolution was still ten years away, and for the younger
generation socialism was becoming a more and more attractive
alternative to what they viewed as their continent's increasingly
anachronistic realities. Many thought that perhaps some sort of
revolution was inevitable; the idea that the state would remain under
the sole control of the most backward Latin American landowning
families was not only undesirable, but also, they reasoned, unlikely.

What was particularly unique about April 1948, as described by
Mark Bowden in his book *Killing Pablo*, was that it was the month
of a historic summit. All the foreign ministers of the North and
South American countries met in the Colombian capital to form the
Organization of American States, the OAS, a United States–sponsored
pan-American collaboration project. The official objective of the
organization was to give South and Central American governments a
bigger voice, but an equally important goal was to fight communism,
a lightning-rod topic that for these few days transformed the city of
Bogotá into a hotbed of all sorts of political debates. Confrontations
broke out between institutionalized establishments and young
revolutionaries, similar to the protests that would occur 50 years later
at economic summit meetings in cities such as Seattle, Prague, Genoa,
and Gothenburg. Thousands of critics of imperialism—one of them
a 21-year-old student called Fidel Castro and another a 20-year-old
freelance writer called Gabriel García Márquez—marched on the
streets, organized protests, and held public meetings in which they
blasted the OAS as a tragic tool invented by Uncle Sam to promote
capitalism. The day before the conference a furious mob attacked
the Ecuadorian delegation; 24 hours later, newspaper headlines
sounded alarms about "terrorists" after the police arrested someone

in the process of priming a bomb; and not long after that, soldiers, members of the police force, and angry demonstrators began to flood the streets.

With all these new political tensions as a backdrop, Colombian politics had also started to change. The Liberal Party—the leftist party of the day, bolstered by urbanization and industrialization—had elected a new radical leader, who would soon go down in history as one of Latin America's most beloved: Jorge Eliécer Gaitán. For the first time Colombia had a politician who had managed to rouse the urban working classes as well as the traditionally ignored peasant population (most of whom were practically serfs). All opinion polls for the upcoming 1950 presidential election predicted victory for Gaitán, a 49-year-old attorney. During the OAS conference he happily took his place in the revolutionary drama, fervently criticizing the new organization and addressing the people in the streets. Gaitán used his great oratory talents to speak out against the Colombian landowning elite and against capitalism like no one had ever done before. The CIA, as Bowden notes, later called him "a staunch antagonist of the oligarchical rule and a spellbinding orator."

The young Castro, already self-assured, requested a meeting with Gaitán to discuss politics, the future, and the possibility of a new Latin America. Around midday on 9 April, just two hours before the scheduled meeting with Castro, Gaitán and a group of people left his office on Seventh Avenue in Bogotá, the scene where most of the day's violence would later unfold, to go to lunch. Not long after setting off they encountered a disheveled man, who let them pass but then suddenly turned around and, revolver in hand, ran right into the middle of the group and fired. He did not say a word. Gaitán quickly broke away in an attempt to seek refuge in a nearby building but failed, and soon it was too late: the new hope of the Colombian left had been shot multiple times through the head and chest. He was dead before 2.00 p.m.

The crowd that witnessed the incident lynched Juan Roa Sierra,

Gaitán's assassin, on the spot and dragged his corpse up and down the street until his limbs fell off. Theories about who else was behind the assassination weren't in short supply, and soon came to include every entity imaginable, from the CIA to hot-headed communists— who perhaps saw the postponement of an inevitable revolution had Gaitán's reformism reached the presidential palace. A theory with more credentials is that right-wing extremists from the conservative party paid Roa Sierra to carry out the deed.

Murder mysteries in Colombia are rarely solved, and the events of 9 April 1948 remain an open wound that has continued to generate sadness and anger in the soul of the country. But more than anything else, the violence lingers. During that morbid afternoon it was not only Gaitán and his assassin who died, but also all hope for a peaceful future. Since that day in the late 1940s the traumatic cycle has taken place at intervals: a new, popular politician with a social agenda suddenly rises to prominence, only to be murdered.

Gaitán's assassination ushered in the most violent decade in one of the most violent countries in the world. Dreams of happy and prosperous times ahead were dashed, and the massive rioting that ensued in Bogotá after Gaitán's death—some of the worst in recorded history—is referred to as El Bogotazo. The wave of violence that followed, as later meticulously described by Colombian writers Arturo Alape and Orlando Fals Borda, was so devastating that even those who had been involved in it were shocked. President Mariano Ospina called for military action—but when troops fired shots into the crowds rather than at individual rioters, they only made matters worse. It was not long before violence spread to other parts of the country, and soon Colombia entered into a brutal ten-year period in which more than 200,000 people were murdered, a period that soon came to be known simply as La Violencia.

Gaitán's assassination led to antagonism and fighting between interest groups across the nation, culminating in a furious war, with everyone against everyone else—the military against the peasant rebels, big corporations against labor unions, the government against the opposition, and conservative Catholics against liberal atheists. Killing became a morbid form of art, a ritual. The Catholic Church, which played a key role in the aestheticization of violence, used its authority and influence to spread the idea that liberalism was extremely dangerous, not only because it would lead to political reform but also because it would end in widespread atheism and the dissolution of social norms. Liberals were viewed as ideologically contagious, and killing became an absurd way to deal with the blasphemous plague. Children were murdered slowly in front of their parents, men's testicles were cut off and shoved into their mouths, and women were raped and killed, after which their stomachs were cut out and pulled over their heads. Such methods—soon copied by all parties—took on different connotations and became a sort of signature for various groups. One of the many grisly killing procedures entailed cutting the throat of a victim and pulling the tongue out through the opening, leaving the mutilated body with a "necktie."

It was in this environment that the two phenomena were born which would play the most decisive role in the fate of modern Colombia: Pablo Escobar and the FARC. During the Violencia era the conservatives set the military on anything that smacked of progressive liberalism or communism. Later, however, the elites in the two dominant parties, the Liberals and the Conservatives, realized that the outrage this was causing could potentially lead to a popular uprising among the nation's poor majority. Consequently, the military seized power in 1953, and in 1957 the two parties entered into a treaty, establishing the National Front. With this pact the two groups agreed to share power by alternating the presidency and allocating an even number of government mandates between them. The Front was necessary, temporarily at least, to subdue the violence, but it soon became a permanent fixture, which in practice meant that all opposition became illegal. It remained in effect until 1974—the height of the marijuana bonanza—when the parties re-instituted the democratic system in which candidates campaigned in open elections.

During these years of violence the army was also waging war against small, isolated peasant communities in Central Colombia, who were demanding social and economic reform. As time went on, the people in these peasant communities—under the guidance of men such as Pedro Antonio Marín, later known as Manuel Marulanda or Tirofijo—took up arms in an effort to defend themselves against military attacks and to declare their status as independent republics. The government, using Cold War logic and supported by the United States, responded with renewed military campaigns, which caused many of the peasants and their leaders living in the "republics" to flee the central mountains and establish new communities elsewhere, mainly in the southeast valleys close to the Amazon. Sixteen years after Gaitán's assassination, in 1964, these peasant movements evolved into the FARC. Half a century later, this guerrilla group, the oldest in Latin America, still controls vast parts of rural Colombia.

But things changed over time in regard to strength and values: if the FARC in the 1960s was a weak military movement whose political objectives garnered strong support, today the FARC is, in contrast, a military machine whose political ideas are vague and whose practices are supported by virtually no one. Over the years, the guerrillas became dependent on the Soviet Union, and when support from the Eastern Bloc began to dissipate, the FARC, a self-identified party of war, became heavily involved in just about any sort of activity that could help it to generate the resources needed, activities that included kidnapping—but, most of all, producing cocaine.

VIRGINIA VALLEJO AND Pablo Escobar became a couple in 1982, the year they met, and their relationship lasted until 1987. She helped him to further his political agenda, and in April 1983 Escobar celebrated with champagne after Colombia's leading weekly newspaper featured a story that portrayed him as "the Robin Hood of Medellín."

Vallejo was Escobar's mistress during the period in which he was transformed from a mere local politician to the most notorious terrorist in the world. And, in the beginning, she loved him. Like everyone else who fell under Escobar's spell, she enjoyed his sense of humor and his sheer wildness. (Years later, once thousands of people had been killed and all of Medellín had been besieged by the American and Colombian militaries in pursuit of "the most dangerous man in the world," Escobar's calmness and sense of humor were intact. In the very last interview before his death, when asked by Colombian journalist Germán Castro Caycedo if he thought he was "bigger" than Al Capone, he responded: "I am not very big, but if I recall correctly, Al Capone was five centimeters shorter than me.")

When he was young, Escobar and his friends used to occupy themselves by emptying Marlboros of their tobacco, refilling them with high-caliber marijuana and selling them to unsuspecting customers on the street. They would follow them around until the innocent victims succumbed to hallucinations, causing the boys to double over laughing; this was the sort of thing he found amusing.

In the 1960s, when both he and Virginia were teenagers, the country was still reeling from the aftershock of La Violencia, and the Church's hypocriscy regarding values, such as the sanctity of life, was getting more and more obvious to a new generation. One day it was morally sanctionable to kill, the next day it was the worst sin. Life, many young people concluded, seemed absurd. This quite rational rejection of rationality would later not only be integral to Nobel Prize–winning literature, but would also contribute to the fact that the very concept of reason later developed into somewhat of a national joke; people who expected or attempted to determine the outcome to anything by using logic or rationality always seemed to end up losing in Colombia.

In Medellín, the apparent absurdity of life and a seemingly wildly changeable system of values gave rise to a subculture known as Nadaismo, "nothing-ism"—the Colombian answer to the Beat generation in the United States—and to the chagrin of his God-fearing mother, Pablo became one of the movement's most active members. Nadaist doctrine was based on the books *The Right Not to Obey* by philosopher Fernando Gonzáles and *The First Manifesto of Nadaismo* by thinker Gonzalo Arango; both men were from the province of Antioquia, of which Medellín is the capital. The credo of the movement was a sort of irrationality of contrasts that vacillated wildly between pronounced atheism and profound spirituality, and in whose cultural practice the term *locura*—madness—was central. Nadaists were leftists, oppositional, and dirty, and did everything they could to shake up the establishment. But most of all, they smoked dope.

One night the year after Virginia and Pablo had met, Nadaismo by then a thing of the past, the two sat down with some men in one of the open bars in Hacienda Nápoles, where a gentle breeze offered some relief from the heat. It was a special gathering. Pablo had brought together those men who, in 1983, were Colombia's foremost mafiosi, and they were all impressed when he introduced his new companion.

"Virginia, this is Gonzalo, a loyal *compañero* who loves food and enjoys the best things life has to offer."

As Alonso Salázar relates in his biography of Escobar, in front of her sat a man who seemed to be trying to conceal his hick background by forcing his most noticeable attribute onto the group without realizing that it was having the reverse effect. Wearing a sombrero decorated with a gaping snakehead and rooster-feather tassels—with a little horseshoe stamped on the right side as a good-luck charm—he scoured the scene with an uncertain gaze and uttered some words in a strange dialect. A thick silver chain with a medallion in the shape of Christ hung around his neck, and his wrists and hands were adorned with bracelets and a ring set with a giant emerald. But what set him apart from the others most was his bad breath.

José Gonzalo Rodríguez Gacha, El Mexicano, was Escobar's ally in the construction of one of the most extensive cocaine-smuggling empires in the world. While Escobar was a diplomatic man from the city, anxious to distinguish himself as a politician with leftist sympathies, El Mexicano was a staunch right-wing conservative whose sensibility reflected his origins in rural Colombia, with its propensity for violence; he was brusque in temperament and had a reactionary distrust of all that was modern. Having no faith in the banking system of the new world, Gacha buried his money in various hiding places in Magdalena Medio. After his death, millions of dollars were discovered by the police and by cunning peasants—though most of his fortune still, to this day, lies rotting away in the vast open spaces along the Magdalena River.

In another armchair sat Gustavo Gaviria, Pablo's cousin, who Virginia already knew since the two men were as close as Siamese twins. They not only did everything together, but also did it in the same way. If Pablo bought a new house, Gustavo bought one just like it. If Gustavo's airplane landed at Nápoles, you could bet your bottom dollar that Pablo's was not far behind. If one became interested in motorsport, so did the other. And so on. Gustavo was a calm man, driven more by common sense than unadulterated passion, and much later—after the CIA, DEA, and the Colombian army had seized Medellín in pursuit of Escobar—he tried to convince his beloved cousin that the two of them should trade all the bloodshed for a life of peace and tranquility. "Pablo," he said, "we have so much money that we'll never be able to spend it. Why don't we just move to a different country?" But Escobar would not hear of it. Medellín, he felt, was his.

Also at Nápoles were the Ochoa brothers and Carlos Lehder. The former represented an entire family, an upper-class clan with a high social standing in Medellín. The Ochoa family had earned their fortune well before the coca boom by breeding and selling thoroughbreds. Lehder, a vain man who spoke fluent English and had refined taste, was the most important and eccentric character in the group. The 33-year-old was arrested in the United States in 1974 for smuggling marijuana, but released in 1976. After that,

he contributed more than anyone else to the industrialization of
the cocaine trade by creating a sophisticated logistics network from
Colombia to the United States, causing both production and income
to increase simultaneously. Before meeting Lehder, Pablo Escobar and
Gustavo Gaviria had been nothing but a couple of car thieves. The
clever half-German was the visionary of the group and had all the
necessary contacts in the United States. One day in 1978 he put down
190,000 USD in cash on the largest house on Norman Island in the
Bahamas, and the year after, he took control of the rest of the island,
on which he built a kilometer-long runway. The whole island was
transformed into a hub for refueling and repacking, where cocaine
could be transferred from one plane to another, or to a boat, which
would carry it the 120 remaining kilometers to Florida. Lehder took a
percentage on all shipments and soon became one of the richest men
in the world. His innovations led to improved cooperation between
the production, smuggling, and distribution segments of the cocaine
industry, and his organizational skills expanded the Medellín Cartel's
capacity dramatically.

The most curious thing about the young man, however, was not
his financial ambitions in relation to cocaine, but rather his political
aspirations. Like Escobar, he was also a radical, in a twisted sense, and
his hatred of the United States fueled his desire to turn cocaine into a
sort of insidious weapon against the empire of the north—one could,
he thought, undermine Uncle Sam from the inside by turning him
into pathetic drug addict, while at the same time stealing his money.

The last man to whom Virginia was introduced was Fidel Castaño,
the father of Colombian paramilitarianism—a man who, in his own
way, would factor into Colombian history as much as Escobar himself.
By 1983 Castaño had already ceased working as a drug smuggler and
had become involved with a scheme that, in comparison to Lehder's
grandiose ambitions of a global political enterprise, was actually quite
local and down-to-earth. Castaño had unusual mannerisms: he was
soft-spoken but firm, athletic but refined, wealthy but restrained. He

had no class complex with which to contend and, unlike the others, opted not to travel to Nápoles by plane or in a gold-plated Ferrari, but instead by bus or on foot. He had purchased Montecasino, an architectural wonder and the most beautiful building in Medellín, and the enormous art and wine collections he housed there were the envy of connoisseurs everywhere. What Castaño needed was not more money, but a strategy to hold on to what he had.

Every year it seemed as if a new guerrilla movement was forming, mutating, being resurrected, or expanding, and the landowning families, such as the Castaños, watched as uniformed revolutionaries either kidnapped or killed their relatives on nearly a weekly basis. In 1981 the FARC took Fidel's father, Jesús María Castaño, hostage and Fidel, the eldest son, immediately started negotiating for his safe release. The FARC demanded a ransom of ten million pesos, 200,000 USD. After it was paid, the rebels announced that the sum had been increased to 50 million pesos. After scraping together this money as well, Fidel sent it to the guerrillas via courier, after which the Castaños waited on pins and needles for their father's return. But the old man was never released. After they received the money the FARC killed Jesús María Castaño, and when Fidel found out what had happened, he made a vow both to himself and to his country that he would not rest until Colombia was completely liberated from "the pestilence that goes by the name of communism." If no one would help him, he was prepared to do it alone.

With this, a Rambo was born; in the coming years, Fidel and his younger brother Carlos would kill thousands of people—initially mainly guerrilla soldiers, but soon an ever-increasing number of civilians. The Castaño brothers came up with a two-tier strategy in which they would not concentrate on the "fish" itself, but on "draining the water from the lakes in which the fish swim"—trade unions, leftist parties, student movements, social workers, women's organizations—all entities of society in which guerrillas could be imagined to be cavorting would be eradicated. The other aspect of their strategy was based on the knowledge that this war would be extremely expensive and could only be won if enough money was raised—and they already knew that there was only one activity that could generate the funds they needed: narcotics. The armed contra war would be based on the enormous returns from drug trafficking and on the traffickers' eternal need for protection. Fidel became Pablo's military right-hand man.

Virginia only had sketchy information on all of this, and no idea of what was really going on. Despite the fact that by 1983 crack and cocaine addiction were already major problems in the United States, most people in Colombia were completely oblivious to this knowledge; using cocaine was certainly looked down on, but the notion that it could be extremely dangerous, and could destroy individuals and their families, was not widely known. With a shrug of the shoulders, average citizens and politicians alike declared that the white gold was something gringos simply seemed to want in massive quantities, and because it was apparently in such high demand, many Colombians figured that, in a way, it wasn't all that big a deal if someone opted to produce it. Another widely held belief in Colombia in the early 1980s was that cocaine was well on its way to becoming legalized, and that the recent rush was a way for those already involved in the industry to position themselves for an upcoming legitimate market. The example Escobar used to illustrate his own aspirations was the Kennedy family, who had made their fortune on liquor smuggling during the Prohibition Era, a fortune that later helped to establish them as one of America's most powerful political dynasties. The first generation criminals, the second generation presidents—that was his dream.

Most of the eccentric men around the table that evening were in their thirties, and it was impossible to imagine then that such a tight-knit fraternity would dissolve in a national bloodbath, and even more difficult to fathom how the rest of the story would play out—that all of these friends, one by one, would stab each other in the back.

ON 17 NOVEMBER 1986, Colonel Jaime Ramírez Gómez was executed in front of his family. He was a key witness in the murder trial of justice minister Rodrigo Lara Bonilla, who had been assassinated by a motorcycle-riding gunman on 30 April 1984. Exactly one month to the day after Ramirez's murder, the editor-in-chief of the newspaper *El Espectador*, Guillermo Cano Isaza, was shot dead after leaving the editorial offices in his humble car.

As Fabio Castillo establishes in his book *Riders of Cocaine*, the three men, Ramírez, Bonilla, and Cano, had three things in common. Unlike most other people at that time, they had not only decided to name and shame people such as Escobar and Gacha, but they had also dared to speak the truth: that the drug mafia was intent on buying the entire country, a goal they were well on their way to achieving. Between 1976 and 1980 total deposits made at metropolitan banks across the nation more than doubled. Several political movements founded with drug money were on their way to making it into Congress. The justice system was bought. These three had made this information public, and it was the same type of individual, a unique character, that had killed each of them. He was a sort of traveling salesman in death, a central figure in modern Colombia—*el sicario*.

When Escobar began to suspect those such as Bonilla and Cano as potential obstacles in his climb to the top, he responded with a strategy that is still practiced by his disciples in Mexico to this day: all opponents must be killed, every last one of them. But high-status victims—including politicians, journalists, police chiefs, and prosecutors—were just a mere drop of blood in the ever-growing bloodbath of Medellín in 1985, a year in which 1698 murders were committed. A year later the already shocking death toll in the city had doubled, reaching 3500. Yet another term—*el sicariato*, contract killing—made its way into the Colombian lexicon, and it was in the midst of this chaos that Escobar's minion Isaac Guttnan, one of the most sinister characters in history, founded the most effective killing machine Colombia had ever seen: a killing academy for motorcycle-gunmen in Medellín.

The demand for murder had quite simply exceeded the supply of hit men—or at least competent hit men. Boys living in the shantytowns needed the skills to commit murder flawlessly, and in order to teach them all they needed to know, Guttnan purchased an estate on which he began educating young men in the art of riding a motorcycle at top speed while firing a machine gun at a target with absolute precision. The trick was to time the two activities perfectly and to do so with confidence—to shoot at a 90-degree angle relative to the movement, the ultimate goal being to ensure that the trajectory of the bullet and the direction of travel together formed a perfect perpendicular cross. The final exam was to make a perfect hit, and the criteria by which the hit was assessed included whether the subject died immediately, as well as how fast the getaway was made. Alias Quesito—the *sicario* who killed Lara Bonilla, the murder that launched Escobar's full-scale war on the state—had attended the academy and would later say in an interview with British journalists James Mollison and Rainbow Nelson that he, like many of his fellow hit men, "was just a kid looking for money."

Most of those who fell victim to Guttnan's students, however, were other poor boys: *sicarios*, smugglers, guards, and others, who killed each other in fits of paranoia and clashes over rank and money in the dollar-driven hierarchy. The fact that cocaine was starting to boom in the United States and Europe just as developing nations were becoming increasingly urbanized was integral to the Colombian drug trade's ability to continually recruit new members, since the value of life was plummeting in overcrowded shantytowns across the nation. Eventually the lives of all policemen—not only the chiefs, but also the local officers—were at risk, and the violence reflected an even more obvious class pattern, since police officers came from the same proletarian background as the hit men. After some time the national police force had to build a number of chapels dedicated exclusively to police funerals just to keep up with demand; El Profe, one of Pablo's men, would later say that it had been a mistake to start shooting officers, since the police force "is an institution with an endless supply of manpower."

Generations of young people with *no futuro* grew up in a "live today, for tomorrow you'll be dead" culture, which was becoming a way of life in all the big cities, but most of all in Medellín, where it spawned a particular style. Certain brands of sneakers, jeans trimmed with fur, and an extreme kind of slang all became associated with that culture, but the most distinguishable feature to emerge, which is still seen in Medellín today, is a particular hairstyle: the mullet, "business in front, party in back," with a clipped head and a bushy foxtail down the neck. Twenty years after the cartel's violent heydays, once cocaine tourism had spread to the Andes, backpackers embraced the haircut; in the 2010s it is not uncommon to see Brits, Swedes, Spaniards, and gringos sitting on their laptops in espresso bars in Medellín sporting "the sicario." But, less privileged than the backpacker and scarred by history, many Colombians still get chills whenever they hear the screeching of a motorcycle over other traffic. Thousands of families residing in the shantytowns have lost at least one son or daughter to the motorcycle-gunmen. When Isaac Guttnan was himself shot down from his place in the hierarchy in 1986, his assassin, ironically, was a former student—who shot him dead in a perfect perpendicular cross, no less.

El sicariato exemplifies very well the sort of religiously coded violence that characterizes gang-related phenomena in Latin America, where "murdering" and "mothering" paradoxically go hand in hand. The fact that death—either someone else's or one's own—is always lurking around the corner is simply accepted as a fact of life. No *sicario* imagines himself living very long. And the only person a *sicario* truly loves and reveres, a sort of emblem for him, is his mother. She who gives life; the caring individual, normally deserted by the drifting father, who must be supported at all costs and must never be abandoned.

This is exactly how the relationship between Pablo and his

mother, Doña Hermilda, developed; the fact that he supported the family financially made him his mother's favorite son, and a mutual idealization ran throughout their lives. Escobar built a church in his mother's honor, and until her death in 2006 Hermilda insisted that her son's life had been nothing but a long list of good deeds sanctioned by God. The Catholic Church refused to bless her chapel, however, and in a desperate attempt to convince the religious powers that her son's altar was holy, she sent not only annual letters of prayer to every bishop in the country, but also figurines of saints. They refused to accept them, fearing they were letter bombs.

ACCORDING TO JAMES Mollison and Rainbow Nelson's *The Memory of Pablo Escobar*, by mid-1984 the Medellín Cartel controlled 80 per cent of all the cocaine consumed in the world, a figure that to this day no crime syndicate in the global drug market has come close to matching. The fundamental business concept was neither production nor distribution but control, and in order to control anything in Colombia, it is essential that the organization, whatever it happens to be, has three branches: one financial, one military, and one political.

Gacha, the Ochoa family, and Gustavo managed the finances, while the Castaño brothers, assisted by people such as Guttnan, handled the military. Lehder and Escobar—mostly the latter—tended to the political ambitions of the cartel. Virginia Vallejo had helped them to produce an image of Pablo's political career as the perfect mix of Messianic populism and nationalistic anti-imperialism, both highly marketable attributes in Latin America. But underpinning the quasi-revolutionary surface was a more fundamental political need: to engage with policy-makers at all levels to ensure the smooth running of the business. Escobar courted everyone from mayors and governors to senators and administrative managers, from directors-general to presidential candidates, and most were easy to manipulate for the right price.

By 1984 Escobar was running the city of Medellín like he was a CEO and it was his own company, while Bogotá, the center of power, was a different matter entirely. In Bogotá a number of upstanding, uncorrupted ministers, senators, editors, and colonels made it a point, much to the surprise and consternation of the cartel, not to accept bribes, and Escobar soon realized that the hallmark of his working method—*plata o plomo*, money or lead—had to be adjusted so that there would be more of the latter. Many of those who refused his bribes had already been shot, but it became increasingly apparent that much more of this sort of language would be needed.

In the beginning the cartel functioned mostly as an illegal insurance and logistics company, which Escobar used to ensure that no cocaine left Colombia without his knowledge. He took 35 per cent of the earnings on all shipments against guarantees of their arrival, but business quickly expanded, and he and his partners, encouraged by escalating profit margins, began to step up production. They created the largest cocaine laboratory the world had ever seen, located on the Yarí River along the Peruvian border, to which paste was flown in from Peru and Bolivia for industrial-scale processing. "Tranquilandia," as it was cavalierly called, was a conglomerate consisting of 14 labs, plus a barracks for 40 workers and the capacity to produce 20 tonnes of pure cocaine every month. If Nápoles was where Escobar spent money, Tranquilandia was where it was made.

But both playgrounds were about to be taken away from him. Justice minister Rodrigo Lara Bonilla not only arranged a debate on the mafia's foray into politics around the time Escobar was running for Congress, but it was also during Bonilla's ministry, in March 1984, that the police seized almost 14 tonnes of narcotics, all packed and ready for shipment, in the little cocaine jungle republic of Tranquilandia. The biggest Colombian drug bust in history was a fact. Escobar realized that Lara Bonilla was a new kind of politician with a potential entourage, and one month after the raid the justice minister was found dead.

Yet Escobar underestimated how difficult it would be to silence his opponents. On 28 July 1985—coincidentally, five days after the

murder of Tulio Castro, a judge who had signed an arrest warrant for
Escobar and Gacha—Guillermo Cano of *El Espectador* published a
scathing editorial:

> Mafia leaders begin offering money and if the bribe is rejected,
> threats are made. If threats go unacknowledged, hit men start
> executing using machine guns, pistols, and grenades. The judge who
> refuses blackmail is issued an immediate death sentence without the
> option to appeal. This is the terrifying situation our judicial system
> now finds itself in.

The following year Cano was also found dead, but his and Lara
Bonilla's murders gave Colombians something new to fear, and what
remained of Escobar's popularity—stemming primarily from the
poor and excluded inhabitants of Medellín—was starting to fade.
Fabio Castillo, an investigative reporter for *El Espectador* at the time,
exposed Escobar just as he won a seat in Congress for the Liberals, and
in this hardening climate both Escobar and Lehder went from having
high-flying visions of an ideal society funded by drugs to having to
defend themselves with every sort of violence imaginable against
increasing demands for their extradition to the United States. For the
drug barons, the ten-year span from 1983 to Escobar's death in 1993
was characterized by the fear of ending up in a US prison, and that
was reflected in the homicide rate for 1991, which reached record
proportions. That year in Medellín alone, a city with a population of
no more than 1.5 million inhabitants, 7081 people were murdered.
Seventeen years later, in 2008, Mexico, a country with a population
of 108 million, experienced a total of 6000 murders, a fact that led
the rest of the world to talk about it as a nation on the verge of total
collapse, under attack from a drug mafia. Yet in terms of drug-related
violence, Colombia is a nation that knows no equal.

By the late 1980s all but one of the people who had distinguished
themselves as Escobar's most outspoken enemies had been killed.

Luis Carlos Galán was not just the Liberal Party candidate for the 1990 presidential election whose victory had been predicted by every opinion poll in sight; he was also was a staunch defender of extradition. For Galán, who was more social democrat than liberal, the drug mafia was just the latest link in a long chain of Colombians who had become accustomed to buying their freedom from national politicians, and this was a phenomenon he despised. Escobar knew that if Galán were elected president, the entire Medellín Cartel would soon find itself sitting in North American prison cells.

FOR 17-YEAR-OLD JUAN Manuel Galán, 18 August 1989 was a Friday like any other: gray skies, school, and an upcoming weekend. He was a senior, had a new girlfriend and, when love was not on his mind, was thinking about which university he would like to attend.

At 5.00 p.m. he got a call from his father, who scolded him for visiting his girlfriend rather than coming straight home as promised. The family had special safety provisions that were not to be ignored. Juan Manuel kissed his girlfriend goodbye, went home and, three hours later, he was sitting around the television with the rest of the family: his mother, Gloria, and two brothers. On the news that evening, he and the family would watch his father deliver a campaign speech in Soacha, one of Bogotá's poorest suburbs, before an enormous crowd of supporters.

Climbing into the bed of a truck among cheering proletarians, Galán reminded many of the late Gaitán; he was also a politically passionate man and a brilliant orator who thrived among the people and despised the inherited privileges of the elite. Once again a cautious sense of optimism was in the air; Colombians were more hopeful than they had been in a long time that a new era was on the horizon—one that would prove fairer, more democratic, and less violent.

But just when it looked like a change for the better was about to happen, an all-too-familiar sound rang out on television sets all across Colombia.

While a call on the family telephone just a few minutes before the news broadcast spared the children from seeing the grisly images, the rest of the country watched their hero go down in a shower of bullets. A guard in a light-blue suit was close to his side; both were shot. As the gunfire continued, and images of chaos and screaming bystanders flashed across television screens, the bodies lay there like two motionless piles of clothes. A few minutes later Galán's bloody body was loaded into a black car and driven to the nearest hospital. Juan Manuel, Gloria, and the brothers jumped into a taxi and headed there too. But all hopes were crushed—for Galán, for his family, and for Colombia.

The assassination of Luis Carlos Galán was Pablo Escobar's most costly mistake: on 18 August 1989 all of Colombia turned its back on him, and the Medellín Cartel began its downward spiral. Virginia Vallejo had long since left him. Carlos Lehder was arrested. Escobar was now the world's most wanted terrorist. And he was desperate. As the Berlin Wall came tumbling down, the United States was called in to clean up the most turbulent corner of South America, and the only means by which the cartel could defend itself was unadulterated violence. Between 1989 and 1991 US expenditures for the global anti-drug war increased from 300 to 700 million dollars, with the lion's share going to Colombia. An unholy alliance of forces was established between the CIA, the Colombian military, the DEA, and Cali Cartel drug lords (keen on taking over the Medellín Cartel's routes and markets), and in December 1989 they were all able to toast in celebration of their first victim: Rodriguez Gacha, El Mexicano, killed in an operation on the Caribbean coast.

Gacha's downfall was largely brought about by a former ally, who had crossed over to the rival Cali Cartel and tipped off the police. This not only led to the loss of numerous lucrative routes for Escobar, but also to several paramilitary groups in Magdalena Medio, Gacha's home region, following suit and turning their backs on the drug lord to start complying with police.

Bombs went off in Bogotá and Medellín every day that fall, and the only people happy about it were the glaziers. The more pressure put on Escobar, the worse his methods became. In Bogotá, a city with a developed sense of gallows humor, old boozers sat chuckling every time an explosion went off. Each burst sent shock waves through the alleys, resulting in entire glass walls of skyscrapers falling to the ground. In September, a bomb went off in the editorial offices of *El Espectador*, blowing out an entire floor; in November, Avianca Flight 203 exploded, with 107 people losing their lives; two weeks later, on 6 December, the security-police headquarters was bombed, killing 89 employees and leaving 500 injured.

But Escobar was on the loose.

During a raid, Hacienda Nápoles estate manager Hernán Henao, one of Escobar's right-hand men, was arrested. In August 1990 the police, using new surveillance technology from the United States, were able to trace Escobar's cousin, Gustavo Gaviria, to a house in a suburb of northern Medellín from which he was running cartel operations. He was executed on the spot, and with this death Escobar's empire was sucked into an even faster downward spiral; the drug routes, essential to the cartel, lost their control officers, and the demise of the cartel was a fact. Escobar desperately tried raising taxes on the smuggling routes he had been able to retain control over, but he was increasingly turning to kidnappings and extortion. The Cali Cartel watched contentedly as the state dismantled their competition, and El Patrón slowly came to the realization that it would be impossible to win after the United States, which he now despised more than ever, had entered the war in earnest.

But despite a temporary advantage, the Colombian state was also down for the count. In the early 1990s Escobar and the state were like two heavyweights who had somehow knocked each other out at the same time: both sides were exhausted, and the referee was counting down. Virtually all of Escobar's enemies working in the government were killed; the 1990 presidential election went down in history as the bloodiest ever after four candidates were assassinated; and with 7000 murders in Medellín in 1991 alone, the government concluded that a wounded terrorist, if cornered, could actually pose more of a threat than a healthy one. No one doubted any longer Escobar's ability to do whatever it took to keep his business afloat and, especially, to avoid extradition. Negotiations for his surrender were initiated, and Latin American history was about to enter into one of its most bizarre chapters yet.

IN MAY 1991 the enormously popular priest Rafael García, serving as mediator between Escobar and the government, proclaimed on his television show *God's Minute* that Colombia had a fantastic future in store: "With Pablo's surrender the country is going to start a divine life. This country is going to be wonderful!"

The state had conceded to a number of Escobar's demands— including that he would not be extradited to the United States, as well as that he would have a "prison" of his own, overlooking Medellín— and, to the despair of many, on 19 June a police helicopter flew him up into the beautiful mountains surrounding his beloved city, where he would be detained on house arrest.

As author Mark Bowden notes, many stakeholders would have rather seen Escobar dead. The United States feared that the Colombian legal system was too incompetent to cope with such a criminal financial mastermind, and that it would not be long before Escobar, through bribery, managed to get his sentence reduced to a few short years. Politicians who had been involved in the drug trade from the beginning were terrified that he would expose them, and Cali drug barons, now happily taking over, worried about the prospect of his reviving the Medellín Cartel from behind bars.

The prison, nicknamed "La Catedral," initially a Spartan high-security institution worthy of being the "home" of one of the most internationally recognized mass murderers, would soon become one of South America's greatest embarrassments. While the police and military at first took their responsibility seriously, upholding strict security measures outside the prison, the guards on the inside were hand-selected by none other than Escobar himself. Under the augur of Father García's pious enthusiasm, Escobar succeeded in reestablishing a sense of hope and peace in the country, a feeling the media—an entity that Virginia Vallejo had tried to help him master—significantly magnified, thus allowing him to ride the crest one last time. The government was so relieved to have him under lock and key that it agreed to a whole list of concessions, the repercussions of which were not taken into full consideration at the time. The guards inside were Escobar's closest friends, manipulative drug traffickers and seasoned *sicarios*, and with all this talent for bribery and smuggling under one roof—the sort that had made it possible to illegally import giraffes and transport them to Nápoles—it was not long before all sorts of goods and services from Medellín came streaming into La Catedral. Escobar continued to garner a monthly salary of over one million USD from the routes he had managed to maintain control over, and Popeye, one of the notorious killers, who was by now more or less the housekeeper on the premises, later said that he had a monthly budget of 500,000 USD which El Patrón would regularly embellish.

Monthly bribery expenditures came to roughly 100,000 USD, but there was still a lot of money to play with. After buying off the man responsible for delivering food to the prison, as well as those who manned the six police checkpoints surrounding La Catedral, the floodgates were opened for anything Escobar's heart desired: prostitutes, preferably around the age of 15; a bar stocked with 18-year-old whisky; potent marijuana from Sierra Nevada de Santa Marta. Plus furniture, artworks, artillery, appliances, and the latest in home electronics. In just a few short months the austere building, with its drab, concrete exterior, was dripping with luxury within the confines of its walls. Escobar purchased a motorcycle for his son and a playhouse for his daughter, for use whenever the family was visiting. According to his sister Luz Marina, this was a fantastic time: "La

Catedral brought everyone together again, all the family," she said later in an interview for *The Memory of Pablo Escobar*. "There were lovely family gatherings."

By the end of his first year of imprisonment, Escobar had managed to revive his once invincible empire. He had also won back one of the classic cartel routes, La Fany, partly through a new agreement with two of his old companions, Gerardo "Kiko" Moncada and Fernando "El Negro" Galeano, both of whom were still at large. Each month, more than ten tonnes of narcotics made its way by ship from Buenaventura to Mexico, where it was transported by speedboat for the last leg of the journey, to its final destination in Los Angeles. In just one year La Fany generated 240 million USD, of which Escobar received a monthly cut of half a million. Yet this was not enough for him, so one day he lured his two companions up to La Catedral, where he had "prison guards" execute them on the spot. From a short-term perspective it was a stroke of genius; in the long term, however, it was nothing short of disaster. If the assassination of Galán was Escobar's first irreversible mistake, the assassination of Moncada and Galeano was his second-greatest blunder, and one that would bring him closer to his own grave.

By now even those closest to him were starting to regard Escobar's behavior as irrational and dangerous, and were fully aware that he could just as easily have any of them killed at any moment. From this point on, several allies began seeking refuge with former enemies. In Colombia, virtually every aspect of one's social, criminal, and political life is impacted upon by whichever armed authority one chooses to align oneself with—the guerrillas, the state, the paramilitaries, or one or another drug cartel. This implies a generalized paranoia and a state in which everyone needs permanent protection; the most dangerous situation to be in is to be "alone." Survivors of the Medellín Cartel were thus forced to seek refuge with the Cali Cartel.

As a result of the bloodbath at La Catedral, the government was beginning to suspect that the situation was getting progressively out of hand. An inspection was ordered, and the results were shocking. The report revealed that the prison was "completely lacking in security"—the stream of lawyers, drug dealers, journalists, doctors, beauty queens, and killers who wished to sell their services to Escobar was infinite. A gym, a go-cart track, and a soccer field had been built to entertain his family; several new apartments had also been built in the space created after blasting underlying rock, and it was from here that Escobar was able to run his business with state-of-the-art communications equipment. La Catedral was also replete with artillery. César Gaviria, the president of Colombia, was horrified by the images from the report, and plans for Escobar's transfer to another prison were set in motion.

But it was too late.

Early in the morning of 22 June 1992, when the military at long last received the order to enter La Catedral and collect Escobar, the greatest security risk to South America was sipping coffee with a friend in Envigado, the area of Medellín where he had spent his childhood. The soldiers killed a guard on the way into the prison, and in order to locate the cell they were convinced Escobar was hiding in, they blasted out walls and floors, and ultimately destroyed the entire building. Yet all efforts were futile, as Escobar had escaped. Or "just walked out," as President Gaviria would later admit to Mollison and Nelson: "It's incredible, the way he escaped. He just walked out. What mistakes did we make? We basically underestimated the capacity of Escobar, his capacity for corruption."

When the news of Escobar's escape got out and spread across the world, the Colombian government became a laughing-stock. All credibility was lost. And people in Medellín were laughing especially hard. They loved the way that Pablo was provoking the United States. What was paradoxical about the situation was that many people, particularly those living in Antioquia, interpreted Escobar's atrocities as the fault of the Colombian and US governments—those who had chased him down, those who wanted him extradited. On the one hand the United States was demanding all those thousands of tonnes of cocaine, but on the other it was punishing those who were simply trying to satisfy that demand.

When Escobar found out a few days later that extradition to the United States had not been on the cards—that the intent had just been to transfer him to another prison—he contacted Alberto Villamizar, a liberal politician who had been one of the mediators when Escobar turned himself in the year before, and explained that he had misunderstood the situation but was now ready to surrender. But when Villamizar reported El Patrón's "offer" to the president, the government's patience had evaporated. Escobar had disgraced the state for the last time. Gaviria just shook his head and, according to Villamizar, fired back with a curt response: "No, no, no. Not this time. We are going to kill him."

ON 31 JANUARY 1993, with Escobar still at large, an estate owned by his mother was burned to the ground. Shortly after that, two car bombs went off right in front of his cousin's house.

Then one of Escobar's properties, in which an aunt and his mother, Hermilda, had sought temporary refuge, was blown up; both women were injured but survived. Soon after, yet another of his estates went up in flames, along with his entire vintage-car collection.

In May Escobar's nephew was kidnapped, and a month later his brother-in-law Carlos Henao also met a similar fate. Two weeks after he disappeared, Henao's body was found.

All of these criminal acts were aimed at Escobar's relatives, who had not committed any crimes themselves. A violent campaign had been launched against everyone around him. The terrorist cell Los Pepes—with the slogan *"perseguidos por Pablo Escobar,"* "people persecuted by Pablo Escobar"—was formed by individuals who had fallen victim to his wrath and had now decided to do what the government apparently couldn't: kill him.

After Escobar had escaped from La Catedral, Gaviria had asked the DEA and CIA to take a more active role in tracking him down. The Pentagon deployed several planes from the US Air Force, while the Navy sent a P-3 espionage plane to supplement what the CIA and the American reconnaissance unit Centra Spike already had. The hunt for Escobar was the perfect way to test American war equipment, and in the spring of 1993 the air space over Medellín was full of all sorts of military aircraft. While this was going on, Escobar, assisted by his US-loathing sympathizers, relocated from house to house within the city's urban center. He would prove impossible to find.

Almost.

The DEA, formed in 1973, had a new head in Joe Toft, whose career was in need of a jumpstart, according to Mark Bowden. Capturing Escobar would be the perfect way to do it. By now the United States had so many units and commanders involved in Colombia that internal rivalry arose as competition ensued over who would do what and, especially, who would get the credit—the winning unit to receive a greater cut of funding in future defense budgets. Colombian law forbade foreign troops on national territory, and the Colombian military had all sorts of assistance except that which it most needed: an effective, high profile commando on the ground. It was a dilemma. Delta Force, the top-secret US Army anti-terrorist force, was what was really needed. But the law would not allow it.

Yet the constitution was not the only obstacle; there was also public opinion. The sordid history of the United States in Latin America was hardly forgotten, even if the Cold War was over, and if César Gaviria was going to have any sort of future in politics it was important that the already enormous US military presence in Colombia remain hidden from the public. Delta Force lay in wait as Gaviria mulled over what to do. Twenty-four hours passed. Then came a historic decision, which reinforced a tradition that would later become the most devastating hallmark of many Colombian institutions, manifest in all the human-rights tragedies of the coming decades: it decided that the end justifies the means.

Four days after Escobar made his escape, Delta Force touched down in Bogotá. According to *Killing Pablo*, the Colombian government and the White House concluded that the special American force was practiced enough in operating incognito that the Colombian media would never discover it. The risk for scandal, they calculated, was minimal.

In 1989 the Colombian government had created the Bloque de Busqueda, the Search Bloc, a renaissance force formed specifically with Escobar in mind. To avoid a possible scandal and accusations of an American invasion, the Bloque de Busqueda would stand on the front line, masquerading as the unit in charge. All others would assist—or at least look as though they were assisting. That way Delta Force's involvement would go completely under the radar.

Yet there was one group that was even keener on seeing Escobar dead than George H.W. Bush and César Gaviria. During the dismantling of the Medellín Cartel the Cali Cartel had calmly been lying in wait, and by now had several million dollars to gain from getting rid of Escobar once and for all. Various stakeholders suddenly began to converge, and an alliance that spanned the spectrum from the White House and the Colombian government to Cali drug barons and former partners of Escobar—by now his most sworn enemies— was built around the one objective that mattered. Although no one could have fully imagined the consequences, that year, as revealed in Natalia Morales and Santiago La Rotta's book *Los Pepes*, saw the incipience of a tumor in Colombian military life and politics: the paramilitary complex, whose metastases would spread throughout the state in the 1990s and 2000s, leading to a decade-long bloodbath whose horrors would surpass the Escobar era.

Los Pepes was led by former Escobar allies Fidel and Carlos Castaño, who had been forced to decide whether they wanted to work for or against him following the assassination of Gerardo Moncada and Fernando Galeano at La Catedral. After the FARC had murdered their father, the brothers had become impassioned anti-communists who offered their services as hit men to the military: they offered to execute the sorts of people the state wanted to do away with, but could not do on its own. The Colombian army could kill the green-clad guerrilla soldiers with no legal or moral quandary, but they couldn't kill "the water"—the peasants, trade unionists, feminists, and other potential left-wingers. In northern Colombia the Castaño brothers had built up a large private army designed specifically to combat the guerrillas, and the two of them had, for that very reason, good contacts among the members of the military, who were increasingly coming to view the guerrilla expansion as a problem much bigger than Escobar. Eight years after Escobar's death, Carlos Castaño would explain in his autobiography how he assembled "the six," a group of six politicians and generals of "the highest level," who gave him orders about which people to have executed. Carlos would submit a list of all sorts of "enemies of the state" and inquire about who to kill next, after which the six would disappear into another room and return with their choice. The Castaños carried out the deed, and Carlos, until the day he died, would insist that there were simply certain "types of military actions that others had to carry out so that the state wouldn't have to."

The murders at La Catedral made the brothers ally themselves with Escobar's opponents, and Los Pepes was an illustrative example of Castaño's theses: the Colombian and US governments needed their help. But everything had to remain top secret. They contacted Cali Cartel leader Gilberto Rodríguez Orejuela, the new national cocaine strategist, and a network of money, threats, intelligence, assassinations, extortion, drug interests, and Colombian and US military operations all started to become intertwined. The Cali Cartel offered huge sums of money in exchange for information that revealed the movements of Escobar and his men, and paid handsomely for sanctioned killings; Los Pepes offered protection to the last of Escobar's allies who wanted to switch sides.

Much later, when his career was back on track and everything had cooled down, DEA head Joe Toft spoke to the author of *The Memory of Pablo Escobar*, offering his insights into what the connection between Los Pepes, the Cali Cartel, and the Colombian government actually entailed:

> They all ran up to Cali and worked out a deal with the Cali Cartel. Cali accepted them and provided them with the intelligence that they had been collecting for a long time. In the process there was also a connection made with the government, although it is not clear how that happened. Cali went and said, "We will help you get rid of him," and the government just looked the other way.

Bloque de Busquda, the government's tool against Escobar, had conducted thousands of raids against what remained of the Medellín Cartel and its operations since the 1989 assassination of Galán; 1314 people had been arrested while 1215 firearms, 7000 kilos of dynamite, and 1.4 million USD had been confiscated. The latter figure was surprisingly low, and Escobar's men maintain that the police made off with large sums of money that they divvied among themselves. Popeye, one of the few of Escobar's men to survive, would later claim that on just one of the cartel's sites the police took over there was three million USD.

Today there are an abundance of incredible stories about how certain poor policemen got rich during these years, and it's hard to know which are true and which are myths. More certain are the accounts of all the people whose lives went up in smoke during this time. In the six months that Escobar was on the run, a total of 3479 people were killed in Medellín alone—approximately 20 a day—and the war between the Search Bloc and Los Pepes, on the one hand, and the gangs still loyal to Escobar, on the other, seemed only to intensify. For every policeman shot, large numbers of young people were killed in a series of sweeping purges, and when a human-rights commission began to investigate the wave of violence, the state was forced to come clean about the active role it had played in various massacres.

By mid 1993 Los Pepes and all the military actions were putting Escobar under more pressure than ever before. It became increasingly difficult for him to access money from his stashes and to move about freely. In February several of the men closest to him surrendered, throwing a wrench into his armed network, and what freedom he had been able to retain was further curtailed. In November he took over a house in Los Olivos, a middle-class area located behind the city's bullfighting ring, where he was happily oblivious to just how little time he had left. His mother's cousin Luzmila Gaviria and his last remaining bodyguard, known as Limón, were two of the few people who looked after him. Luzmila felt him to be in good spirits, though "changed."

Escobar was a guy from the streets, and his aim in life was to use cocaine not only as a means to become wealthy but also as a weapon to rebel. Against the United States. Against the Colombian upper class. Against the members of elite society, who gave him congratulatory pats on the back and were happy to spend time with him at the height of his popularity but who, as soon as the United States took over, turned their backs on him. Against the political class, which—unlike him, at least in his own twisted mind—had never lifted a finger to help the poor masses up out of the misery in which they lived and into homes of their own.

While Luzmila made his meals, Escobar kept mostly to himself. He read the papers, watched television, and smoked grass. When US aid to the Colombian army forced Escobar into further seclusion, he gradually began to morph into a sort of warped Che Guevara figure: he started plotting an escape to the mountains, where he would make a temporary home for himself in the jungle and recharge his batteries, after which he hoped to return to society with a vengeance, and with his own guerrilla movement: the Antioquia Rebels.

The Colombian and US governments saw the future of the nation as dependent on how the Escobar story would end and were anxious for a resolution. Meanwhile, the Cali Cartel calmly began setting the infrastructure in place that would revolutionize cocaine production in the 1990s, forging an increasingly intimate collaboration with the military. At one point a tape recording turned up in which Cali leader Gilberto Rodríguez Orejuela explained to a senator that he and the Colombian National Police had agreed to make a payment of ten million USD as soon as Escobar was captured or killed: eight million to the Search Bloc and two million to whoever provided the information essential for a successful operation.

Joe Toft was alarmed by the disclosure. What were they up to? The Pentagon, the White House, the DEA, and the CIA were all now deeply involved in an operation that was apparently infected with the same criminality they were supposed to be putting a stop to. Colombia seemed a hopeless case. Its layers of crime were infinite. A sense slowly developed among those working in various local DEA branches that the excessive concentration on Escobar was actually strengthening structures within the Colombian cocaine industry, rather than weakening them. Los Pepes continued to wreak terror everywhere and with everyone's consent, and the Escobar family watched in horror as those nearest and dearest to them began falling like flies: on 5 November Juan Herrera, a friend residing with the family, disappeared; on 8 November the family's domestic servant was murdered and the manager of one of their apartments killed; on 10 November the children's private tutor disappeared; and, according to Escobar's son, on 15 November police attempted to kidnap their chauffeur. A few years later, Carlos Castaño would boast in his autobiography, to many readers' despair:

> Everybody accepted us. The Chief Public Prosecutor, the police, the army, the Security Service, the Attorney General, and even president César Gaviria Trujillo. No one tried arresting us. Even the journalists secretly applauded our actions. Everything was just as it should be.

But for the United States at this point, there was no other way out. The coup de grâce was near, thanks to the assistance from the Cali Cartel and the tactics of Los Pepes. By the end of November this joint venture between the United States, Colombia, and the next generation of drug lords finally led them straight to Escobar's hideout; now it was a matter of striking while the iron was hot. The only dilemma was whether they should take him dead or alive. No one—absolutely no one—was in favor of the latter option, but both legal and religious law forbade anyone from being killed unnecessarily. Could they not, though, make just one exception?

ON WEDNESDAY 1 December, Escobar had a long telephone conversation with his wife and children from his house in Los Olivos. It was his 44th birthday, and they offered their best wishes. The only people by his side on this special occasion were Luzmila and Limón. Escobar—as the story goes in Luis Cañon's book *El Patrón*—celebrated with wine, cake, and marijuana.

Everything had been going according to plan, with the exception of two incidents, which his friends regarded as bad omens. The day before, a large fly, the type that tends to buzz around decaying bodies, had insisted on circling around Escobar all day; and later, after they had all sat down at the table to enjoy the birthday dinner and Luzmila had poured the wine, a glass fell to the floor but did not break. "What good luck," she exclaimed. But Limón shook his head and explained that this was actually a sign that something bad was sure to happen. Escobar, who was less superstitious, ignored their pessimism and appeared quite content as he reached for a letter from his daughter, on which she had drawn a pink heart, and proceeded to read aloud the words she had written: *Daddy, I love you and wish you happiness on your birthday. You are the heaven, the moon, and the stars to me. I adore you. Your girl.*

The next day he woke around lunchtime and had some lasagna before retiring to his room again with a cordless phone, a move that was cause for jubilation for the chief investigator at the Search Bloc. He was following it all on a monitor from a hotel room in Bogotá, and the phone call confirmed that Escobar was where they thought he was. Los Olivos was teeming with spies, snipers, surveillance vans, policemen, and neighbors who had begun taking orders from the commando. Everything was happening covertly, and all the organizations were present—the DEA, the CIA, Delta Force, Centra Spike, the Colombian police force, the military, and the security police, but most of all the elite force, which had been distilled from all available resources, the entity that would now close the deal: Bloque de Busqueda. The operation was ready to commence.

Escobar was wearing sandals and jeans rolled up over his ankles when a man in charge of one of the mobile units, Hugo Martinez, coasted down the street in a white van. They knew which block Escobar was on but were unsure of the exact house. Suddenly Martinez saw a man he recognized, but at the same time did not, standing at a second-story window holding a telephone. He had only ever seen Escobar in photos and on television, and he had always appeared well kept and clean-shaven, except for his famous mustache. This man in the window, on the other hand, had thick, curly hair and a full beard. Nevertheless, he was absolutely sure who it was. Something clicked: it was Escobar.

Hugo Martinez, together with his father—head of the Search Bloc—had been working on the case for a long time, so it was quite exciting for him to get the chance to see Escobar in person. After so many years of hard work and effort, thousands of deaths, hundreds of failed police raids, several false alarms, millions of dollars, and all the humiliation experienced by the police and military, there he stood before them. Within reach. The most wanted man in the world. The street gangster who had become one of the richest men in the world, and for almost 20 years had reigned over an entire underworld. The godfather of Medellín; Colombia's biggest living legend. He could hardly believe it. He was so close—just a shot away, in fact.

"I see him," Martinez exclaimed to his father by radio, and then he dispatched two armed men, who carefully crept their way to the front door, pressing their backs up against the outside of the house on either side when they reached it. He called for reinforcements, circled around the block, and parked in the back. Escobar's building was connected to the neighboring houses on both sides, but in the back there was a possible line of retreat over the roof of one of the bungalows. But Martinez now had backup, as Bowden reports, with all spots covered. All possible escape routes were blocked.

He gave the orders to begin.

Martín, one of the commando lieutenants, broke through the front door with a sledgehammer and barged in, accompanied by five other men. They immediately began shooting. One after the other commandoes ran up the stairs; but just as Martinez had predicted, the thugs tried to escape out the back window. Limón was the first to attempt a getaway, jumping two meters to the bungalow's roof, which would give him access to the street. He didn't make it far, though, and was shot dead just as he began to bolt.

Then came Escobar. After kicking off his sandals, he heaved his now rather corpulent body out the window and slid down the roof. Having witnessed Limón's fatal error, he stayed close to the wall, which offered temporary protection. Commando marksmen, deployed like scattered birds, sat on the neighboring rooftops, but Escobar's position made it difficult for them to find a good angle from which to shoot. They held their fire momentarily. With two revolvers in hand, Escobar slid barefoot down the roof, coming to a stop at the edge, but from there his only option was to try and make it to the other side. With his next step he suddenly found himself in the line of fire, and the shooting resumed. The first bullet went through his chest, the second through his leg, while a third entered through the left ear, exiting the other side. The drug baron fell headfirst.

Once the shooting stopped, one of the marksmen climbed up onto the roof and shouted: "It's Escobar! It's Escobar!" Crowds formed in the street, and men from all the military units on the scene craned their necks to get a look at their catch. Major Aguilar, one of the Search Bloc officers, rolled the body over to get a look at his face. With his thick beard and the curly hair sticking out from behind his ears, Escobar, despite his obesity, resembled the world-famous image of the dead Che Guevara, also killed with help from the CIA. Aguilar called Bogotá and conveyed his message as loudly as possible so that everyone who had gathered on the street could hear: "We have killed Pablo Escobar! Viva Colombia!"

MORE THAN ANYTHING else, Pablo Escobar was a product of the country. When the agrarian society, with its deep class divisions, became urbanized rapidly in the 1970s and 1980s, injustices and inequality became even more visible than before. In this social soil of religious yet poor people with no prospects, the door was wide open for all kinds of people claiming to be saviors. Escobar was one of many. A little smarter. Definitely a lot wilder. The fact that his personal and political objectives were funded by illegal activity had very little, if any, bearing for the working class, which had never seen either the state or the oligarchy respect any laws other than those of economics. To the inhabitants of Barrio Escobar the conclusion was obvious: their Pablo had been opposed and pursued not because he was a drug dealer, but because he was not an organic part of the Colombian upper class—and because he was a threat to the United States.

People liked him. At least in the beginning. The oligarchy supported him as long as he was successful, but were quick to turn their backs once things turned sour and they felt they had to protect themselves. Large parts of the working class, on the other hand, were faithful up until the very end. It made more sense for them to back an unadorned anti-hero from the hood than a member of the Bogotá elite. In Barrio Escobar today, many people living in the small single-family homes built by their savior still have his portrait hanging next to paintings of Christ, and some of the older generation, who had the chance to shake his hand, insist that he is still alive and will show up one day with the refrigerators he promised them in 1984.

But there is no doubt that Escobar was the worst perpetrator of violence to ever emerge from the global cocaine trade, and the romanticizing of him and his deeds is sometimes shockingly distasteful. Yet what's much more tragic is that Escobar's downfall actually intensified a number of existing maladies in Colombian society, and there appears to be no cure for them. It was during these years that intimate, often secret relations between the Pentagon and the Colombian military—the latter notorious for human-rights violations—were established, an alliance that soon became a force to be reckoned with, and by the 2010s would come close to triggering a major war in Latin America.

The intense focus on one individual, Escobar, instead of on the structures of society also made it possible to depict evil in an overly simplistic way, which has had devastating consequences for Colombia's political development ever since; so many different representations of violence and barbarism were projected onto him that many became blind to just how sick the state and its internal organs were in their own right. General Miguel Maza Márquez—the security police chief during the Escobar era and depicted in all historical accounts as an unwavering public servant, as well as an incorruptible hero, for having brought down Escobar—is just one of many examples. "Of everyone Escobar wanted to kill, I am the only one who is still alive today," Maza Márquez has been quoted as boasting. His words have circulated over the years and been used to reinforce the image of a black-and-white dichotomy in which good and evil are mutually exclusive in an unadulterated, almost biblical way; the Lord sentenced evil to death and allowed goodness to live on. Such was the case at least until 18 August 2009, when Colombians were shaken once again. On the 20th anniversary of the assassination of Luis Carlos Galán, the attorney-general made public the disturbing news: General

Maza Márquez, one of the national heroes of the 1990s, had been arrested and imprisoned, as mounting evidence implicated him as a participant in Galán's assassination.

Another phenomenon, for which Escobar is more directly liable, and one few other countries have experienced to the same extent, is the practice of making murder a business. The 1990s as well as the 2000s saw the emergence of a number of scandals, and when news of *falsos positivos* exploded, it only confirmed the deep structural problems. This *confusión de valores*—confusion over values—is still a greatest problem in parts of Colombian society, and its roots in poverty and an historically violent rural elite go back much further than the Escobar era. What Escobar did, however, was to propel ethical chaos to levels from which the country has never recovered. His Nadaismo, with its fierce oscillation between absolute atheism and absolute spirituality, combined with cannabis, revolutionary radicalism, and the confession/forgiveness logic of the Church, was in the beginning just an innocent part of a Wild West mentality. But when the dollars from the cocaine trade started pouring in and gradually infiltrated most institutions, the consequences of a get-rich-quick culture, dominated by arms, quickly rose to the surface, posing a threat to society.

Once the images of Escobar's body began circulating all over the world, the United States, Colombia, and even Europe assumed that the hub of the global cocaine wheel had been destroyed. This conclusion was drawn through simple but naïve logic: the Medellín Cartel controlled over 80 per cent of world production, and the collective belief was that if Escobar, the CEO, could be killed, then the entire enterprise would simply crumble. Yet this is not what happened. Other presumptive CEOs were waiting in the wings, and in terms of production, the pursuit of Escobar actually had the reverse effect. Between 1990 and 1994 presidents Bush and Clinton invested more millions of dollars than ever before on combating cocaine, but the global price during the same time fell by one-third. While the quality just got better and better. In only a year's time, between 1993 and 1994, production doubled.

Those who came out on top after the Medellín Cartel was toppled were not the state or its citizens, but Escobar's adversaries: Gilberto José Rodríguez Orejuela, the Castaño brothers, and the man who founded Los Pepes, Don Berna. From this point on, the latter would be the new leader of Medellín's crime syndicate, and he and his men would never repeat Escobar's biggest mistake—making an enemy of the state. Nor would Escobar's successors repeat his over-the-top and violent megalomania. After his murder, keeping a low profile and cooperating with the state became hallmarks of the modern cocaine industry. While the Cali Cartel, like the *marimba* kings, had always striven for peace with the political class, and in doing so had won every battle, the Medellín Cartel, which had mostly sought out war, had always lost in the end. So it was after Escobar's death: his adversaries took over all his routes and created a smuggling machinery five times as lucrative as the former drug king's empire.

Although the Escobar era left a vast number of problems in its wake, the two most devastating phenomena, which quickly started to infect politics and culture, were: for the state, the military's tendency to believe that the ends justifies the means, and for the citizens, the development of a fast-cash culture. While the defeat of Escobar didn't reduce cocaine production and consumption, it strengthened the ties between the criminal Castaño brothers and the military. Los Pepes came to rewrite Colombian history, and with the help of expanding drug revenues, Carlos, the middle brother, was able to transform the small right-wing militias into a single giant organization called Autodefensas Unidas de Colombia, the AUC: a national, albeit illegal, communist-hunting commando unit equal to the FARC in size, which by the late 1990s and early 2000s was wreaking havoc, with military approval. Over 30,000 people, mostly civilians, were killed. An entire left-wing party, Unión Patriótica, was eliminated after 3000 elected representatives were assassinated. The number of refugees, displaced from their homes during the three-way war between the AUC, the FARC, and the military, would skyrocket to four million by 2010, a number of internally displaced people surpassed only by Sudan. The military refined the Castaño brothers' "everything goes" strategy and cooperated with the AUC, which the European Union labeled a terrorist organization due to its involvement in a number of massacres.

Just as devastating as the state's merger with the successors of Los Pepes was the idea about fast and easy money, a seed planted in Colombia by the cocaine bonanza. The notion that working, saving, and planning were necessary for achieving wealth was negated by the thousands of people who had succeeded in making their fortunes by participating in one or another link in the drug chain. At the time of Escobar's death Colombia was producing 120 tonnes of cocaine a year, and ten years later it was producing 550 tonnes annually. Gustavo de Greiff, attorney-general during the hunt for Escobar and one of the key people interviewed in *The Memory of Pablo Escobar*, revealed that it was during the second cocaine wave he decided to reconsider his entire approach to the war on drugs, an evolution that eventually led him to become one of Latin America's most outspoken proponents of legalization:

> In terms of the drug business, when Escobar died, the same thing happened that had happened when Gacha died—absolutely nothing. This was one of the things that made me think about the hopelessness of the fight against drugs and prohibition. When they extradited people, when they put Escobar in prison, when they killed Gacha, when we put more than a thousand smugglers in prison, nothing happened to the drug-smuggling business. The cocaine kept arriving.

AT 6.00 A.M. on Tuesday 18 July 2006, three bulletproof vehicles dispatched by the US ambassador stopped outside Virginia Vallejo's mother's apartment in Bogotá. And Virginia was ready. The night before, security personnel from the embassy had given her strict rules to follow, including not to stand in front of or look out the window, and under no circumstances to open the door.

Still a diva, she had packed her Gucci and Vuitton suitcases full of designer-label clothes by Chanel and Armani, but knew that from that day on her life would never be the same. She would be a refugee, a lot in life which was becoming increasingly common for all kinds of people who, like her, dared to do the most dangerous thing imaginable in the country: speak out about the past.

The historic crimes committed in the 1980s—the attack on the Palace of Justice and the assassination of Galán—were still unresolved. While Escobar's involvement had been assured, the role the state and the political class had played in the bloodbath had not. And the deeper investigators and journalists delved into the case, the more convoluted things became. The military clammed up, lies were concocted, and truths went untold.

Over 20 years had passed since the Palace of Justice tragedy and Virginia's time with Escobar, and after having watched his old friends come to power one after the other, she decided that she had had enough of the hypocrisy. Álvaro Uribe—one of Escobar's early partners, according to Vallejo—had been elected president, and a third of the Congress was now made up of individuals with ties to the mafia. She thought it was time to give her side of the story. Galán's widow and sons were convinced that the head of the National Intelligence Service at the time of the assassination, General Maza Márquez, had been integral in Galán's murder, but in a recent interview with *The Miami Herald* Vallejo had maintained that the original architect of the crime was in fact Alberto Santofimio, former justice minister, senator and, on two occasions, the Liberal Party's presidential candidate.

Just 24 hours after the interview was published, the seemingly endless dark forces of Colombian society—those who had killed

Gaitán, assassinated the justices at the Palace of Justice, and killed 3000 representatives of the Unión Patriótica—had descended upon the park located directly across the street from where Virginia was staying. The investigator for the US government had discovered several suspicious men lurking around her building, and because they knew she could be killed at any moment, they decided to fly her out of the country. Neither the United States nor Colombia wanted to have yet another drug-related scandal on its hands that could be directly traced to the state apparatus. Before Vallejo had given her account against Santofimio, two other people had done the same; both were now dead.

She took her place in the caravan of vehicles and was driven to the airport. A car equipped with machine guns led the procession through the city, snaking its way in Bogotá's smoggy morning traffic. Once there, she marched right up into the DEA's specially chartered plane in her usual elegant way, in the presence of a throng of security personnel, and nine hours later, following a stopover at Guantanamo, they landed in what would be her new land of exile. Ironically, it was the very place where the now 30-year-plus modern cocaine drama had begun: Miami, Florida.

Carlos Lehder had by now already been in prison for several decades, and Norman Key—just 120 kilometers out from Miami, in the Caribbean—was in other people's hands. It was somewhat typical, even telling perhaps, that the little plane Virginia was flown in took almost the same route that so many young men of the cartel had made use of to become immensely wealthy: from central Colombia, via Sierra Nevada de Santa Marta, around Cuba, over the Bahamas, and landing in Miami.

Virginia had never taken part in any illegal activity, but she could not bring herself to despise Escobar completely, however much she wanted to. He had a double nature; her head was spinning now as she considered her adventures with him and how all of these disparate images could come together in a book. Hundreds of films, books, documentaries, and television programs had already been made about the mafia honcho she had once loved, but to her they had all been too cliché. In her mind the little man with the soothing voice, the occasionally sensitive guy who treaded a fine line between monster and hero, had never been accurately portrayed. She felt that her depiction of him would be better—a picture of both sides of the man. She also wanted to draw attention to the tumors within the Colombian state.

In October 2007 Alberto Santofimio was sentenced to 24 years in prison for instigating the assassination of Galán, with Escobar's help. To the despair of Virginia and the Galán family, the higher courts acquitted him just one year later. Some of the testimonies were not credible, according to the court. The case was still being deliberated in the early 2010s, though showing signs—like most other major political assassination cases since cocaine began to reign—that the country would end up with yet another huge scar. In Colombia it is very hard to prove things. No one is credible. And often the truth comes at much too high a price. Twenty years was not enough time to clarify much more than that the head of the National Intelligence Service had most likely been involved. Virginia was disgusted by the terrible chain of events in her country and had started to feel contempt for her homeland, although her personal story was also replete with paradoxes.

Virginia Vallejo's account of one of the most notorious criminals in the world was released by a major publishing company the year after she landed in Miami, and the title reflected the paradoxical obscurities, demonstrating that not only did Escobar, Colombia, and the never-ending cocaine drama have two sides, but also that the author might herself. At least when it came to her romance with Escobar.

The book was a bestseller, but came at the cost of the loss of her homeland. It was called *Loving Pablo, Hating Escobar*.

THE WAR ON DRUGS

From Nixon to Obama

'Everyone here is a whore to statistics. We're fighting over criminals.'
— GUSTAVO GUEVARA, GOVERNMENT PROSECUTOR

HEAVILY ARMED HELICOPTERS carrying 30 soldiers plus a prosecutor advance rapidly over Colombia's hilly green landscape. Operation Third Star has begun. Major Quiroga and his men have been allocated a Black Hawk and two Bell 212s. The aircraft are now crossing over the mountains that conceal many of the *cocinas* in the nation, though exactly how many is anyone's guess.

"That's coca," says Juan Carlos Rivera, one of the soldiers, gesturing with his gun to one of the light-green slopes, which quickly passes by below. He only wants to point it out. It is not just any poor man's cultivation plot they are looking for today, but a *cocina*, a lab where highly concentrated cocaine is produced—the final export product, known as cocaine hydrochloride (HCl).

"Worst-case scenario, there will be people at the target site who are armed and will open fire." Rivera seems somewhat concerned about how the day's mission will go, but then lowers his sunglasses and gazes out into the distance.

This is the front line of the war on drugs. Around 165 tonnes of cocaine are seized every year in Colombia, more than in any other country, and every year the narcotics squad and the DEA destroy more than 2000 labs. Today's military target—if it is found—has, like almost everything else, come to police attention by way of a well-paid tip-off, and the DEA and military intelligence have concluded that the information is probably correct. The lab was reported with coordinates provided: it is located within a radius of one kilometer from the little village of Mulatos Arriba, in the municipality of Sansón. According to the informant, the lab is quite large, with 40 employees. Guerrillas are not on site at the moment, but the outfit has its own security force of eight guards.

Operation commander Major Quiroga clears his throat. "The lab we're targeting today has people working on the premises right now. We'll be there in half an hour."

But Quiroga is overly optimistic. The whole morning was a washout, a storm keeping them from setting out at the appointed time, and it is already 2.00 p.m. By 5.00 p.m. it will start to get dark, so if the lab has not been discovered by 3.00 p.m. they will have to pack it in for the day. If that happens, not only will they have missed out on a major bust, but they will also have revealed to the lab owner that the police are on his tracks, which will simply make him pack everything and set up business elsewhere. "Today, there are labs that only operate three or four months in any one place before moving," says Quiroga. "That way, they avoid discovery and losing their investments."

Running a HCL lab is both simple and complex. Provided that there is access to coca paste and all the necessary chemicals, no more than an elementary infrastructure is needed: a filtering table, a press, a generator, and a few microwave ovens. Plus labor. The latter is easy to find, as unemployed people looking for work are everywhere, and the equipment can be purchased hassle-free from any local hardware store. The problem is logistics. Practically, a HCL lab should be close to the coast, by the Caribbean or the Pacific, to export the drugs cheaply; but the exportation of the final product is relatively simple compared to the import of chemicals. The average lab produces almost two tonnes of cocaine a month, and the only thing limiting their capacity is their ability to obtain the necessary quantities of paste and chemicals. The ratio of coca paste to the final product is almost one to one—1.2 kilograms of refined paste, *base*, is needed to make one kilogram of cocaine—whereas for the chemicals, the ratio is ten to one: in order to produce a tonne of cocaine in a month, an excellent transportation system is needed, efficient enough to bring in almost ten tonnes of chemicals each month without arousing suspicion.

"The people who run this lab," explains Quiroga, "were organized into paramilitary groups three years ago and joined the government's demobilization program, but then opted out to form new criminal groups."

Belts of machine-gun bullets lie on the helicopter's floor like writhing boa constrictors, and the pilot suddenly gets the order to circle. At a low altitude the three helicopters fly around an ordinary house on a ridge, surrounded by pastures and livestock.

"We're there," says Juan Carlos Rivera.

As the helicopters descend, a herd of cows and three horses runs off in a panic. A cloud of terror descends over the mountain as all remaining livestock flee the scene, and when the platoon lands, rotor blades rip branches and leaves from trees in a furious whirlwind. No one is around. Major Quiroga's men disperse on foot, and once the helicopters ascend again to survey the surroundings, peace is restored in the area. There is no counterattack.

"This is what usually happens," says Quiroga. "The sound of the engine scares off the workers. They just run away. The guards, too."

And so the search begins. It is 2.30 p.m. No one knows the exact location of the lab, just that it is somewhere in the vicinity. That is, if the intelligence is correct.

Inside the house there is hot food on the kitchen table, and next to the plates sits a deck of cards, which has been dealt. Toys are strewn along the foot of the stairs.

Ten minutes later, *los cambuches*, the shelters where the lowest-ranking workers sleep, are discovered. Poorly concealed blue oilcans and chemical drums, scattered in ravines across the ridge, prove that the intelligence was correct. But, increasingly bewildered and sweaty with exhaustion, anti-drug soldiers keep searching for the target, to no avail.

Time is flying. It's getting late, and there is still no lab in sight.

WHILE THE EXACT year to which the start of the war on cocaine can be traced varies depending on perspective, it is clearly associated with two very decisive years: 1989 and 2001, the fall of the Berlin Wall and 9/11.

When in 1972 Richard Nixon appointed the Shafer Commission to assess the consequences of US drug policy, the findings indicated that there was no link between cannabis and other criminality. It also concluded that alcohol was more dangerous than marijuana and that personal use of the latter ought to be decriminalized as soon as possible. Nixon, a devout Christian with a furious temper, was livid when the commission presented what he felt were "anti-American" conclusions, and he lashed out by voicing one of his many deep-rooted beliefs: "Every one of the bastards that are out for legalizing marijuana is Jewish."

After the Shafer Commission reported, the White House acted in opposition to its recommendations. Just ten years subsequent to this, the US fight against cannabis would not only launch the global war on drugs, but also, paradoxically, the cocaine industry—which, in the coming years, would itself become the primary US target.

The story is complicated and contradictory. Sometimes this proclaimed "war" has followed shifts in military threats; at times it is colored by religious paranoia; often it is rooted in genuine fear of widespread social misery. But mostly, and sometimes quite unintentionally, it is the result of political strategies that have very little to do with its expressed goal of fighting drugs.

When Bill Clinton and then Colombian president Andrés Pastrana negotiated Plan Colombia in 1998, they agreed that the fight against guerrillas and the fight against drugs were two completely different battles. The FARC, of course, had become dependent on various layers of the drug trade—as had many other aspects of society—but the historical development of the guerrillas had nothing to do with drugs; or, as Pastrana expressed it, "Colombia is fighting two totally different wars: one as a result of an attack from the drug industry on the state and the entire world, the other an attack on the guerrillas, whose principles are based on the belief that society is unjustly organized, corrupt, and only benefits the privileged."

But not long after that, during a meeting in Washington, Pastrana changed his stance and suddenly came out on the side of what would later be called the "narcotization" of the Colombian conflict—that is, the idea that drug trafficking is the only real problem hampering Colombia today. "The only peace agreement that both myself and the Colombian people are willing to accept is one that is built on strengthening our ability to eradicate the cocaine production in Colombia," he announced.

This was a dramatic shift. Before Plan Colombia, every Colombian president going back to the 1960s had been elected on promises of negotiating peace for the country, and although Pastrana had tried harder to reach a compromise with the FARC than most previous heads of state, his turnabout marked the beginning of the end of all negotiations. From this point on, all major problems in Colombian society were explained in terms of cocaine. The successive governments saw injustices, corruption, violence, impunity, and every other problem as stemming from the same source, and thus it was thought these problems could automatically be solved if only the country could do away with narcotics.

After the attack on the World Trade Center on 11 September 2001, the FARC and the ELN were branded as terrorist organizations; and with George W. Bush now in the White House, not only were Colombia's two domestic wars united, but the war on drugs was also made synonymous with the US war on terror. Washington's official policy under Clinton had focused on the fight against the Colombian "narco democracy," but under Bush this morphed into a fight against Colombian "narco terrorism." Clinton's policy had mostly concentrated on what had transpired in the aftermath of Pablo Escobar's assassination—how the cartels had cosied up to politicians and the military, a process that culminated in the revelation that the Colombian president from 1994 to 1998, Ernesto Samper, had accepted campaign funding from the Cali Cartel. From 2001 on, the policy line disregarded that side of the problem and focused exclusively on the guerrillas.

For the new president of the country, the right-wing populist Álvaro Uribe, the war on terror was a gift from the gods. He came to power in 2002, with the promise not to negotiate with the guerrillas but to crush them with military force, and to do this he needed money. It was thought that both drugs and terror could be eliminated by doing away with the incarnation of these two evils: the FARC.

Plan Colombia became the military and judicial framework for this operation. On the geopolitical map, Colombia was looking more and more like Afghanistan all the time. Money was pouring in from Washington, where an increasing number of Colombian domestic policies were being decided, and the nation's armed forces were growing so fast that it would soon be the greatest military power in Latin America, and the world's third-largest recipient of US military support (after Israel and Egypt). The FARC, whose practices are now rejected by nearly all Colombians but whose original demands were supported by most, had been effectively debunked as a guerrilla movement. By the mid 2000s they were being presented to the rest of the world as something even worse than a terrorist organization: from this point on, the Colombian government, the United States, and much of the European Union would regard them as nothing short of a drug mafia.

Uribe's strategy, the process of acquiring money under the banner of fighting drugs and using it in anti-guerrilla warfare, had a number of consequences with which Colombia continues to struggle—or in which it takes delight, depending on the perspective. These new resources during the first decade of the 2000s enabled the government to go after guerrilla strongholds more effectively, and not only did they succeed in freeing some of those who had been kidnapped by the FARC—one of the most famous being the French-Colombian politician Ingrid Betancourt—and assassinating a number of feared guerrilla leaders, but they also succeeded in regaining power in many parts of the country previously under rebel control (a prime example was Putumayo). By the early 2010s the FARC was politically unfocused and militarily weaker throughout the country than it had been for a long time. Today the FARC may have—though statistics vary—only 10,000 soldiers left in the ranks.

During the first decade of the new millennium, many of the paramilitaries—the illegal death squads in the anti-guerrilla war, formed under the leadership of Fidel and Carlos Castaño—were also demobilized. This controversial program, which ran from 2004 to 2006, was criticized: not only because it allowed mass murderers, responsible for the deaths of thousands, to go free after serving just seven years in prison if they cooperated with the courts, but also because it ignored the pervasive social problems, which were the primary driving force behind the war. The program appealed to many of the destitute and the young homeless masses in rural areas, as it offered them education, financial support, and housing assistance. Consequently, thousands of teenagers who had never joined any armed group started to collect old weapons and head to the registration offices to enroll. By the time the program ended, over 30,000 people had "demobilized" themselves; that was twice the number of paramilitaries there had been when the program started. And many of the "real" soldiers simply turned over their weapons, gratefully accepted financial support, and promised to begin pursuing normal, everyday civilian lives, only to go back on their word and to join one of the many new criminal groups that were established in the wake of the demobilization program.

The strange thing was that, despite the successful fight against the guerrillas and the demobilization of the paramilitaries, the cocaine industry carried on as usual. Although the FARC—the group that, according to the Colombian and US governments, was nothing but a drug-dealing organization—was now half its original size, drug trafficking continued. Moreover, even though the AUC, 70 per cent of whose funding stemmed from drug activity, no longer existed, global demand was still being satisfied. A remark by a frustrated Alfredo Rangel, co-editor of the book *Narcotráfico en Colombia*, sums up this development: "This plague has a very unique quality: it is one that is constantly mutating, and not only does it persevere after every attempt to eliminate it, but comes back even stronger as a result of each and every strategy used to combat it."

Plan Colombia had thus borne fruit in a number of ways, but not in any of the ways for which it was intended. Although the AUC had been dismantled—in the sense that the organization no longer fought in standardized units throughout the country, and that its leaders had been imprisoned—in reality the criminal syndicate had only abandoned its political project, not its financial one. The paramilitaries no longer existed as an anti-guerrilla army, but they continued to live on as a drug-trafficking network. In some ways this was also true of the guerrillas, though in reverse: the FARC had been severely crippled as a guerrilla or terrorist organization, but its role as protector of the farmers, transportation routes, and laboratories remained intact in many areas, or was taken over by the mutating powers of the paramilitaries.

It was in many ways a stroke of genius on the state's part to forge attacks on guerrillas under the guise of fighting drugs. Outside remote areas, support for the FARC is now practically non-existent. After the kidnappings of strategic individuals from the oligarchy, as well as, in the early 2000s, many others, loathing for the politically misguided rebels spread throughout the land, a hatred that persisted among all social classes. The fact that Álvaro Uribe had started out in the circles of Pablo Escobar's mafia—and that he was personally responsible for the growth of the paramilitary element—was of little importance to Colombians, as long as he kept the FARC in check. No one cared about drugs; all that mattered was the FARC. Uribe's policies had resulted in a reduction of the number of kidnappings and various other crimes, and by the end of the decade—when command of his Uribismo, a sort of right-wing version of Argentina's Peronismo, was handed over to his defense minister and protégé, Juan Manuel Santos—he was the most popular president the country had ever had.

Popularity went to Uribe's head, and in 2008 the war on drugs went international in a way that turned the entire region into a ticking time bomb. With US support, the Colombian military initiated full-scale bombing of one of the guerrilla camps—in Ecuador. A diplomatic crisis ensued. At least 20 people were killed; Ecuador's sovereignty was compromised; and the Brazilian foreign minister proclaimed that Colombia had, by taking military action within other nations, "put the countries of South America in a situation in which the security of the entire region is in jeopardy." Most of the world condemned the attack, but the United States, under George W. Bush, stood up for Colombia's right to defend itself against "drug terrorism."

Under mounting pressure, Uribe apologized, but it was too late. The political paranoia associated with the war on drugs was so great that the nightmares of the bordering countries appeared to be coming true. Colombia, the only lasting trouble spot in South America, had started to infect its neighbors; the guerrillas were spreading, the coca was spreading, and even the contra war was now spreading to the surrounding regions. In December 2009 Venezuelan president Hugo Chávez recommended to the United Nations that it send troops to Colombia, because Caracas regarded the domestic unrest in its neighbor as "a serious threat to international peace and security."

Colombia took the opposite stance. Although the attack within

Ecuador had admittedly been a mistake, the Colombian government, surrounded by politically hostile neighbors, was feeling more and more like Israel every day: alone, vulnerable, and misunderstood— but militarily superior, and with the United States on their side. The fact that the FARC had camps along the other side of the southern border was seen as proof that the socialist government in Ecuador was actually supporting the Colombian guerrillas in its war on the state, and the fact that guerrilla fighters moved around Venezuela easily supported Uribe's conviction that Hugo Chávez was more than just an ideological brother of the jungle communists. The FARC leaders, exhausted from repeated defeats, were pleased with this escalating tension, convinced that nothing would be better for their historic struggle for revolution than a full-scale war between Venezuela and Colombia. They set aside their rivalry with the ELN, a competing guerrilla group, and in January 2010 the two rebel movements announced that they had formed an alliance with "Latin America's other left-wing forces" to combat the threat that they still, to this day, regard as an overarching problem: US military expansion on their continent (now being deceptively administered by a smart black president with support from virtually the entire Western world).

The Colombian right, which, in the early 2000s, had consolidated its power, now looked on with apprehension as troops guided by Marxism made moves on both sides of the border. The political climate that was thought to have brought about a historic victory for Colombia during the first decade of the new millennium—leading to less violence, fewer kidnappings, stronger institutions, and an improved investment climate—was again under threat. The war on drugs had, in the view of the right, saved the country. The alliance between Bogotá and Washington was absolutely essential to Álvaro Uribe's political career, and the only way to motivate the United States to maintain its presence was drugs. A war with Venezuela, the government feared, would make the FARC immediately send all of its remaining troops to serve on Chávez's side, and Colombian democracy would be attacked at the same time both from within and without, with such brutal force that all the US resources in the world would not be able to stop it.

All sides now depended on cocaine, in rhetoric and in politics. The Colombian right wing believed that if the United States did not continue to provide military aid for the nation's war on drugs, Colombia would be attacked by Venezuela, the FARC, and Ecuador, and be dragged into the Bolivarian Revolution. On the other hand, if the United States were to change the course of its anti-drug policy, opting to pull its military support out of South America, Hugo Chávez would have lost his strongest rhetorical weapon—that is, the idea that "the empire" was increasingly closing in each day, and could intervene against his revolutionary nation at any time. The same forces were at work in Bolivia, where the president, Evo Morales, a coca-cultivator-cum-politician, had based his entire career on opposition to the US war on drugs, and he took the DEA accusation that Morales' government had been involved in drug trafficking as a simple confirmation that he had always been right: Washington would never, not even under Obama, allow a social and economic uprising in Latin America.

Colombia's activation of six flight battalions, the construction of a new military facility along the Venezuelan border, and an offer to let the United States use the nation's military bases—all of this decided in the early 2010s—was the ultimate proof for the new and emerging revolutionaries in Latin America. Álvaro Uribe and Juan Manuel Santos attempted to counter their growing unpopularity in parts of the region by asserting that the only thing they intended to fight was drugs, and Washington agreed. The problem was that, ten years after Plan Colombia had been put into effect, cocaine was no longer just a drug. It was everything.

THE WAR ON drugs was formed not only by regional turmoil, but also by major geopolitical changes. Following the collapse of the

Berlin Wall, the FARC lost all financial and ideological support from the Soviet Union, after which taxes from cocaine trafficking and kidnapping became its primary sources of income. Meanwhile, in the United States drugs replaced communism as a threat to the West, and just one year into the first round of Plan Colombia, 9/11 took place.

In the beginning—when Richard Nixon coined the term the "war on drugs"—the policy was also a reaction to revolutionary political trends of the hedonistic 1960s, which Republicans feared posed a fundamental threat to family values in the United States and other parts of the world. Debates about abortion, homosexuality, euthanasia, drugs, and a number of other issues pertaining to bodily autonomy were beating down all political doors and rocking the very foundation of American Christianity. Moreover, Nancy Reagan's "Just Say No" campaign in the early 1980s proved completely ineffectual, not only against the propagation of crack among the poor, but also against cocaine use among the more affluent. In the 1970s 16 million USD were invested annually in the fight against drugs, a number that 35 years later—after George W. Bush had given his support to Plan Colombia—had grown to 18 billion USD per annum. Today the United States has spent a total of 500 billion USD on what Dick Cheney, a key strategist for the war on terror, in 1989 already viewed as a geopolitical matter and called "a high-priority national mission."

Until George H. W. Bush took office, the White House's formal strategy had always been to stop the entry of drugs into the United States at its southern borders, but as the Berlin Wall came down, a number of events coincided, causing sweeping changes throughout the entire narcotics complex. In Colombia, Pablo Escobar and his men not only assassinated Rodrigo Lara Bonilla and Luis Carlos Galán; they also caused the explosion of Avianca Flight 203, in which two American citizens were among the 107 people killed. Just a year before that, a bomb had brought down Pan Am Flight 103 over Lockerbie, Scotland, resulting in the death of all 259 passengers, and as international air travel was perceived as an integral part of the free

Western lifestyle, demand grew to punish those who had attacked an open and vulnerable system in cold blood. Three years earlier, in 1986, Ronald Reagan had declared that drugs were "a threat to US national security," and this defense-oriented definition would soon be vital to the military expansion of the war on drugs.

After the collapse of the Soviet Union, the imminent threat of drug-funded criminality somehow gave the disoriented US military new relevance. Above all, the intelligence units, which had lost a clear mission, were reorganized. When Escobar's attacks, a domestic cocaine epidemic, and the fall of communism all coincided in the one year, Cheney was not alone in formulating a possible future direction for the military: "narcoterrorism," at the time a completely new concept, turned into the impending threat to the West.

Escobar became the bin Laden of the era. Between 1989 and 1991, US military spending on international anti-drug operations more than doubled, and virtually all of this funding went to Colombia; in the eyes of Washington, the bombing of Avianca Flight 203 had transformed the Medellín Cartel into a direct threat to US citizens, which in turn turned its drug lords into legitimate military targets. Until 1991 Executive Order 12333, an initiative to curb human-rights violations by the CIA, had limited the United States' right to kill citizens of other nations outside of the States, but not long after George Bush senior took office, the order was amended to ensure that such actions could be carried out if US national security was felt to be under threat. The fact that cocaine was spreading like wildfire among America's youth, along with the frustration that there were now apparently individuals who could be blamed for the suffering, was instrumental in the government's decision to rouse public opinion in favor of legislative change, giving the United States the green light to attack individuals in other countries with or without the consent of that state.

If 1989 was the year drugs surpassed communism as the ultimate threat to the West, 9/11 would—indirectly—play an even greater role in the evolution of the anti-narcotics war, particularly in Colombia.

The war on drugs was a legal and geopolitical precursor to the war on terror, and the rhetorically effective term "war" has been crucial to both. The word promises a temporary state that will eventually end, a psychologically potent pledge that in both cases has been central to mobilizing resources and galvanizing public support. But it is, critics argue, a highly misleading concept, because while both these of "wars" can be fought, neither can ever truly be won. The war on drugs prompted the United States to increase its military and judicial authority in order to take military action in other nations over threats to "national security," while the war on terror made it possible for Washington to drastically extend these actions, though this time in reference to the right to defend the nation against global terrorism. In neither case has the "the war" been won or even ended, though in both instances it has led to significant changes in global power relations—such as the United States' takeover in a number of weaker states, as they become the de facto government.

In Colombia, the combination of 9/11 and the ongoing war on drugs led to the perception that the nation's century-long internal conflict could only be solved by the military. Until 2001 the White House, much of Colombia's political elite, the European Union, and the majority of ordinary Colombians were of the opinion that one of the longest civil wars in the world could only be solved politically—through a dialogue, in which negotiations between the government and the guerrillas would lead to a peace accord whereby the guerrillas would surrender arms in exchange for basic social and political reforms. The introductory negotiations for Plan Colombia, which the European Union played a central role in, simply outlined how such a peace process could be strengthened and improved. But then came the change in the world order following 9/11, and the war on terror was born. The role of the European Union became marginal. The Colombian mafia was able to gain congressional seats, while the US and Colombian militaries fought against terrorism with the new conviction that guerrilla war, drug trafficking, and terror were synonymous. Most of the massive sums built into the military budgets earmarked for "fighting drugs" went exclusively to funding military attacks on the FARC, and by 2010 the world was faced with a dismal situation that surprised some more than others: the Colombian guerrillas were decimated, the concentration of landownership in the country increased dramatically—and the number of tonnes of cocaine transported from the Andes to the United States and Europe remained unchanged.

THE PLATOON TROOPS let out a sudden exclamation. Helicopters circle in the sky like venomous flies, keeping a lookout for potential enemy units. The hastily abandoned house is located on a small ledge in a beautiful valley, where white waterfalls tumble between cliffs and terracotta-colored roads wind through the green hills. Now all of the soldiers, except the ones on guard, rush out with crackling walkie-talkies, down to the little ledge overlooking the ravine. "Here, here! We've found it!"

Juan Carlos Rivera stands up and gasps. "Check out these hoses." He catches his breath. "And the buckets there." He points to a pile of sacks hidden in the bushes. Then to a stack of white plastic buckets a bit further back. It is 30 degrees Celsius, and beads of sweat from the inside of his helmet stream down his cheeks.

The soothing buzz of the helicopters from above adds to the good feeling. An armed attack is no longer on the cards. The area is secured and everyone who works in the lab has fled the scene.

Major Quiroga arrives, along with Colonel Correa and the rest of the men.

"Here are 12 55-kilogram bags of active charcoal," says Rivera. "There are three 25-kilogram bags of caustic soda. And these buckets are full of sulfuric acid and acetone."

But what is interesting here is not the bags or buckets, but the three thick rubber hoses tied around a few trees and aimed down into what appears to be a never-ending ravine.

"The lab's down there, camouflaged in the jungle," Rivera says with absolute certainty, even though he has not seen a trace of the building. "The liquid chemicals are stored here and then pumped down. That way nothing has to be carried. Now all we have to do to find the lab is to follow the hoses."

It is 3.00 p.m. The hoses are such a sure indication of the presence of a lab that Major Quiroga at once gives the order to complete the operation. The soldiers exhale. They will be rewarded in one way or another. Today's war on drugs is completely controlled by statistics: the number of blown-up labs, sprayed hectares, seized kilos, or dead guerrillas. The soldiers are rewarded with wages, promotions, vacations, and benefits, depending on how well they fulfill various quotas. This piecework system has made quantity more important than quality, a situation that has—according to certain critics—not only generated *falsos positivos*, but also led to a number of other systemic failures in the fight.

IN *COCAINE POLITICS*, Peter Dale Scott and Jonathan Marshall suggest that the global cocaine trade has increased since the 1980s not in spite of, but *thanks to*, the US war on drugs. The authors argue that because actual drug traffic is subordinated to other strategic interests, the consequence is often that the CIA and the DEA are more than willing to cooperate with the drug-funded anti-guerrilla networks that have been essential to the opening up and running of various routes from the Andes to the United States and Europe: "In country after country, from Mexico and Honduras to Panama and Peru, the CIA helped set up or consolidate intelligence agencies that became forces of repression, and whose intelligence connections to other countries greased the way for illicit drug shipments."

As to what the legal obscurity that arises when US and Latin American militaries enter in an alliance with strategic paramilitaries to catch a bigger fish—whether it is an Escobar or a FARC leader—actually means to the global drug trade is hard to say. Not surprisingly,

CIA involvement in drug trafficking has led to a number of wild, often leftist, conspiracy theories, put forward by people who routinely hold the United States responsible for all of the misery on the planet, but there are also a number of scholars more seriously devoted to the issue. Adriana Rossi, a prominent investigator of Latin American drug-trafficking, is one of those who argues that there is clear evidence that the United States has either facilitated or been directly involved in trafficking on a number of occasions throughout the 2000s. However, the image that the CIA and the DEA present of themselves today is of organizations that have been purged of corruption, the drug scandals among their ranks history. Following a debate in Colombia about whether the Colombian anti-narcotics police had any genuine interest in putting a stop to the flow of cocaine, Jay Bergman, Andean regional director for the DEA and one of the world's top anti-narcotics officers, stated that such suspicions are myths created by people who don't understand the realities surrounding the war on drugs: "Let me be clear. If you have been doing operations with the anti-narcotic police here for a while, then you have seen so many police officers being killed, that have no legs because they walked into landmines, have been blown up in attacks, or have lost colleagues in combat, that it becomes obvious that that's just a myth. I have been to more funerals and I have had more tears in my eyes in this country than anywhere else. Trust me, there is not a police officer in this country that doesn't want to see an end to this."

The same month in which Bergman made these comments, the Colombian government was forced to fire 25 police officers, including their commander, in Bahía Solano, a village on the Pacific coast. One day they were working against the trafficking, the next day with the traffickers. But this was nothing new, and not at all unique for Colombia. Interaction between the mafia and the police has a long history in Latin America, and in November 2008 it was revealed that Noé Ramírez, one of the highest-ranking Mexican police chiefs, had accepted 450,000 USD a month from the cocaine clan Beltrán Leyva, and that both the head of Interpol in Mexico and the head of a special organized crime unit, as well as four other police officers, had been on the cartel's payroll.

The authorities' schizophrenic relationship with the war on drugs, and with drug trafficking itself, plays a key role in Adriana Rossi's theories about the paradox in which governments whose militaries have been funded by anti-drug money often become better drug exporters than they were before they had the financial means. Colombia is just one example. Its experiences may, some fear, be repeated in the West African states that are now being infiltrated by new and old cocaine-smuggling networks, who are in the pursuit of new routes to Europe; states whose police forces are benefiting from substantial foreign military aid.

Everything is a result of the corrupting influence of drug trafficking and the mafia's demand for good infrastructure. When Don Mario, an anti-communist warlord and one of Colombia's biggest drug barons, was arrested in April 2009, the government was forced to replace the police officers along the coast, all the way up to Panama. All were, or were assumed to be, links in the drug king's efficient transport chain. Just like the police officers in Bahía Solano, drug smugglers were disguised as anti-drug soldiers, and were superbly equipped in both roles. After they had been replaced a new cycle of corruption began, and a couple of years later, Don Mario's successors had bought so much loyalty that it was time for a new raid. And so, according to the critics, it continues: more corruption, more military, more trafficking.

A 2001 report by Human Rights Watch gave a detailed account of the dynamics at work between the military and the mafia in cocaine production in Putumayo. Payment to the officers rose according to rank. A lieutenant received 1500 USD a month and a captain up to 3000 USD, while the colonels received their dollar transfers via intermediaries so that if the system was discovered, they would not be directly responsible. Or, in the words of Scott and Marshall: "Aiding foreign military and intelligence forces in the name of fighting the war on drugs risks empowering the very forces responsible for protecting organized criminal syndicates."

This is exactly what happened to one of Colombia's biggest drug lords, Pedro Oliverio Guerrero, alias Cuchillo, who controlled large regions in the eastern plains. When the DEA and the narcotics police launched a major operation in 2008 to arrest him, they failed, for reasons that gave rise to a number of concerns about how armed forces with funding from the war on drugs actually operate. Like many of the nation's most successful Mafiosi, Cuchillo was a former officer in the Colombian army. In 2007, in his ambitions to take control from the law-enforcement authorities and to eliminate the guerrillas in the area, he doubled his own private army—the paramilitary group Ejército Revolucionario Popular Anticomunista Colombiano (ERPAC), Colombia's Anti-communist Army of the People—to 2000 soldiers and successfully made the government's regional soldiers work for him. When the DEA-led operation was launched, Cuchillo was nearly killed in a shootout, but because so many of the members of the army in the area were now on his payroll, the drug king eventually managed to elude the special commando. Moreover, when an investigation later explained how and why the operation had failed, despite all its resources and meticulous intelligence, a familiar yet revealing trend became known: a large amount of the arms seized from the ERPAC had come from the army, and Cuchillo's five closest guards, who died in combat, had all been former soldiers and officers. But most disturbing for those arguing that the army was "clean" was a satellite-phone conversation that the operation commando eavesdropped upon three hours after the shooting. An indignant Cuchillo was heard asking someone in the army: "How in the hell could three Black Hawks get in here without anyone informing me?"

IN BUENAVENTURA—FAR FROM Cuchillo's arid plains—the Coast Guard searches among the city's poor canoe-borne folk, and Captain Edwaer Picón and his men will soon, they hope, find a big amount of pure cocaine, perhaps tonnes. Gasoline vapors from all sorts of boat traffic mix in the warm coastal winds as the military boats pass through the entrance to the harbor and take aim at one of the hundreds of creaky wooden piers surrounding the downtown area.

"The negro is the problem. Crazy by nature." Captain Picón blocks the sun with his right hand and gazes out at the city.

This is the most cocaine-dense area in the world. Of the almost 500 tonnes of cocaine Colombia exports annually, a quarter passes through Buenaventura, an over-populated urban island. A month ago, almost 3.5 tonnes were seized in the commercial harbor. Alongside the concrete pier belonging to the Coast Guard is a turquoise *volador*—a boat with four 250-horsepower engines—that was confiscated two weeks ago with almost two tonnes on board. On a nearby litter-strewn beach is a steel-hulled vessel, which was recently seized with 160 kilos onboard. In the course of a year, between 15 and 20 tonnes of cocaine are confiscated in the district of Buenaventura—perhaps a tenth of everything that goes through—but as to exactly how many thousands of kilos are hidden here among the other traffic on any given day, it's anyone's guess. Maybe three. Thirteen. Or 30. No one knows.

"Just look at them," says Picón, squinting and pointing at all the hustle and bustle around the piers.

The city, circular in shape and linked to the mainland by a 200-meter bridge, is divided into three sections. In the north is the main port, whose thousands of different-colored containers resemble a huge mosaic laid out over parking spaces and cargo ships in the gated area. In the middle is the commercial district, with its damp-damaged concrete buildings. In the south is "the problem"—the African-Colombians and their ramshackle housing, a chaotic maze of traditional, rudimentary wooden houses on rickety posts that manage to treacherously obscure the boundary between land and sea. In reality, large parts of the city are built right on the water. It has expanded—like a spontaneously swelling social and economic amoeba—because the armed conflict has meant a population migration from rural to urban areas.

On the surface *los esteros*, as these poorer areas are called, look like total anarchy: a jumble of shantytowns with too many inhabitants stuffed into spaces far too small. Yet beyond that first impression of chaos lies a sophisticated community completely and rationally organized by the marginalized masses of the new urban proletariat. Despite all the city's bloodshed—this is the most violent part of the country, one of the most violent places in the world—almost everything happens against a backdrop of levity. Happily playing children. Open doors. Laughter. Beautifully decorated homes. Gossiping neighbors.

Every once in a while men loosen their canoes from the posts that support their houses, and as they paddle out into the bay they look like black specks against the slowly moving walls of red, green, yellow, black or blue container vessels. "They may give the impression of poor fishermen," says Picón. "But in reality they're often informants, who'll start texting from the moment we arrive."

The Coast Guard is white, Buenaventurans black. The former are here temporarily, stay in hotels, operate big military boats, and spend time and money at brothels in the city at night. The latter are here for good, live in shantytowns, paddle canoes, and sell their nightly services to those visiting the city's brothels. The gap between people of European and African descent is nowhere more pronounced than on the Colombian cocaine coast—the entire region along the Pacific Rim—and it is here that the war on drugs has also been gradually transformed into a war between cultures, in which a particular life-style has come to be viewed as a symbol of the nation's drug industry and become subject to eradication. The war on drugs is no longer a fight against the flow of cocaine, but a fight for what is usually called progress, modernization. It is large scale against small scale. Shopping center against fishing family. Square concrete buildings against scattered wooden structures. Cars against canoes. Industry against craftsmanship. The government claims that all they are doing is fighting poverty, but many inhabitants argue that what the state is actually fighting is them. Their lifestyle. And the guerrillas, always ready to exploit the tension between people and state, are lying in wait.

"Over there," says Picón to one of his men. "Steer over there."

THE HISTORY OF those who have suffered the most at the hands of the global cocaine industry is as old as the boom itself. As the country's largest port, ever since the 1980s Buenaventura has been seen as an attractive area, over which many have vied for control. It was from here that those taking La Fany, the classic route of the Medellín Cartel, departed for Mexico with almost ten tonnes of cocaine a month; it was here that the FARC took over when they became reliant on the drug trade in the 1990s; and it was here that civilians were killed by the thousands when the state regained control in the 2000s, with the help of the paramilitary death squads.

The flow of cocaine has continued to grow irrespective of which armed group has been in control, and since the early 2010s an ever-increasing importance has been placed on the aesthetic aspects of the war on drugs. Like every other place in Latin America in which the drug industry has gained a foothold, the government has ignored the Colombian coast along the Pacific for as long as Colombia has existed as a nation. The commercial port in the city from which 40 per cent of the nation's exports are shipped has been the central power's only object of interest, while the Afro-Colombian inhabitants next to it have been left to fend for themselves to the best of their ability, without state support. This has resulted in a peculiar, but in many ways functional, settlement along the southern part of the island; as the number of poor though picturesque pole houses has increased, so has the amount of trash, gravel, and other debris in the water beneath them. This has caused the island to expand in an organic way, a process that has been uncomplicated for two reasons: because the sea and small-scale fishing have been the only reliable means of livelihood, and because, since the water belongs to everyone, there is never a need for anyone to purchase land they cannot afford. Over time, the city's destitute have established a strong cultural identity, and many residents proclaim that, were it not for the poor health care, the absence of schools, and the ubiquitous violence, life here would be paradise.

The problem is that cocaine strategists have found this type of environment ideally suited to their needs. When the tide rolls in, there are thousands of homes just above the surface of the water; and when it rolls out, the wooden seaside shacks look like dancing storks. This odd convergence of nature and culture has made these houses the ideal stations from which small amounts of illegal cargo can be shipped north on a nightly basis. The hundreds of brushwood-covered islands scattered just off the coast are infested with *caleteros*: people paid to collect small packages containing a few dozen kilograms and gather them until there is a decent quantity, never more than three tonnes, that can be picked up by a *volador* continuing on to Panama or Mexico. By no means all, and likely only a fraction, of the families in the southern shantytowns work, voluntarily or at gunpoint, by providing feeder services to the collection points; but for those fighting in the war on drugs, these distinctive residential areas have become synonymous with the cocaine trade.

Yet it is not what is actually being done, but what it *looks like* that is the central problem in the modern-day war on drugs. A large part of the economic growth promised by Plan Colombia is based on the concept of an impending tourism boom in this exotic and colorful yet largely uncharted land. Colombia, the idea goes, will be restored, and presented to the world with a new image in which wars, guerrillas, massacres, death squads, kidnappings, and even poverty are history. If only the country dares to embrace free trade fully, the logic holds, both foreign investments and tourists will be drawn here in droves. The only problem is all the visible misery caused by the cocaine trade, and that has to be eradicated. Cities such as Buenaventura not only need a fresh new image, but new inhabitants as well. People that are, in the words of the drug police, less "crazy."

After the paramilitary takeover, the government, military, and municipality have started construction on "the new Buenaventura," based on the Western ideal of the southern European seafront boardwalk. Rather than channeling resources into schools, health care, and security for long-time residents, a mega-project with the intention of pleasing the rest of the world has gotten underway; the original inhabitants of Buenaventura will, according to the urban plan, be relocated and their homes razed, in the hope that in a few years' time one of the most notorious cities in the world will attract sophisticated tourists who will stroll along the seafront, among chic hotels and cafés, with lattes and frozen yogurts in hand.

This will be painful for the thousands of families who will have to see their homes bulldozed, but the project itself would not be completely unreasonable if there were a potential customer base. However, Buenaventura has none of the attributes that attract the more picky travelers from the wealthy corners of the world, in their pursuit for postcard-perfect tropical experiences—no white sandy beaches, no crystal-clear waters, no steady sunshine. Here it rains every day, and the port, which is the focal point of the city, gives the entire island an implacably industrial feel. If the city has anything to offer the global leisure industry at all, it would be its distinctive social life and culture, its people.

But the Europeanization of Colombia's African roots is already underway, and the war on cocaine has become an effective tool to bring about the city's new face. Sections of the boardwalk are under construction, and a number of cafés have been decorated in the style that the owners believe the wealthy of the world expect. But most places have already been abandoned for lack of patrons. Today Roxette blasts from a deserted concrete desert and Marlboro and Absolut memorabilia dangle in empty bars, while the remaining wooden shanties vibrate with their own rhythms and neighborhood parties. According to Aida Orobio, a nun from the Buenaventura Diocese, the transformation is typical: the city's most basic problem is, she says, not drug trafficking, but the fact that the state stubbornly insists on investing in everyone except the people who reside here.

But as always in Colombia, there is a parallel story on another level, one that is both related to and separate from drugs. The vast majority of the unfathomable tonnes of cocaine passing through this little town of 300,000 inhabitants every year does not go out through the roughened hands of fishermen from *los esteros*, but in containers via the main harbor: in coffee sacks, boxes of tuna, bags of sugar, crates of bananas, and loads of timber. And at every level, from loaders and unloaders to customs chiefs and city councilors, there are people working under contract with the mafia. The fact that the Coast Guard and the narcotics police put such emphasis on these marginalized residential areas and their canoe trafficking cannot be explained in terms of quantities of powder; it is due to something else. In the earliest years of the war on drugs—during the Nixon, Reagan, and Bush administrations—elimination was the main objective, with the support of bans, and this was validated on a global scale at United Nations conventions. Eradication was key. Yet since then the lack of results has forced Washington to lower its expectations, and elimination is no longer the goal. Instead, what is essential to the DEA and White House today is which kind of powers are strengthened and which weakened by the drug industry. The new goal is merely to make sure that the amount of drug production going on is not so prodigious that it becomes "a threat to national security."

But just what qualifies as a threat of this kind is determined by the United States and is interpreted in completely different ways throughout Latin America. In Bolivia the democratically elected government is, according to the DEA, a threat to Bolivian national security, whereas in Colombia the democratically elected government maintains Colombian national security, despite the fact that both governments have ruled over national institutions and authorities that played key roles in streamlining cocaine production in the 2000s. In Buenaventura's case, drug ambitions and priorities are both closely related to the new emphasis on the *function* of drug trafficking in society, and what the city has been through recently is, in many ways, a consequence of this emphasis.

When in the 1990s the guerrillas strengthened their positions in this strategic city—Buenaventura is in the province of Valle del Cauca, just two hours from the sugar and cocaine metropolis of Cali—the elite classes throughout the entire region began to smell a rat. Paramilitaries were in full bloom in other parts of the country, and as the guerrillas made advances in the largest port off the Pacific Coast, the need for a counterattack grew. Various stakeholders financed the AUC's arrival in the city; landed proprietors, drug lords, sugar magnates, and a whole range of industrial sectors with interests in Buenaventura's harbor entered into an alliance with the provincial political clans and unscrupulous military officers, and the first of several purges were carried out during the early years of the new millennium. One of Carlos Castaño's brothers in arms from Urabá—Ever Veloza, alias H.H.—took it upon himself to make changes in the balance of power in Buenaventura, and seven years later, after he had demobilized his private armies, he would confess to having ordered the killing of over 1000 people in the city between 2000 and 2001—and that the murders had been carried out "in cooperation with representatives of the state." Since then several mass graves have been discovered, confirming Veloza's version of the story. The authors of *Parapolítica*, the investigation that includes the most extensive analysis of the connection between the private armies and the state apparatus, maintain that "the establishment of the AUC in the central parts of Valle del Cauca went hand in hand with a weak police response, which for the most part accepted the actions."

The "actions," which were carried out in the 2000s and continue to this day, often took place in *los esteros* of Buenaventura. The wooden hovels and their inhabitants were synonymous, in the eyes of the elite and paramilitary groups, with guerrilla-controlled territory—an assessment that has sometimes been correct, but many times hasn't. Over time the idea took root that a sustainable guerrilla remediation of the city could not be achieved with anything less than an elimination of the cultural traditions and housing conditions that were perceived to be an essential part of the social "water" in which the guerrilla swam. War between the FARC and paramilitary groups raged in the neighborhoods until the latter eventually proved victorious, after which the plan for "the new Buenaventura," with its clean seafront instead of "crazy" neighborhoods, was presented. The fact that several districts in *los esteros* were controlled and often terrorized by urban branches of the FARC was nothing new, but after thousands of innocent people were murdered before the eyes of a passive army and police force, distrust developed between the people and the state—a distrust which has remained the hallmark of the city ever since. And the seafront, which has only just begun to be built, has become a highly charged political symbol of white against black in Buenaventura. A symbol of the future against the past. Drugs flow as effortlessly through the harbor as through *los esteros*, but the government and the DEA view drug trafficking as more of a hazard to society when it moves through the poor area, with its dirty waters and seeming chaos, than when it has to do with corporate boardrooms and the main harbor. And for the FARC, it is becoming easier and easier to convince the city's Afro-Colombian majority that the focus of the war on drugs is not primarily on the flow of drugs, but on what kind of people are involved in it.

IT IS 10.00 a.m., and a great deal of commerce is taking place down by the piers when the Coast Guard pulls up beside two abandoned boats, each loaded with three large plastic oil drums. In a sea of chatter, quantities of goods both large and small are being bought and sold on the nearby boats, but these two have suddenly been abandoned. No one wants to take responsibility for them.

Quite undramatically, Captain Picón's subordinates simply loosen the punts before the merchants' trained eyes, making no other seizures, and tow them behind their patrol boat toward a little island in the bay, which functions as one of many military bases.

"See here," says Picón, once the six drums have been rolled out into a large hangar. He points to a semicircular incision at the bottom of each large drum. Nothing can be seen from a distance, but if you look closely it's obvious that someone has cut out a sort of a lid in the hard blue plastic and then glued it back in. This, he says, is what they always look like. Picón's staff break open lid after lid and start to pull out tightly packed rectangles of cardboard, all carefully taped and labeled either "Scrooge McDuck" or "Batman."

"This means that the goods originate from two different labs," says Picón. "McDuck is one producer, Batman another. They are like logos for the cartels. Had the packages been sent unmarked, absolute chaos would ensue once everything arrived in Panama. Distributors and producers always double-check with each other just to make sure they know whose goods have arrived. So the labels are essential."

Kilo after kilo is arranged in endless rows on the shiny concrete floor, like dominos, while technicians, chemists, prosecutors, and more police officers arrive. In the retail sector cocaine is dealt in grams, though here a kilo is the smallest denomination. A soldier in a blue uniform, crawling on all fours, numbers each brick with a squeaky felt-tip marker, and after a couple of hours of tedious work he scribbles out digits on the last three Batman packages: 390, 391, 392. "Phew."

The chemist takes out a scalpel; he cuts open a dozen or so arbitrarily selected packages and digs a bit with a spoon into the crosshatched surface of the densely packed powder. He sprinkles a few drops of solution in a couple of places, which stain like piss marks in the snow. "Cocaine," he verifies.

"And the quality?" asks Picón. "Good or junk?"

"*Puro*," says the chemist.

Then something strange happens. Signs, banners, and pennants are dragged into the hangar. They bear large coats of arms, that of the

Coast Guard and of the security police (Departamento Administrativo de Seguridad, DAS). A makeshift stage is quickly constructed behind the orderly rows of packages. "A little more to the right ... There. That's good," says a police officer.

The empty plastic drums are arranged in a small pyramid, under a banner reading, "We are quick and transparent in our efforts to make peace and a better future along the coasts of our fatherland—The Army." The DAS emblems surround the whole display, but as it turns out, the most important thing is not that the DAS, the Coast Guard, or the army has acted, but that the local and regional entities, Puesto Operativo Buenaventura and Seccional Valle del Cauca, have made the confiscation. Yet as the cameras are hauled out and the seizure of the 392 kilos is about to be documented for the media and officials, one police officer nudges his colleague, telling him to stop: "It doesn't look big enough. Thin the rows out a bit, so it looks like there's more."

The packets are reconfigured, an additional half-meter or so created between each row, and when the new arrangement is complete the plastic-coated cardboard packages glisten like gold ingots throughout the entire hangar. With machine guns in hand, platoon soldiers line up in front of the placards and banners so that the picture can finally be taken.

"Good, very good," says Picón.

The notion that more is better, and that it is absolutely essential the quantity looks greater than it is, is so self-evident to Picón that he does not understand why a question would even arise. But why was the whole capture at the pier so straightforward? Why didn't they do some intelligence work on the two boats when they realized they were carrying cocaine, so the perpetrators could have been caught? Why didn't they try to find out exactly what was going on, to reveal the entire chain? And why was it so important for the local police entities to front for the photos?

Captain Picón looks uncomfortable, and his response is difficult to interpret. "That's not how we work."

ON THE OTHER side of the harbor, in an office where files and toy cars are jumbled together on bookshelves, is a man who is in a better position to answer such questions.

"Whore-mongering. Excuse the expression, but that's what it boils down to."

Gustavo Guevara, whose life is in constant danger, is the region's most senior government prosecutor, and of all the words passing through his mouth on a daily basis, "problem" is the most frequent. He has worked in the court system for 20 years and apologizes for his disillusioned tone, but says that it is difficult to remain cheerful after so many years in the field.

"Of course it would be more desirable to have better policing. More reconnaissance, to search for links, to see what supplies are being used, which people are involved, where they're going, where they're leaving the goods, to clear things up—to get at the root of the problem. But that seldom happens. Because here in Colombia, what it all amounts to is 'el positivo'. It's terrible. When a confiscation is made, it's all about the media. It's about taking the credit fast; taking a good picture with law enforcement in front of whatever happens to have been confiscated, notifying the officials that you've been diligent. Window dressing."

Gustavo Guevara has a dimple in his chin and a gap between his two front teeth, and he is wearing a blue shirt with the sleeves rolled up. The stacks of papers on his desk are all about drug smuggling, and after clarifying that what he is expressing is his own personal opinion, nothing necessarily supported by the state prosecution office, he explains that the prioritizing of quantity over quality is due to "the damned statistics." "We're all whores to the system. It's pathetic. Different divisions within institutions are all fighting over criminals. If it's proven that someone who is arrested comes from another region, the police authorities in that province demand that the person be registered as having been arrested in their district. That way they can take credit for a *positivo*. I detest that term most strongly.

But the performance of every police officer and soldier is measured according to statistics. I am a prosecutor and, thankfully, am assessed according to other standards; it's more serious at our level."

Few people have seen as much of the ins and outs of drug smuggling and the war on drugs as Gustavo Guevara, and he says that it is difficult to have a clear idea of what should be done after so many young people have been put behind bars, so many hundreds of tonnes have been confiscated, and so many new military and police resources have been acquired—without any fundamental change having occurred.

"When we ask for a 100 police officers, they send 300. But with poverty as bad as it is here, it doesn't make any difference, because people will do anything for money. No one is afraid of winding up in prison. Many see it as a place where you can at least get fed and clothed. They think they'll either succeed and get rich or they'll get caught by the police, but at least then they'll get something to eat and have a roof over their head. There are no jobs here. People are desperate," says Guevara.

"Those operating the boats are usually paid half their cut before the trip and then the remainder after, but the latter rarely ever materializes; they are taken in by us, arrested by police in Panama, attacked by the guerrillas or a paramilitary group. Or go missing at sea. They're taking an enormous risk. We have no idea how many people have gone under. The kids just disappear. The attackers cut up the bodies and throw the parts overboard, where they immediately become fish food. The sea devours everything, even boats."

Another of the many problems Guevara brings up concerns the flow of resources, especially know-how, from the government to the mafia. The latest innovation used to escape the Coast Guard is the so-called semi-submarine, a small homemade craft that can travel a few meters below the surface. It is typically made out of old hulls and other marine debris. A trip to Panama on a *volador* takes eight hours; by semi-submarine, up to a week.

"It's like being in a prison cell in the middle of the ocean. Some have made it all the way to Mexico. For over a week you're in a rickety little craft under the surface of the water. You're going to the bathroom there, eating there, never knowing if you're going in the right direction, and risking getting pulled off course by a strong current. It's sheer insanity. We've seized 12 of them. But what's most tragic is that it's always our own people who make the semi-subs. Three former officers from the fleet had made the last one we took in, and they've all worked for us. Most semi-subs are made by soldiers who've learned boat-building at the expense of the state and then afterwards sold their skills to the drug dealers."

Opposite Guevara's office is La Estación, the city's only luxury hotel and the place where people dispatched by the war on drugs stay, along with everyone else in the aid industry that claims to want only the best for Buenaventura. In addition to the DEA and USAID, there are members of the European Union, the UN Office for the Coordination of Humanitarian Affairs (OCHA), the Organization of American States (OAS), and the United Nations Development Programme (UNDP). Fortunate locals who have found work at the hotel have succeeded in the laborious task of learning how to pronounce all the complicated abbreviations while serving muesli, yogurt, and eggs sunny side up every morning. Giant palm leaves sway gently by the pool, and black hands tend to brooms and white hands to silverware, as two enormous vessels leave Buenaventura and slowly move out toward the Pacific horizon. One is steel blue, the other mustard yellow. Each has its own checkered heap of containers.

In *los esteros* children jump around with crabs they have caught, dangling them like yoyos on strings, and at the mouth of the harbor a canoe chugs out to sea, carrying two men with fishing gear.

"We never catch the people who own the goods," says Guevara. "The ones we catch are at the bottom of the ladder, kids who don't even know who they work for. The trafficking will never end. The industry generates way too much money. The government's strategy is to fight trafficking every way it can, and with Plan Colombia we've gotten a lot more funding, which helps; in the past, we hardly had any equipment at all. But every time we catch one person, ten others are brought in. We can keep on fighting this, but it's a labor of Sisyphus. Something that makes money knows no end."

He runs his hand through his stiff hair and sighs. "I and everybody else who works here will retire, but boats will continue to depart from here, regardless, on a daily basis. One or two will be caught, and we'll keep on filling up the prisons."

THE HOSES HANG like lianas down into the ravine. Their weapons rattling, Juan Carlos Rivera and his platoon stomp through rapids and waterfalls in the hope of arriving at their destination soon. But time is flying. The hoses just keep going. And going. No lab.

"They've done a really great job of hiding it," says Rivera.

Yet he is not worried. Hoses are the best indication of a lab, and now four pack-asses arrive down below, panting and bewildered after having been abandoned by their owners. Every day these animals lug cocaine all the way from the lab up to the gravel road, where it is transported elsewhere by car—in this case, Major Quiroga says, to Venezuela, the new transit hub for supplying powder to the expanding European market.

In the past it was common just to load the cargo onto the back of a pickup truck and drive it to the nearest coast or airfield, but with the modernization of the war on drugs the cartels have become more advanced, and today there is an entire industry based on illegal logistics: there are companies that specialize in purpose-built jeeps and trucks that can bring in several tonnes hidden in extra gas tanks or in the chassis. The hiding places are becoming more sophisticated every day, like the whole industry. When the fleet of vehicles belonging to drug baron Daniel "El Loco" Barrera was seized some time ago, it was discovered that he had over a hundred trucks at his disposal, all especially constructed for the concealment of cocaine.

"Phew. Finally."

After working their way down for an hour, Major Quiroga and his men have reached a pretty clearing in the jungle. The area hums with life. Water ripples. A streak of sun makes it through the thick rainforest and, like a mirage, the camouflaged lab appears at the bottom of the valley. Three separate wooden structures, linked together by short, narrow piers, rest on poles over a gold-colored creek. All is quiet, until the platoon fills the area with shouts of joy.

"*Hijoepucha!*" yells Rivera. "Damn, it's big. One of the biggest I've ever seen."

The lab has no walls at all and just a black tarp covered with dried palm leaves for a roof. It is about 200 square meters in size. The building in the middle is filled with yellow plastic tanks, a dozen bathtub-like basins, and filtering tables with seating for 16 workers. On the other side of a long jetty is the drying room: eight microwave ovens, three drying lamps, and a long table, on which sits a white mound of about ten kilograms waiting to be packed into "condoms," the rubber casings that are used to ensure a waterproof journey around the world.

"Here are their stamps," puffs Rivera, as he eagerly holds up a pair of molded leaden weights. "Every cartel has its own trademark, and the workers stamp the emblem right into the cocaine when they press it. Here are the hydraulic presses. A normal lab has two. This one has four."

The individual supervizing the work in every *cocina*, just as in the larger paste labs, is the chemist. It is he who draws up the schedule, keeps in touch with the outside world, and makes sure that none of the raw materials ever run out. And he is the only one who earns really good money; the others work for minimum wages.

"Hurry up now," says Major Quiroga. "We're losing daylight."

The platoon troops disperse across the site like ants. A couple of men stick their knives into bags to take samples, while others keep a lookout. The officers supervize as four soldiers start wrapping explosive wire around the entire construction.

"We gather our evidence very quickly," says Rivera. "Then we blow it up."

The high point of the day's activities is drawing near. Exactly 40 years have passed since the war on drugs was first declared. At the turn of the new millennium, when socialists were coming to power in country after country in Latin America, the project became the very symbol of the constant need for North American imperialism to renew itself in order to continue its dominance over its old backyard neighbor. When the DEA and the UN produced reports in the early 2010s declaring that production was increasingly being moved to Bolivia, while Venezuela was becoming the new transit hub, the socialist administrations of Evo Morales and Hugo Chávez saw these documents as building up information to legitimize an invasion of the rebel states, with Colombia serving as a military base.

Barack Obama has now removed the term "war" from the vocabulary of Washington's anti-drug efforts, but after yet another big military budget for Plan Colombia was drawn up and the United States had been given the green light to use the country's military bases, Bolivia's red president Evo Morales sarcastically stated the pattern looked familiar. The concept of "drug terrorists," he said, had been updated and transformed—the prefix now no longer needed—into a tool the White House could use to obstruct Latin America's left wing and to prevent the continent's increasing economic integration: "So now we're narcoterrorists. When they couldn't call us communists anymore, they called us subversives. Then traffickers. And since the September 11 attacks, they call us terrorists." It seems, he concluded, "that the history of Latin America repeats itself."

The White House had a different view. The DEA was not thrown out of Bolivia and Venezuela because the organization had conspired with the state's right-wing forces, but because so much incriminating evidence had been gathered to indicate that both nations were deeply involved in the cocaine business that it was easier for the presidents just to kick the DEA out than to deal with the problem. Today Bolivia is not only a state in which cocaine production is on the obvious rise, but also, according to Washington's global narcotics investigators, a nation whose government is increasingly being overtaken by a drug mafia. And after the doors to the outside world have been slammed shut, collaboration between the state and drug traffickers will, they argue, flourish undisturbed.

But the hub of cocaine production and the war on drugs remains Colombia. In the last decade the police have blown up 20,000 labs in the country, and over a million hectares of rainforest have been sprayed. During the same time period, a resilient system of production has continued to satisfy the world's growing demand and Colombia's armed groups.

However, while John Freddy Sanchez, one of those participating in today's operation, admits that he has lost count of how many labs he has blown up, he remains hopeful that he will be able to make a difference. "I think our method is working," he says. "It's expensive for those involved in cocaine production. It costs a great deal to get all the equipment and chemicals out to the boondocks, and when we blow up the labs they're put at a severe financial disadvantage. They lose a lot of money."

He adjusts his machine gun and straightens his bandana. Nightfall is near. Birds are chirping in the tall shadows of the glade, completely unaware that the entire site is about to be blown up. Just as Edgar, Nelcy, Graciano, Andrea, Solin, and César make up the lower stratum of the global cocaine industry, Sanchez, Rivera, Quiroga, and the rest of the soldiers find themselves at the bottom of the counter-war hierarchy. They are just doing their job. Satisfying demands.

The platoon is on its way up to the crest of the hill when the jungle gives a start, as if it has been given a fright. The blast fills the entire valley, transforming the glade into a giant black hole. Today's quota has been met.

A cloud of smoke rolls out across the rainforest while animals cry out.

MAÑANA

The Future of the Powder

'The very idea of drugs being illegal is an extremely recent one,
dating back less than a century.'
— MIKE JAY, HISTORIAN

SHADOWY CLOUDS FLOAT over the mountains of Bogotá as Melissa, 17, takes her mother by the hand on their way to the Plaza Bolívar to take part in a demonstration against what Melissa calls "the rise of Christian dictatorship." "Prohibition is abusive. If it's not warranted," she says.

The megacity is tucked away at the foot of the green mountains like a tattered rug: while the lower classes reside in the shantytowns scattered along the southern fringes, the wealthy make their homes in the well-planned neighborhoods in the north, and between them lies the chaotic city center, with its skyscrapers and hubs of highways. Accompanied by friends, mother and daughter turn off onto Seventh Avenue, right where Gaitán was shot down in 1948, and walk past the Palace of Justice, rebuilt like a garrison after the fatal military attack in 1985. It is 6.00 p.m. The demonstration will commence as the sun sets in Soacha, the western suburb where Escobar's men assassinated Galán in 1989.

"I never think about drug abuse. I always think about war." Ivonne, Melissa's mother, is hardly even able to say the word "abuse" as she explains that she feels an unfathomable disconnect between North

197

and South America with regard to drugs. Prohibition perpetuates wars and corruption; legal drugs may of course generate more consumption and abuse, but what she cannot understand, she says, is if neither can be eliminated, why war is not seen as the greater evil. "I honestly don't think drug abuse would increase if drugs were legalized. I really don't think so."

The House of Congress is located by the historic Bolívar Square in the capital city, along with the statue of Simón Bolívar. The plaza, covered with pigeons as usual, quickly fills with other people who have come to take part in a demonstration over the "right to enjoyment."

"Cannabis is my drug of choice," says Melissa. "It's safe, a plant. Cocaine is different, a powder. All chemicals. Up your nose. Huh. I worry about what it can do to me. But I respect the rights of others who want to use it."

It sounds a bit like Ivonne and Melissa, a mother and daughter from the lower middle class, are simply marching in yet another nostalgic flower-power demonstration over the global legalization of marijuana, but in fact this isn't the case at all. They are not demonstrating for more-liberal drug laws, but instead in defense of their national constitution, written in 1991, which is "secular, libertarian, democratic and anti-authoritarian in its entire spirit," according to the country's supreme court. In 1994 this documented "spirit" led to a historic decision in which Colombians were given the right "to give meaning to their lives" without state intervention, as well as the right to "freely develop their personality," which included the entitlement to do drugs as long as it did not harm others. It legalized the so-called "personal dose," specified as 20 grams of cannabis or a gram of cocaine. The left supported the change, whereas the Church was up in arms.

The 1991 constitution came into existence after negotiations with several of the guerrilla movements in the process of demobilizing, and it was an unparalleled victory for Colombian socialists and liberals. While it has certainly not delivered social justice or land reform, it has, by virtue of its judicial influence, improved the lives of millions of Colombians, especially women, indigenous peoples, and black citizens: the progressive wording pertaining to pluralism and human rights has challenged the economic cornerstones of racism, judicial boundaries between sexual identities have been erased, and women are permitted a number of new rights, including abortion in certain cases.

"It's non-paternalistic," says Ivonne. "I think that's what they can't stand."

Yet when the more radical Christian right came to power in 2002, they declared war on the constitution, and the clauses they targeted were mostly those pertaining to secularism—the one on *dosis personal* in particular. A symbolic eight-year battle ensued, and when it came to an end at the closing of the decade, the government's new policy line had proven triumphant: the clause on legal use was removed from the constitution. The president's new strategy borrowed from the Scandinavian concept that there is no difference between drug use and drug abuse, that national unity and political emphasis are crucial in the fight against drugs, and that the only ethical and logical aim of the war on drugs is elimination. In fact, in the religiously charged debate prohibition was not just seen as possible but also as a duty. A moral obligation. The more military budgets for the fight against drugs were increased, the more emphasis was placed on the war on terror; and the more closely united the Bush and Uribe administrations became in their joint efforts to fight evil, the more difficult it became for Colombia, the epicenter of the drug war, to uphold a hedonistic constitution that permitted drug use.

Prior to tonight's demonstration, liberal newspaper editorials across the land have been lavishing praise on the secular ideals expressed in the constitution and damning the recent change regarding personal use. The government's decision to criminalize drug use was explained in *El Tiempo*, Colombia's most widely read newspaper, as an "empty populist gesture" that "runs counter to global trends." This

latter comment referred to the new wave of criticism of the US war
on drugs, which, in 2009, spread from Buenos Aires to Washington:
as the first decade of the new millennium drew to a close, Argentina,
Mexico, and several US states adopted policies similar to the one Colombia had implemented 15 years earlier, decriminalizing personal use
of some or all drugs, and similar reforms were being considered in a
number of other South American nations. By the 2010s the legitimacy of global prohibitionist policy was being looked at more critically
than ever before, with Latin America at the center of the contemporary drug-policy debate. Today, a number of nationally celebrated
authors and intellectual heavyweights from all over Latin America are
proponents of legalizing cannabis, at least, and the same goes for a
number of former presidents from the larger countries, along with an
increasing number of former prosecutors, politicians, police chiefs,
and former military officers. Or, in the words of Mario Vargas Llosa:

> Legalization of drugs is assuredly not without risks; thus, in order
> for it to work, the enormous funds that are now being spent on
> repression must be redirected toward information and rehabilitation,
> two approaches that have worked in the context of tobacco addiction.
> The argument that legalization would lead to greater consumption,
> particularly among young people, must of course be taken very
> seriously; even so, as all evidence shows, that phenomenon would
> probably just be temporary—provided legalization is accompanied
> by effective prevention campaigns.

Evidently, many places in Latin America are now doing what
Colombia did in 1994, and Colombia—the country in the world
most affected by drugs—is doing now what its neighbors were doing
then. This signaled a reversal, an about-face in relation to time and
politics, a move influenced by ideology, Colombia's relation to the
United States, and a different perspective on the national trauma. Is
the nation ahead of or left behind the times?

Colombia's decision also exposes wider questions now that the entire drug complex is subject to a new global debate. How will it end? Will it end? Is a drug-free world, if possible, desirable? Is cocaine simply a parenthesis in the history of narcotics? If not, who will produce the powder of the future? Will Colombia, still the supplier of the lion's share of all the cocaine consumed in the world, be able to satisfy the current boom in demand in Europe, Asia, Brazil, and Australia? Or is Bolivia now taking over? Peru? If so, will the war on drugs relocate?

In short, what is the future of cocaine?

Melissa was just two when Escobar was killed, a time when the entire world was rejoicing that the war on drugs was about to be won. Since then, cocaine production in Colombia has quadrupled, and those involved in the drug-fueled conflict have grown from small, lacerated groups of rebels to formidable and prosperous armies. She says she has only come to defend the constitution, but she does believe that complete legalization of all drugs is inevitable. Everything, she thinks, is moving in that direction. Yet considering that she is only 17 and already knows people who have succumbed to cocaine addiction, she is also concerned about what such a change could bring. "Of course I am. But I think what we're going through now with drugs is what we have already gone through with homosexuality and abortion—when those were legalized, the same concerns were raised. The fear was that everything would end in disaster. Everybody would become gay. No children would be born. It would, they said, be a total catastrophe. But it wasn't, and I don't think there will be one over drugs, either. Maybe consumption will increase for a while, but all the same, I don't think that can justify all the misery caused by banning it."

SEVENTY BLOCKS NORTH, in one of the city's more affluent districts, Colombia's foremost advocate of legalization strokes his well-trimmed beard. His tinted office windows look out over Bogotá's economically vibrant urban topography, a place where a sparkling new shopping center opens each month, cranes are continually completing new skyscrapers, and, in a maze of evenly dispersed alleys, chauffeurs wait in SUVs for members of the growing upper class to finish lunch in the ever-increasing smorgasbord of exclusive restaurants. "Colombia has a very strong and sophisticated economy. The cocaine industry is just a fraction, making up no more than two or three per cent of the GDP, but what it does produce a lot of is misery. That's the first thing you have to understand in this debate."

Despite his attitude toward drugs, Alfredo Rangel—a columnist for *Semana*, Colombia's equivalent of *Newsweek*, and head of a leading Colombian think tank—is not overly critical of the right-wing government. On the contrary. For a long time he was president Uribe's adviser, and he belongs to a long list of right-leaning intellectuals who believe that the nation did indeed make great strides during the first decade of the new millennium, in terms of reducing violence, curbing corruption, and weakening the guerrillas. Yet on his desk are piles of books with titles about the topic he has, to the chagrin of the government, come to devote much time to, a subject whose adherents are otherwise leftists and liberals. In his most recent book in the field, written in conjunction with three other of the country's top scholars in crime and conflict, he argues that the global approach to drugs in the future must strive to achieve an in-depth "understanding of prohibitionism." "The use of psychoactive drugs, everything from coffee to heroin, is as old as mankind," says Rangel. "People of all cultures and time periods have attempted to find ways of altering the mind, and always will. Creating a completely drug-free society would require us to change man's genetic makeup, something I don't think many of us would want to do. If you look at history, you will also see that all the widely popular drugs have gained social acceptance sooner or later regardless of their legal status, and this is what makes bans impossible to uphold. That's exactly what's now going on with cannabis. The attempt to keep on defending the bans with military action has led to a completely failed policy, if the goal in the first place was to reduce use. Prohibition is an absurd denial of all of these facts, and thus is ultimately doomed to failure."

Rangel represents both of the quite different perspectives that dominate the legalization trend in Latin America. The Colombian constitution, in the process of being dismantled, expresses the libertarian notion that everyone has the right to do with their body what they wish, provided it does not hurt others, while the resolution to decriminalize drug use in Mexico in 2009 was based on *consequential* ethical principles: the Mexican lawmakers were not primarily concerned about where to draw the limitations of state control but about pragmatically estimating the degree of suffering, and came to the conclusion that some bans generate more misery than they prevent. Hairsplitting, one might think, but this distinction is essential in order to understand the constantly changing role that drugs new and old play in all cultures of the world.

But the libertarian and pragmatic traditions almost always coincide in hands-on politics—as they have for Rangel—and today their mutual counter pole is prohibitionism: now making a comeback in Colombia and already strong in the United States, Scandinavia, and the Muslim world, but support for which is on the rapid decline in much of Europe and Latin America. The philosophy behind the bans originates in a religious or Kantian imperative in which it is simply morally wrong to do drugs, regardless of the consequences. Harm-reduction initiatives such as methadone and needle-exchange programs, or recognition of the existence of "unproblematic drug use," is, in this tradition, very hard to accept, since the imperative is absolute and loses meaning as soon as it is made relative; the so-called warning signs carry more weight than the factual consequences, in the same way that it is always wrong for those who oppose abortion to terminate a pregnancy, irrespective of the circumstances.

It is exactly the economic and social consequences of Latin America's entire bitter experience with cocaine—including the counter war—that have prompted several of the continent's nations to abandon prohibitionist standpoints. In the 40 years since the war on drugs began, supply and demand have only increased, and the costs of the counter efforts have also increased continually, if counted in drug-war killings, swelling prison populations, escalating corruption, and democracies eroded by the mafia.

"The basic idea behind the war on cocaine," says Rangel, "was that if supply could be decreased then the going rate on the end markets would increase dramatically, after which a significant decline in overall consumption would occur, the ultimate result being the complete elimination of demand. But after decades of employing this strategy, the results have been exactly the opposite. Today, there is more cocaine in the world than ever, the prices have fallen, and more people than ever before are consuming. To this already mounting list one could add all the problems directly attributable to the actual ban: organized crime, violence, corruption, and loss of quality control over substances. After taking everything into consideration, I believe that decriminalization of drugs and total legalization is, in the long run, all included, the least damaging option. Drug trafficking is a hydra that can sprout a new head at any time and has the ability to withstand every attack through a new mutation."

The notion that the industry has the ability to reinvent itself constantly is a key factor in why an alternative policy is emerging in Latin America today. When in the 1990s Washington managed to dismantle Escobar and Gacha's routes through the Carribean—the quickest way from Colombia to the United States—it only meant that the majority of trafficking relocated to Mexico, the next-most economical route. In 1991 50 per cent of all cocaine from Colombia entered the United States through Mexico, a figure that increased to 90 per cent 15 years later, and as a result of that development, the country absorbed a large portion of South America's organized crime. Today, the whole Mexican democratic system is under threat, and since 2006 more than 20,000 people have been killed in drug-related purges.

Unlike the big Colombian cartels of the 1980s and 1990s,

Mexican traffickers—now in control of the entire North American market—have diversified the business and today deal in cocaine and cannabis as well as heroin and methamphetamines. A slight decline in the demand for cocaine has been detected in the US market in recent years, but the gap has been filled in abundance by rising demand for methamphetamines. And when the land designated for cocaine cultivation in Colombia decreased after years of heavy herbicide spraying, cultivation in Peru and Bolivia increased correspondingly. Yet the fastest thing in the business to undergo a mutation has been human capital. The Mexican cartels, which alone employee 450,000 people, generate sales of 20,000 million USD per annum. One kilo of cocaine costs 2000 USD in Colombia, 12,000 USD in Mexico, and between 30,000 and 50,000 USD in the United States and Europe. That same kilo can cost up to 90,000 USD on the streets of New York, Madrid, London, or Sydney. The people who oversee the later stages of the exponential value curve—Mexican cartels control the US market, while the Colombian and Italian mafias cover large parts of the European—earn astronomical amounts, and thus the inflow of people willing to risk their lives on the carousel is infinite.

"Wars shouldn't be declared on what cannot be won. The story of drugs is never-ending." Alfredo Rangel's conviction that the war is "never-ending" and that decriminalization is necessary—in some domains, at least—is now widely shared among former politicians and officers who have been involved in the anti-drug war but have stepped down or retired and are now able to speak freely. The major names in this category—Ernesto Zedillo, Fernando Henrique Cardoso, and César Gaviria, former Mexican, Brazilian, and Colombian presidents respectively—published a report in 2009, in which they supported the legalization of cannabis for pragmatic reasons. (Since then Cardoso has taken it a step further, proposing the same for cocaine.) For the first time since the war on drugs began, high-profile politicians openly defended the idea not to crack down with sporadic military action, but to pull the rug out from under the mafia by structural and economic means. Although cocaine is the substance that helped to build up the Mexican successors to the Medellín and Cali Cartels, today cannabis—by far the most common of all illegal drugs—is responsible for much of the revenue to organized crime. In Mexico a significant proportion of all the resources invested in killing prosecutors, corrupting politicians, and maintaining mafia extravagances comes from cannabis, and the former presidents consider this much too high a price tag in light of the relatively limited adverse effects of the drug. A pan-American or global legalization of cannabis, goes the argument, would move almost all production to the United States, the world's largest consumer of both cannabis and cocaine, where it would be manufactured more effectively and closer to the market. But above all, such a measure would cut organized-crime profits in half.

However, Rangel's perspective is more radical. As a Colombian, his focus is on cocaine, and he believes that the 6.8 billion USD the United States has invested up to now in ending coca production in the nation should have been allocated differently—or, more correctly, that the anti-drug operations have done much more harm than good. In his most recent book he outlines a three-step approach many would call naïve, but which he believes is the only way. "This isn't something one country can do on its own. The issue of narcotics is regulated at the international level, and everything done from this point on must happen there. Colombia has signed a global agreement, which of course cannot be breeched, but there are things that can be done. Herbicide spraying has brought only perverse consequences—socially, economically, environmentally. It has also been counterproductive: coca cultivation has spread to every corner of the nation, and production has doubled. Consequently, I think efforts have to target a completely different link in the cocaine chain—that is, the point at which it leaves the country. This would cripple crime organizations directly, instead of the small farmers, which is important, as state attacks on the poor peasants have had disastrous consequences in terms of increasing guerrilla support. Concentrating on export routes would keep large amounts of cocaine from getting transported out as planned, which in turn would disrupt things for those working in the earlier stages: the labs would produce less, the farmers wouldn't be able to deliver as much raw material, and many middlemen would lose their jobs. Once the oversupply is greater, the cash value on coca leaves will plummet, and then alternative crops would be able to compete with coca. But this isn't a solution, just the first step.

"The second is to make cocaine a central issue in peace talks. Drugs were never part of the peace negotiations carried out with paramilitary groups during the first decade of the 2000s, and this was a major mistake. This issue needs to be discussed, and an agreement reached; the guerrillas have to assume the responsibility for certain things, and the state for others. For instance, the FARC—in consultation with its troops and social bases—would commit itself to eliminating coca cultivation, and in exchange, the government would agree to invest heavily in alternative crops and to provide new infrastructure, subsidies, micro credits, and land reform. Today, many farmers grow coca solely because small farming here has failed, since their markets have disappeared with globalization. They have to be given the chance to make a comeback. Obviously this is a huge issue that demands cooperation at all levels of society, but with this method I believe we can bring down production much more dramatically than has previously been the case.

"Thirdly, at the international level, we need to bring an end to prohibition within the global framework of regulation. Implementing legalization in one country without consulting other nations would be an enormous risk, not least because the country in question would be isolated and condemned. But a first step is to decriminalize consumption, at least of smaller amounts, which is exactly what is happening now in Latin America, some US states, and certain EU countries. After that, gradual steps will be taken, depending upon those results. You have to try new things. Experiment. Evaluate. Take

a step back. Try something else. The problem with today's global
policy is that exactly the same methods are being applied again and
again, but with the expectation that the outcome will be different.
Every scientist knows that if all the circumstances are identical, it's
sheer stupidity to expect new results. A reorganization at the global
level doesn't require a consensus in the UN, but what is important
is that cocaine-producing nations, transit nations, and nations of
consumption are all in agreement. Colombia is the country with the
most combined experience, and if such an agreement can be reached
between, say, Colombia, the US, Brazil, Mexico, Peru, and the EU,
then I believe that the entire course can be changed on a global
scale." Alfredo Rangel speaks as if he is absolutely certain that the
future is on his side, but he does not deny that the transformation he
advocates comes with great social risks. "Obviously there are many,
such as the risk of a marginal rise in consumption. But with awareness
campaigns and better supervision, I don't think the number of drug
abusers will increase simply because the number of those who use
drugs responsibly does. If six out of ten users today have to seek help
for drug abuse, it may well be that only four will need help even if
there are 12 users. All you can do is to speculate about what the risks
could be, compare them with the enormous costs we have today, and
then to take a stance. As far as I'm concerned, those costs cannot
possibly outweigh the ones we're already paying now, at least in the
case of this country. It's important to be pragmatic and weigh in on
both the positives and the negatives."

Yet the prohibitionists think that legalization would not only lead
to a marginal increase in consumption but to an extreme one. The
example most often used is legal drugs: despite all the difficulties in
controlling today's illegal narcotics, the fact is that these drugs yield far
fewer victims than legal drugs such as tobacco or alcohol. However,
Rangel is not impressed by this argument, since on that perspective
the only "victims" are those who have been directly created by the
drug; it forgets all the victims—mostly poor people in the south—of

the wars and crime structures created by the bans.

He also believes the idea that consumption would increase dramatically is far from given. "One can never be sure. But there have been attempts we can learn from. In Portugal, consumption of all drugs was decriminalized and abuse didn't go up but down. In the Netherlands, cannabis was legalized and consumption increased, but not to the extent expected. And much of the increase was, and still is, owing to all the tourists who go there to buy legal marijuana. If you look at the number of people who abuse drugs, there is no correlation between the increase in consumption and the number of abusers. There are so many other variables involved: tradition, culture, poverty, level of education, social maladjustment, spread of organized crime, and what kind of awareness campaigns the politicians carry out. Drug abuse is an extremely complicated social issue, and you can't expect to have the same results in every country. Every society reacts differently to decriminalization, and must respond with different social and educational measures."

Sometimes it sounds as if he believes that a global or semi-global legalization is inevitable, but this isn't the case. "No, I don't think so," he says. "On the contrary—I think it will take time for such an approach to receive wide support. It's important to recognize that general truths don't automatically generate the same outcome in all environments. While it's certainly true that drugs cause violence and corruption, it doesn't necessarily mean that more drug trafficking will always lead to more violence. Sometimes it does, sometimes it doesn't. In Colombia, violence and corruption escalated on a par with production, but in more recent years both violence and corruption have actually fallen, while drug trafficking hasn't. Today, Colombia produces more cocaine and fewer murders, whereas before we had less cocaine but a much higher homicide rate. There's no direct connection. What has happened is that the mafia has changed, evolved. The drug traffickers have learned that it's a bad idea to declare war on the state, since such wars can never be won. They have learned to use no more violence than is absolutely necessary, no overly demonstrative violence. This is a new phenomenon. A phenomenon of the future."

He shoves his hand between two buttons on his shirt as he takes in the view. Bogotá's chaotic mixture of skyscrapers, cranes, highways, and low buildings sparkle in the light, and in the distance the mountains in the south provide a visual border to what everyone knows is guerrilla territory. Still. Rangel is aware that many intellectuals in Colombia support his views on this topic, but also that he is heavily criticized in one respect. Some of the books he has published tend to convey the notion that Colombia just has one problem—narcotics. That legalization would not only eliminate a great deal of the world's organized crime, but also lead to peace in Colombia. Yet in that respect he is not supported by many academics.

"Peace may be too much to expect," he says. "But violence and misery would never have reached such levels here had it not been for drug trafficking. In the early 1980s the FARC had 900 soldiers, but because of the drug industry that figure grew to 18,000. I believe the number could have been stopped at around 4000 had it not been for cocaine. We would have just a fifth of the guerrilla problem we have today, a problem which is a gigantic scourge. In terms of the paramilitary groups it's all more complicated, since they were set up almost exclusively with drug money. Add to that the war between the two, which created unprecedented violence and so many internal refugees. And that's just the armed conflict. To that should also be added all the other types of crimes generated by drugs. My response is that a Colombia without the drug industry would be an entirely different country. A completely different nation."

IN A CORTÈGE of cars with tinted windows, Juan Manuel Galán, son of Colombia's own Kennedy clan, watches the buildings roll by while he wonders what his assassinated father would have said about his son's present stance on drugs. "I can't speak for him, but if he'd seen the historical balance sheet I think he'd have been all for a change of focus. The battle has to be fought with the weapon that will do the most damage to the mafia—we have to get at their money. My stance is all about focus. We'll fight them more, not less."

Juan Manuel Galán was introduced to the Colombian people on 18 August 1989 when, at 17, in a moment of passion just a few hours after the assassination of his father, he grabbed the microphone during the live television broadcast and pleaded to his father's successor, soon-to-be-president César Gaviria, "Please, save Colombia!" The nation was in shock yet again, though Colombians were becoming increasingly accustomed to these unwelcome surprises. Once more, a left presidential candidate heading to a certain victory had ended up in a pool of blood as he was about to cross the finish line. Many leftists drew their own conclusions; some joined the guerrillas, others abandoned politics, and thousands went into exile.

It seemed that whoever—a political party, a trade union, a social movement—dared to organize a political project threatening the landowning elite, the drug mafia, or a corporate interest would sooner or later end up dead. The dead bodies were counted in their thousands and all hope for a better future seemed lost; but when the pimply teenager, who, a few hours after his father's brutal death, had enough insight to call for reconciliation, the entire nation took him into their hearts. He symbolized a ray of hope. Some thought that perhaps—perhaps—there might just be some sort of peace in store for the future after all. Many years down the road. With a new generation in power. In different times.

Since that day Juan Manuel Galán, his brothers, and his mother have been to Colombia what the Kennedys were to the United States after John F. Kennedy's assassination in 1963. Today, the family is a symbol of a liberal, enlightened, and progressive political tradition. In Congress Juan Manuel—he is a senator and all his brothers are politicians—continues to fuel their father's furious battle against the nation's violent landowning elite, and whenever a Galán takes the floor, he does so with a very special moral weight. All Colombians know it was Luis Carlos Galán's vehement struggle against cocaine that led Escobar to assassinate him, as part of an alliance with Galán's political adversaries. This is exactly why so many people became disillusioned when Juan Manuel, the son of the biggest opponent of drugs, came out as yet another Latin American politician in favor of legalization.

"I changed my mind when I began studying the issue more scientifically," he says. "And the first thing you have to admit is that there are no simple answers. There's no magic wand you can simply wave. But it's important to come up with an alternative to prohibition. Of all the 40 billion dollars spent on fighting drugs each year, 38 billion go to repressive measures, to hunt down and punish those who live on this business. The mere thought about the sort of good that money could do for prevention and treatment instead is very appealing."

Juan Manuel Galán is one of those—Noam Chomsky being another—who think that there is no actual war being fought against narcotics, but that the war on drugs has increasingly become a rhetorical tool to serve other purposes: territorial control, defense of religious values, the war on terror, and the undermining of socialism. If it were really about drugs, Galán says, there is plenty of evidence to show what really gets results, and almost all of it has to do with prevention, rehabilitation, and reducing poverty.

Critics such as Galán and Chomsky base their conclusions on a vast number of studies, but on one major investigation in particular: "Controlling Cocaine," carried out by the RAND Corporation in 1994, in which four methods to curb drug use in the United States were analyzed. The most effective measure, by a significant margin, was prevention and treatment, followed by the much more costly policing, and third, the even more exorbitant implementation of stricter border security. Most demanding in terms of resources but least effective were operations carried out in other countries, such as herbicide spraying in Colombia. Nevertheless, the United States continues to channel its resources in opposition to these results: the majority of funds go to the latter options, the least to the former.

The fact that most of this continues—even under Obama—may, according to Chomsky, be because the actual goals of the war on drugs differ from those expressed publicly. When this is taken into account, the argument goes, the fact that these methods repeatedly fail to achieve their purported objectives does not matter, since they succeed in the way they were actually intended. So why, if Chomsky is correct, is the resistance to the war on drugs not more evident among those governments, many of them socialist, that do not exactly share the same concerns as Washington?

One response relates to economic power. In 1986 the US Congress passed a resolution on "decertification," which means that Washington can punish nations that fail to comply with the White House's stance on drugs by raising tariffs on agricultural products, putting a stop to air traffic to the country, or voting against loans and aid to the neglectful nation in question in the International Monetary Fund and the World Bank. When Colombia was decertified in 1996, the country fell into a deep recession and took a decade to recover, and in 2009 Bolivia was punished by drastic increases in tariffs on Bolivian goods aimed for the US market—a measure estimated to have resulted in the loss of 25,000 jobs. When in 2001 the Jamaican government appointed a commission to study the possibility of decriminalizing cannabis, it concluded that arresting thousands of citizens for using it was causing more harm than that caused by marijuana addiction itself, but the US Embassy in Kingston made it clear that the White House would not tolerate such legislation—and, following the threat of decertification, the recommendations from the study were scrapped entirely. The paradoxical consequence resulting from this North/South dynamic is that the US government has more power over poor, developing nations than over its own states, many of which have already effectively legalized cannabis.

Juan Manuel Galán runs his fingers through his shiny hair. He is still a young man, maintains a low-key image, and is anxious for his words to resonate. He has absolutely no sympathy for the FARC and is indifferent as to whether they are called guerrillas or terrorists, but does agree with the analysis that the war on drugs is driven by neo-colonial principles and is irrational in terms of its goals. "Prohibition has just turned 100 years old. I think that's old enough. But if there isn't a change in the UN conventions that regulate this issue internationally, nothing can be done. It's a straitjacket preventing us from developing alternatives. The worst thing that can happen is that we legalize without having prepared ourselves with regard to care and prevention. Such a drastic step requires very developed treatment infrastructures, good state control over the substances, and serious prevention. On a global scale. I would like to see a UN convention on prevention and treatment. That would be a paradigm shift."

In the new global legalization movement it's possible—as touched upon earlier—to single out a few different perspectives: pragmatists, liberals, and what could perhaps be called supporters of the normal-ization theory. The first is the broadest category, gathering all sorts of people of various political persuasions together around the utilitarian belief that bans do more harm than good, while the second category consists of classic liberals and libertarian leftists, who claim that what individuals do with their own bodies should be a matter of personal choice. The third school of thought, often a combination of the first two, has been strengthened by the younger generation, who grew up exposed to a broader variety of drugs and have now entered into the debate with their own intellectual spokespeople. This category gained a new representative in 2009 with the publication of Tom Feiling's book *The Candy Machine: how cocaine took over the world*.

One overarching thesis is that cocaine, like many other drugs, is something of a hedonistic reality in postmodern societies and is now undergoing the same normalization process as abortion, homosexuality, and atheism; that the laws dramatizing the phenomenon at present will gradually be abandoned. Scandinavia is an odd fish in the global debate on drugs, with its secular political tradition but harsh drug laws, but in other parts of the world there is a strong connection between absolutist ideas on drugs and religion, and the critics believe that with increasing secularization, the spread of democracy, the victory of the market economy, better education, and not the least the free flow of information, the legislative idiosyncrasies will eventually be pared down—similar to how many countries' anti-abortion legislation has become outdated due to the global evolution of science, ethics, human rights, and availability of services.

Another tenet of the normalization thesis is that the dangers associated with the majority of drugs—cocaine and marijuana in particular—are grossly exaggerated, and that far too often throughout the 20th century these dangers were analyzed in terms of apocalyptic scenarios, instead of within their social and economic context. It's true that cocaine, unlike marijuana, can generate rapid addiction, but Tom Feiling refers to a wide range of research that arrives at one and the same conclusion: the absolute majority of those who use these drugs only do so for a short period of time and do not become abusers. The most common curve for those who use cocaine is the same as that for cannabis or alcohol: users engage intensively for a period, usually between three and six years, when they are relatively young, and as they get older, gain more life experience, and embrace a more mature lifestyle, they quit or reduce their use on their own initiative. However, the fact that more people use drugs responsibly than not does not mean that class, poverty, and psychology do not play major roles in the development of problematic drug behavior; on the contrary. And, as with alcohol addiction, these are often the determining factors, not the drugs themselves. Feiling believes that these arguments will soon be more widely accepted, not least because the schoolteachers who will teach pupils about alcohol and narcotics in the future will often have had their own experiences with drugs:

Hysterical claims about drug use have abounded since the Industrial Revolution, but a more sober assessment now seems possible. Most people don't like most drugs. Most of those who try cocaine do not go on to use it heavily. They don't even go on to use cannabis heavily.

Another commonly held belief in relation to normalization has to do with the psychological relationship between total abstinence and abuse. Various studies show that young people who do a lot drugs often develop low self-esteem, become stressed, and have difficulty forging genuine relationships, but less publicized results from similar studies show that young people who completely *abstain* from all forms of drugs are also often emotionally inhibited or socially incompetent. As Feiling argues, what applies to young people also seems to apply to adults: pleasure and satisfaction are associated with moderate use of drugs, and frustration and anxiety are associated with both abuse and total abstinence.

Another idea in a similar vein is that the terror of increasing drug use is based primarily on religious or nationalistic apocalyptic paranoia, a kind of fear on the part of the authorities of the increasingly malleable nature of human beings and the endless relativism of modern man. When Mike Jay's *Emperors of Dreams: drugs in the nineteenth century* was published in 2000, one of its themes was that religion, more than reason, has guided legislators' efforts throughout the last two centuries to control the human quest for intoxication. Prohibitions against alcohol and other drugs have rarely been based on rational considerations, but have usually been colored by moralistic crusades, or by the fear of cultural or ideological invasions from foreigners.

For the advocates of evolutionary normalization, Mike Jay's comparisons with traveling—tripping, escape from the everyday, transcending—serve well as both a general analogy and a useful hint about the future:

Drug policy may be an immovable object, but drug culture has become an irresistible force which shows every sign of becoming an enduring passion of the Western mind. Just as the pioneering journeys of nineteenth-century explorers have become today's popular travel destinations, so the inner worlds first colonized in the nineteenth century are now visited by more people than ever before.

Paradoxically, however, lawmakers today seem more concerned about protecting citizens from adventure-seeking trips "inward" than to exotic foreign destinations that are far more dangerous to reach. Or, in the words of one of Feiling's informants: "Who's to say you can go up Mount Everest, but not have a line of charlie? It's pushing at the boundaries of human experience, and who's to restrain you from doing that?"

Juan Manuel Galán rejects an incoming telephone call. Bodyguards circle around the restaurant he has chosen for lunch, and outside, congested traffic clogs the streets of Bogotá as he explains that for a long time these issues only applied to the wealthy nations of the world, but this is no longer the case. Globalization has not only brought shantytowns to Europe; it has also brought an exclusive culture of recreational drug use to the developing world. One of the new realities Latin America faces is the fact that the dichotomy between countries of production and consumption is now a thing of the past; today Colombia is also a nation of consumption and the United States also one of production. North America is the biggest producer of cannabis in the world and South America is one of the new and emerging markets for cocaine consumption. Brazil, whose economy is experiencing a rapid boom, is today the biggest cocaine-consuming nation in the world after the United States, and Colombia's sophisticated propensity for criminal activity has turned the country into both a world-leading producer of heroin and a rapidly growing manufacturer of synthetic drugs.

In other words, it is chaos on the drug markets. The landscape is being renewed. But cocaine is still the primary generator of war and corruption, and Juan Manuel Galán thinks that Colombia, with its unique experience as the world's main source of powder, possesses, as he writes in a new book, "the moral authority to propose legalization to the world." "The magnitude of the blood bath we've had to endure puts us in a unique position in the debate," he says. "No other country has come even close to our experience. If you look at the number of assassinated ministers, prosecutors, magistrates, journalists, politicians, policemen, and ordinary people, I think Colombia should be able to stand before the international community and say with a great deal of authority that this just isn't working. We can't go on like this. We have to do something different."

Today's successful advocates of legalization tend to forget—or ignore—one key issue, though. The report from the three former presidents was universally hailed in the American press and persuaded politicians, intellectuals, and officers to "come out" as critics of the war on drugs, despite the fact that their logic was based on one obvious weakness: there is no counterfactual history. The notion that the war on drugs has been a failure is based on the premise that an alternative policy would have generated better results. But would it?

ON MONDAY 8 FEBRUARY 2010, Jairo Villegas bid farewell to the free life. Not even 30, he was a young pilot with his entire life ahead of him when it became apparent that someone in the organization was not to be trusted; information had leaked out from what he believed to be a completely safe network, one with an endless supply of cash that would continue to flow forever. But after just six years it had all come to an end.

At a party in the early 2000s he had met Daniel "El Loco" Barrera, one of the cocaine barons in Colombia, who informed him that he was in need of people who could fly goods from the eastern part of the country to Central America. Jairo did not have a pilot's license but was eager to obtain one, so when Loco Barrera offered to pay his way through pilot school on the condition that he would later return the favor by running "flour" up north, it was an offer he couldn't refuse. He entered a program at a university, and a few years later took his final exam. Upon graduating, he took a job with a local airline in Villavicencio, the capital of Meta, the Texas of Colombia. But the position was just a stop—some practice—on his journey to the real work. In March 2004, Barrera notified him through a contact that the FARC had granted permission to use an airstrip in Puerto Alvira, a remote village in the south of the province.

Jairo Villega's first assignment as a part of the global drug industry was to fly half a tonne of cocaine from a hick town in Meta to a small place on the border with Venezuela. The product he was transporting was certainly cocaine, but the amount was small, as one of the objectives of the mission was to determine if Jairo could be trusted. Upon successful completion of the assignment, he could start to make all his *sueños blanco*, "white dreams," come true. *Sueños blancos* was the pilot guild's slang for cocaine runs: "white" for the cargo and "dream" for the sum pocketed if nothing went wrong: 500,000 USD.

His first international run was in an old Cessna, to take off by the Venezuelan border. Jairo and a young man he had never met entered the sky with a full tank of gas, along with two extra cans of fuel and an unknown number of kilos of cocaine destined for Nicaragua. Not until they were in the cockpit did they receive their flight instructions, which were that they would neither be landing with the cocaine nor flying the plane back. It was a highly unusual procedure, but such was the assignment this time. They were to drop the cargo into the sea at specified coordinates near the town Puerto Cabezas, on the Nicaraguan Mosquito Coast, and continue on to Honduras, where they would land on a deserted highway, an isolated road leading out onto a thin peninsula. There they would abandon the plane and take a bus to Panama, where they could purchase airline tickets back to Colombia. They did exactly as instructed and everything went according to plan. Jairo was thrilled.

And so it continued for five more years, until that fateful Monday in 2010, when the organization in which he was involved—the Pilot Cartel—was exposed, resulting in the arrest of Jairo and seven other pilots. They had 25 planes at their disposal, had flown six tonnes of "flour" a week from laboratories in seven different Colombian provinces, and provided the link between the motherland of cocaine and the cartels in Mexico through a sophisticated network of routes, including runways in Panama, Costa Rica, Nicaragua, Guatemala, Honduras, the Dominican Republic, and Venezuela. Instrumental to the success of this bust was the discovery of the bodies of four dead pilots, which had been brought to police attention: one airline captain who'd been murdered in Medellín three months prior; one who had been found in a plane that had recently crashed near the Dominican Republic; and two who had crashed the previous year, their plane, with 1.5 tonnes of cocaine on board, having run out of gas before it reached its destination in Guatemala. Each incident was yet another piece in the puzzle that the Colombian and Mexican drug squads, as well as American DEA agents, were working on together, and which eventually made it possible for them to carry out what the police later called "the biggest crackdown ever on the alliances between the Colombian and Mexican cartels." Óscar Naranjo, head of Colombia's national police, went even further when he declared that the operation ripped "the heart out of the cocaine industry" and brought "organized drug criminality to the verge of extinction."

Similar proclamations had been heard from the police and the DEA ever since Pablo Escobar was killed, and as production had increased, so had statements concerning the impending death of the mafia—statements that had been made more frequently and with greater emphasis as the absence of success became clear. But perhaps the spring of 2010 would be the time in which the idea of "the lost war on drugs"—a new mantra among liberals and leftists in Latin America and around the world—would be disproven. According to the police, over a thousand drug offenders had been arrested in the last seven years in Colombia alone, and of those, 350 were "high level." This data could, on one hand, be interpreted as a frightening indication of how many "high level" cocaine offenders there actually were or, on the other, that the police, despite all the criticism, were correct in their assessment that an eradication of sorts was imminent.

There is one man, something of a legend, who is particularly pleased these days, as he is not only convinced of an eradication but has also been a spider himself in the web of information that has in recent years led to the arrest or death of a whole series of major drug sharks and kingpins: the regional head of the DEA. And, as it turns out, there are a lot of other things he is convinced about as well.

THE US EMBASSY in Bogotá is a jumble of concrete blocks with roofs full of satellite dishes resembling Mickey Mouse ears. From time to time, black cars pass in and out through the openings of closely guarded barrages, which are made of cement, iron bars, and bulletproof glass, with some 50 meters between every layer so that if one gives way, the second will bear the brunt. This is, people working here proudly say, the second-largest US embassy in the world, after the US legation in Baghdad.

Nestled in the middle of this secure construction is Jay Bergman, a sporty-looking man who launches straight into his primary message: '*Those guys are dead men walking.*' He stutters slightly, but it's not clear if this is due to a speech impediment or is just his way of adding emphasis. 'I, I … give them one year.'

The people Bergman refers to as 'those guys' are the successors of Pablo Escobar; besides Loco Barrera, he rattles off a handful of other names, some of which are Colombia's most recent and notorious drug offenders, and he confidently reiterates his prediction that it will not be long before they are all *dead*. He seems totally certain.

'If you look at how things developed after Escobar was killed, you will see that each successive generation of trafficking cartels has been less powerful than the previous one,' says Bergman. 'And this is thanks to better training, more resources, and better strategies that the Colombian government has been able to implement after military support from the United States. Each new generation has been less able to penetrate the government, undermine the political process, and maintain territorial control. But in terms of success, it's all relative. I'm not saying that the total amount of drugs these groups are now sending out is any less than before, just that their ability to cause damage to society has been drastically reduced."

Another relative success he points out is that the shelf life of these groups has been shortened significantly, from as long as 15 years to something more like 15 months. "There is currently nobody on the Colombian top-ten list of drug traffickers who has any other option than to one, surrender; two, be arrested; or three, be killed in combat. People like Cuchillo, Loco Barrera, Comba: as I've just said, those guys are dead men walking."

Jay Bergman has been pursuing drug lords under the US flag for over 30 years, but because victory in the war on cocaine has been declared so many times, the only reaction such a claim receives in the Colombian press is scorn. Yet this time it seems as if there is more pointing toward an actual break in the trend than just political rhetoric. In its most recent report, the UN announced that coca cultivation has declined by 28 per cent in the last year, and that in Colombia only 390 tonnes of cocaine were produced, as compared with 545 tonnes the year before. When the Pilot Cartel was arrested, it was yet another in a long series of blows against both the Colombian and Mexican mafia and its offshoots around the world, and in July 2010 the Italian police made a historic raid and arrested 320 people from Calabrian mafia organization the 'Ndrangheta, which had controlled a large part of the European cocaine market for a long time. So just when the international intelligentsia seemed to have agreed that the war on drugs was "an absolute failure," in the words of Mario Vargas Llosa, both the United Nations and White House were presenting statistics suggesting that the strategy of cracking down hard on production had finally started to pay off.

The fact is, Jay Bergman says, that during the past two years, the price of cocaine has been going up and the quality down, and not just in the United States, but in Europe as well. This has also occurred during a time in which global demand has gone up in general; today there's a surge in demand in Europe and an explosion of new markets in Asia, Australia, and Latin America. According to Bergman, these trends show that there's now a shortage of supply, which means that the DEA and the Colombian government have been able to successfully slow down production. "The aggressive policy of herbicide spraying and manual eradication have been so effective that it has made it impossible for traffickers to meet the global demand. That's a huge success because if it was up to Colombian traffickers, they would meet that demand. But this isn't just a Colombian issue, it's a South American one."

Jay Bergman draws out his last words, and for good reason. His office is in Colombia—the United States' last ally in an increasingly revolutionary Latin America—and the statistics pointing toward success apply only to this country. As soon as production and cultivation decreased in Colombia, it increased in Peru and Bolivia, and the reduction in consumption discernible in the United States in recent years has been abundantly offset by an increase in the demand for cocaine in Europe—especially in England, Spain, and Italy. Thus, today's calls of victory from the Colombian government and military quickly fall on deaf ears as soon as the issue is viewed from a global perspective.

The problem that the DEA and Colombia will have to deal with in the future is that the other Andean countries have developed different views of the cocaine puzzle than the United States. For Bolivia and Venezuela respectively, there is no question that the white powder is causing addiction and severe suffering, but for the leaders of these countries the problem—measured in addicts—is by no means as dramatic as it is to the United States or the United Nations. Apart from any ideological divide between these nations and the United States, the global aspects of the problem are difficult to address as long as the enormous demand in the West prevails.

But the DEA's problems are even worse than that. The institution that Jay Bergman represents is not, according to the neo-revolutionary analyses, primarily an anti-drug agency with an interest in fighting narcotics, but an organization whose main purpose is to look after the interests of Washington in Latin America, which they do using cocaine as a pretext. The United States' history of working with or against drugs, depending on their strategic needs, is well documented— the Iran–Contra affair, the collaboration with Manuel Noriega, and the alliance with the drug mafia during the pursuit of Escobar. In 2008, with this history as a backdrop, the DEA was forced to pull out of Bolivia after Morales' government claimed to have evidence that Bergman's colleagues had participated in right-wing plots to overthrow the socialist government, and in Venezuela the situation is even tenser, ever since George W. Bush declared the war on drugs synonymous with the war on terror.

Jay Bergman sighs. He does not deny that the DEA has become plagued with a number of emblematic "corruption scandals," but he does believe that times have changed. He says he can guarantee that the organization is "clean" today, and insists that the Colombian state—notorious for human-rights offenses—is increasingly able to rid itself of corruption and abuse thanks to the American aid they have received over the years. "There's a catharsis going on here right now," he says, recognizing that there are so many scandals going on at once that he can hardly keep track of them all: the para-political scandal, *falsos positivos*, criminal acts of the secret service, and so on. But Bergman's point is that they are no longer swept under the rug, that they're being taken seriously, adjudicated. "Today, we're watching Colombia moving itself out of the hell it was going through in the 1970s, 1980s, and 1990s, when the country was being terrorized, in every sense of the word, by the devastation of drug trafficking. What we see is certainly a corruption phase, but this is a healthy phase. Many people here see all of these scandals as a bad thing, but I see it as a cathartic moment. It's a natural progression and evolution as this country tries to get itself out of a very dark place."

The development that today's Latin American politicians see as the worst-case scenario for the 2010s—that the demand for cocaine and the contra war on production are slowly perpetuating a large-scale regional war—is one Jay Bergman sees, if the hypothesis holds water, not as the fault of Colombia but of the revolutionaries. Ripping the problem out by the roots is, according to him, an ongoing job, and it is therefore a historic tragedy that just when the strategy instigated by Nixon and Reagan is starting to show results in the Andes, Colombia's neighbors have governments that try to absolve themselves of responsibility by placing all the blame on demand.

"The old days are becoming the new days," says Bergman, referring to an ever-increasing amount of production gradually being relocated to the socialist country of Bolivia, which, according to the DEA, is also the mafia's reinvented free zone. The "old days" are the 1980s, when the global boom got underway. At that time almost all coca fields were in Bolivia and Peru, and the coca paste was flown to southern Colombia for processing, after which the powder was distributed to the rest of the world via the criminal networks of the Medellín and Cali Cartels. However, when the war on drugs intensified in Bolivia and Peru—a process the farmers read in imperialist terms, and which later brought the revolutionary coca grower Evo Morales to power—the majority of fields were established in Colombia, which became the center for both cultivation and processing in the late 1990s. According to Bergman, production is now emigrating south again, since the climate has tightened in Colombia and loosened in Bolivia. But all this, he says, is happening with one major difference. "The labs in Bolivia today are run by Colombians, not Bolivians. It's Colombians working in the labs, doing quality control, and taking care of oversight, et cetera."

According to the DEA, Colombian traffickers are moving large parts of their criminal infrastructures down to Bolivia, and there is a substantial migration of people from Colombia to Bolivia in order to carry out illegal business. But the old days won't become the new days in the sense that they will bring products to Colombia for export anymore. The vast number of Colombians who are migrating to Bolivia will process cocaine and export the high-quality product directly from there. It doesn't make sense, says Bergman, to bring paste up here anymore. "I mean, considering all the policy, army, navy, air force, and everything you have to deal with in Colombia, why would you? It's so much better to just produce it down there and bring it straight out on the international markets."

Another of the DEA's causes for concern is Venezuela. Under Hugo Chávez, the most important oil state in Latin America also became a key player in the cocaine drama. According to the CIA, more than a third of all the cocaine that now leaves Colombia exits through Venezuela—data that Chávez's government dismissed as a rigging of a future invasion, based on "the well known pattern from Iraq" and its non-existent weapons of mass destruction.

The third displacement, which, according to the DEA, will play a key role in the cocaine landscape of the future, is over the control of new markets. The European, Asian, Australian, and Latin American markets have all been experiencing periods of rapid growth, while the US market seems to have passed its peak, as methamphetamines are taking over. At the dawn of the new millennium the Mexican cartels took over the US market following the fall of the Medellín and Cali cartels, and in the 2010s a key concern is how these criminal Mexican monsters will behave when other markets grow at a faster rate than that of the United States.

"What's really happening now is that the Mexicans are beginning to dominate not just the American distribution market but the global distribution market," says Bergman. And if they manage to dominate all the distribution markets, they will be calling the shots and, in the end, also gain power over production. During the era of the Medellín and Cali cartels the DEA used to say that these organizations had control "from the farm to the arm," an expression that refers to heroin, but the principle is the same with cocaine; someone had a linear organization that owns the distribution in the United States and Europe, the transportation system, and the production. Bergman compares it with the "Detroit model"; the ones who own the production—General Motors and Ford—are in charge of everything. That's why a source country such as Colombia has always been so important. But in the new world it's the other way around; it's the distributor that's in charge. "Like Walmart," says Bergman. "Now it's Walmart who dictates to Colgate, 'this is the price we want per unit, this is when we want it; this is how much we want and this is what we're willing to pay for it.' And it's this position the Mexicans today are reaching."

But no large-scale war is expected between the Colombian and Mexican mafias. In terms of drug criminality, Colombia is 20 years ahead of Mexico, and the cartels' war on the state that is tearing Mexican democracy apart is long since history in Colombia. These kinds of wars cannot be won. In Colombia production could be rendered more effective after Escobar's death thanks to the decentralization of the mafia (the birth of mini-cartels) and the flexibility of the process (mobile labs and smaller units), but first and foremost it was the result of the mafia's adoption of a new strategy: to work with the state, rather than against it. And this model remains in force to this day. The mafia created its own political parties, its own mayors, governors, senators, secretaries, and prosecutors, and integrated their illegal operations with legitimate industries in a way that gave birth to a variety of large companies, which the state has been subsidizing ever since.

Until now deliveries to Europe, long since the fastest-growing market, have been managed by the drug-production emperors of Colombia, but after the historic crackdown on the 'Ndrangheta, the future for the Colombian–European connections is unclear. "The Colombians," says Bergman, "gave up the American market for a number of reasons: to avoid extradition, to avoid prosecution, et cetera, and they already had the European market. At the time, when our focus was elsewhere, the mafia here already knew that the European market was going to be a money-maker. Mexicans never forced the Colombians from the US market; they left voluntarily."

Outside Bergman's office the sun is refracted on the façade of every glass building in the metropolis of ten million, a city that became known in the 1980s as "the global capital of cocaine," something it has in many ways continued to be through elegant mutations across the decades. Both Medellín and Bogotá have undergone so many impressive facelifts since the turn of the millennium that there is not a media outlet in the world that hasn't reported on the story of these urban metamorphoses. Carl Bildt, Sweden's minister of foreign affairs, was just one of the many European leaders to sing the praises of president Uribe in 2006, commenting on how Uribe, with a "firm hand," had eliminated squalor and corruption:

> I remember years ago when Bogotá was seen as so crime-infested and dangerous that one could hardly enter the terminal in the airport when one needed to change planes in the city. That's all gone. Today, charming Bogotá is one of the safest and cleanest cities of Latin America ... This is all associated with the efforts done to combat the drug trade that previously risked totally destroying the country. A program of spraying coca plantations from the air that was once rather controversial has evidently started to be successful.

That same year, in 2006, Colombia produced 545 tonnes of cocaine, six times as much as during Escobar's time, and the nation's share of global cocaine production rose from 12 to 62 per cent during the same period (1993–2006). How could Bogotá and Colombia be so loved as a large-scale producer, but so feared and despised as a small-scale producer? And how could Carl Bildt describe a 600 per cent rise in drug trafficking as an evident success in the fight against drug trafficking?

The answer is that a great deal of time has passed since the DEA, the United States, the European Union, the United Nations, the Colombian and Mexican police forces, and other institutions stopped fighting drugs and crime and chose instead to fight the aesthetics of drug criminality. Nothing is about narcotics anymore; everything is about appearance—how it is done, who does it, how they do it, and by what means. Or as Jay Bergman puts it: the "holistic policy" for the DEA and the war on drugs is, nowadays, just to make sure that the money generated by drug production "doesn't become a threat to national security in countries like Colombia."

He keeps stressing the importance of *how* things are done, and says that when it's down to a level where everything is only a matter of law enforcement and not of national security, the DEA's job will be done. The struggle today, he says, is to get it down to a level that is "manageable, perhaps even acceptable."

A "manageable level" is thus no longer measured in terms of drugs or crime, but violence; when drug criminality is handled by respected businessmen instead of by guerrillas and street gangs, and so generates selective but not organized violence, the war on drugs has achieved its goal. No other country in the world has seen its narcotics criminality mutate so smoothly according to this principle as Colombia in the 2000s. The guerrillas have been repelled, paramilitary organizations have been demobilized, urban violence has decreased dramatically, and foreign capital has poured in, while cocaine production has only continued. And when it recently came out that several members of Congress had been elected on political platforms financed by the drug mafia, the DEA, along with a large number of US and EU political establishments, also read that as positive: the nation is going through a healthy purge, a catharsis.

In light of this—the fact that the amount of violence, not the amount of drugs, is the deciding factor—it might seem that legalization ought to be more of a standard-bearer for the global war on drugs than one would guess at first glance, but such is not the case. Jay Bergman maintains that he is an "absolute opponent" of legalizing drugs, even cannabis, and he cringes when the report by the three former presidents and the current decriminalization moves in Mexico, Argentina, and several US states enter into the discussion. And of course he welcomes Colombia's new criminalization of the personal dose. "I've been doing this for so long, so it's hard for me to have an objective opinion, but let me just say this: I have a 13-year-old son, and I'm really happy I don't have to explain to him why it's bad—I just tell him that it's bad and, by the way, illegal. Trust me, I like having that helping me when I'm trying to guide my son through life and help him not to ruin his future," says Bergman. "I'm not so concerned about decriminalization itself; I'm more concerned about legitimatizing. By decriminalizing it you're legitimatizing it, making people think it's not harmful."

The endless corridors of the US embassy branch out into an expansive maze. Outside all the security barriers, hundreds of Colombians line up in a curling queue with forms carefully filled out by hand, in the hope of obtaining a visa to the promised land in the north. Jay Bergman prepares to return to his computer, which, over the past 30 years, has been at the helm of much of the work that has resulted in hundreds of dissolved criminal networks, thousands of arrests, and the confiscation of hundreds of thousands of kilos of cocaine, but that, at the same time, has succeeded only marginally, if at all, in altering global demand and production. Yet this latter idea is a fallacy, according to Bergman. The ever-increasing number of academics, intellectuals, and politicians who are calling the war on drugs "a fiasco" are ignoring the good work it has done. Certainly, the goal set by the United Nations in 1998—that the world would be drug-free by 2008—is easy to scoff at, but according to Bergman, had it not been for the work carried out by the DEA, the United Nations, and the police forces of the affected countries, the global misery caused by drugs would have been many times worse than it is today. "But will there ever be zero coca? No."

The cocaine exporters of tomorrow—Colombia remains a main

source for the foreseeable future—will, in other words, not only need to decentralize more and cease using violence, but also to carefully embed all drug activity in legal business operations. The Mexican mafia's violent large-scale model will most likely collapse at some point during the 2010s, just as the great Medellín and Cali cartels did in the 1990s, and once Bergman and his men have killed off Loco Barrera and the others he refers to as "dead men walking," the decentralized landscapes of modern drug trafficking will be colonized by the white knights of tomorrow.

"The smartest people are those who stay under the radar. People moving ten kilos a month to Japan at 100,000 dollars a kilo," says Bergman. If you buy it here, he goes on, nodding toward the outside, for 2000 dollars, and spend another 15,000 to move it to Japan—and you have a route into the country—you still make almost a million dollars every month. "That's more than Cuchillo makes!" he concludes. "Because at the end of the day he has to pay all his people, pay for his weapons, et cetera. While you live as a comfortable businessperson in the nicest neighborhood in Bogotá. So I'm not saying that there aren't a lot of small-scale Colombian drug traffickers staying well under the radar screen making fortunes."

WHEN CÉSAR GAVIRIA became head of state in 1990, after Galán's assassination and young Juan Manuel's plea for him to "save Colombia," the new president looked north and said a prayer: "The demand for drugs is what fuels the drug industry. If the US and the industrialized nations of the world do not find a way to reduce consumption, we will never solve this problem. It doesn't matter how much we fight, how many lives we lose, how many sacrifices we make—the problem will always remain. The industrialized world has to find a way to reduce the demand for narcotics."

Exactly 20 years later María Jimena Duzán—who was in the 1980s a journalist for *El Espectador*, the paper whose office was bombed by Escobar—sits among bookshelves in her home in Bogotá. She says that Gaviria's wishes have not been granted, but also that he was wrong. Or at least halfway wrong. "Demand isn't the reason for our problems. The fact that millions of gringos and Europeans consume cocaine doesn't explain why almost all of it is produced here. Why not in Ecuador or Venezuela? Argentina or Brazil? Colombia's problem is that the inhabitants in half of the country have been used to living outside the law. What needs to be done here is for the state to show its presence in all those left-behind areas—and not just militarily. Most people growing coca in our jungles have never seen anything of the state except its army."

María Jimena Duzán's home was blown up in 1982, and her sister—a young documentary-filmmaker on the verge of revealing liaisons between the cartels and the state—was murdered in 1990. Duzán's adult life coincides time-wise with the country's cocaine drama, and now she sits here in denim and gray boots, surrounded by books on a topic she is familiar with: war. Carl von Clausewitz's *On War*. Jonathan Marshall, Peter Dale Scott, and Jane Hunter's *The Iran Contra Connection*. Norman Mailer's *Why Are We at War?* And her own, a classic in its own right—*Death Beat: a Colombian journalist's life inside the cocaine wars*.

"The progression of the cocaine mafia here is completely logical," Duzán says. "The first generation tries to gain control over the state with weapons and fails. The second generation doesn't make the same mistake and works in a more civilian way. What's unique about Colombia is that we now have a third generation, which has practically taken over. Pablo Escobar never succeeded in his political ambitions, though several of his relatives and allies are in positions of power today."

María Jimena Duzán has followed the growing impact of cocaine on the nation, and the world, for the past 35 years, and is today one of the country's most influential authors and journalists. Her analysis about what happened in the past, what is happening now, and what will happen in the future is both positive and negative: her negative perspective applies to Colombia, her positive one to the rest of the world. Behind the country's polished façade of an exuberant economy, a strong military, a reduction in violence, and a thriving tourism industry lurks a populist dynamic that in some ways resembles that in Italy—a nation whose authoritarian structures have been impressively updated. Just as Italy's political culture has been "mediatized," María Jimena Duzán believes Colombia's has been "narcotized," which has resulted in incalculably negative consequences for democracy: "The alliances between large landowners and the drug mafia have been legitimized. That's what's happened."

All the millions that have been pouring in from cocaine since the 1990s were welcomed with open arms by those rural clans whose power was threatened by the 1991 constitution. When Colombia adopted this statute, a key tenet was the rights of minorities to traditionally inhabited areas, and the nation was hailed the world over for having created a genuinely multicultural state where indigenous peoples and blacks, after 180 years of institutionalized racism, were guaranteed ownership rights in specific territories. But these areas were often in remote and isolated parts of the country—exactly the kind of land that would prove attractive to drug traffic in the coming years—and it was these vast virgin areas that the nation's agrarian elites had long since used however they saw fit, employing a supply of conveniently poor and drifting peasants as day labor in a semi-feudal system. What was new about the constitution, Duzán says, was that it not only gave displaced ethnicities nominal rights to land, but also that it created a new legal order—completely new institutions— intended to implement gradual landownership reforms throughout the country. And this is where it went too far. The elite revolted. And cocaine became their weapon.

"Basically, the problem here is that the national government doesn't govern the entire country. We are still in the process of building a state. Large parts of the country are in the hands of regional elites, who see no reason to abide by the law the way that people in the cities have to. Outside the urban areas is a wild Colombia—feudal, archaic, and reactionary—and it's in those milieus all sorts of armed groups are thriving. The guerrillas, paramilitaries, and drug mafia—they all live in the past. As if the state doesn't exist. The greatest challenge for Colombian democracy is to overcome this. To become a real state. The 1991 constitution was a first step and it saved many lives, but it threatens a certain type of power that is traditionally strong here—the power of the extreme right and the guerrillas. It benefits civilians, not armed groups. It supports people who obey the law. Since the neo-rightists came to power, the constitution has been their worst enemy, and politics just strives to undermine it."

But as usual in Colombia it is much more complicated—or tragic—than that. One progressive objective that the "world's most modern constitution" had was to decentralize politics: to give more power and autonomy to villages, municipalities, and regions. The problem was that this was planned without consideration for the archaic power structures that essentially govern the rural parts of Colombia. Loaded with economic and social strength, large landowners were thus given carte blanche to establish their own political parties in line with their own interests, and after the guerrillas' earlier half-hearted attempt to civilize themselves by launching a political party was quashed by private armies acting in alliance with the regular military—3000 elected socialists were executed in the course of just one decade—the way was paved for what was to come: the auctioning off of local and regional political platforms to the highest bidder. The state's inability to prevent guerrilla attacks on landowners' property made the rural oligarchy increasingly reliant on drug trafficking, not just to fund local armies but also to establish political parties. This was what, by the end of the first decade of the 2000s, became known throughout the world as "the paramilitary political scandal"—a third of the Congress, the majority supporting the government, were funded by drug money. And it soon became apparent that most major elite political groups—not just the rural reactionaries, but many urban liberals as well—had been using drug money in their fight against the FARC.

In June 2010 Juan Manuel Santos—minister of defense in the Uribe administration, responsible for the attack on Ecuador, and a son of the largest media mogul in the country—was elected president. "What has happened in Colombia over the past 20 years," says Duzán, "is that all the major political groups have been united by a common enemy: the FARC. Their frustration over their inability to wipe out this guerrilla plague has led to a tacit agreement to combat the FARC with all the means at their joint disposal. New political classes and parties have been born in this way, and the two old parties have been imbued with the same objective—and they have all entered into different alliances with the drug mafia in order to achieve their goals. This is the political concept about which no one speaks openly, but which today is the root of the efforts of people like Álvaro Uribe and Juan Manuel Santos: to defeat the FARC by whatever means possible. And the immense problem we now have to handle is the fact that large portions of today's political establishment have grown together with the dark forces of the drug trade."

The paramilitary political scandal revealed patterns resembling a huge conspiracy. From above, the White House had showered the government with financial support in the name of the war on drugs, and from below that same government had grown strong thanks to political interests with deep roots in the drug trade. As a result, Colombian right-wing populism—an inverted version of the Venezuelan Chavismo—is today one of Latin America's most stable political forces.

María Jimena Duzán sighs. "The guerrillas demolish, destroy, and murder. The mafia buys. Eighty per cent of congressmen own land, and most often large estates. No one cares about the fact that many of them have built their power by exporting cocaine—no one gives a damn about that. And for them, the important thing is that the government helps them in their struggle for landownership."

That is the Colombian part of the story. As for the future for the rest of the world, she is more optimistic. María Jimena Duzán adheres to the common argument in today's Colombian drug debate, that legalizing cocaine would be the best thing for this country—although not necessarily for others—but she also says that this is a utopian idea, and therefore pointless to discuss. There are simply too many forces working against it. Mainly economic ones: all of Switzerland, she says, would collapse, as well as large parts of the US financial sector, where much of the drug money ends up. An equally important factor in legalization being a non-starter is that global drug-policy collaboration is regulated in UN conventions, and those are not based on reason and science but on dogma—sometimes Marxist, sometimes religious. The growing choir of liberal and secular voices in some parts of the West now calling for decriminalization cannot change the fact that prohibition is strongly supported in every other corner of the world: China, the United States, Japan, the Arab world, Russia, Africa, the Nordic countries, and Eastern Europe; all but a few EU and Latin American countries are against it.

"We waited far too long. It's too late now."

Her argument is in line with what Mario Vargas Llosa writes in his essay "The Other State," in which he suggests that drug-funded criminality is the "greatest threat to Latin American democracies" today, and asks how most governments can continue to support the idea that drugs must be illegal, despite the overwhelming amount of research suggesting the contrary. The answer is, he writes, that politicians the world over in the 1970s and 1980s really did think—in contrast to their views on alcohol and tobacco—that they could not only combat the problem but actually *obliterate* it. That belief has since been abandoned by most analysts, but if a phenomenon is to be legalized it must be done relatively soon after the illegal markets have begun to expand; otherwise it will be impossible, since an ever-swelling bureaucracy with growing interests in keeping the phenomenon illegal will become too strong. According to Vargas

Llosa, this is exactly what has happened with drugs: "The biggest obstacle today is that all those institutions and individuals who are making a living on the repression of drugs are all fighting—which is completely logical—tooth and nail to defend their livelihood."

María Jimena Duzán agrees, but thinks, like most other Latin American politicians—the Christian right being the exception—that there is now a window of opportunity for a new policy, one that defends neither legalization nor the war on drugs, but constitutes a humanization of the fight. Pragmatism. Change.

After the three former presidents sounded the alarm on the consequences of the war on drugs, US Congress appointed another commission whose sole objective is to recommend a new policy to President Obama—and thus to the world. The conclusions are still to be presented, but the investigators started off by listing a collection of facts that can be read as heralding either success or disaster: today five per cent of the world's population lives in the United States, but 17.2 per cent of the world's consumers of illegal drugs; 100 per cent of all cocaine and 90 per cent of all heroin consumed in the United States is produced in the Andes, mostly in Colombia. In the transit countries—Haiti, Ecuador, Jamaica, and Venezuela, but especially Mexico and Central America—drug trafficking is the economic backbone of organized crime, which threatens legal systems, political institutions, and the security of citizens. A war is currently being fought between the Mexican cartels and the nation's security forces, the former overseeing the wholesale market for all the cocaine sold in the United States today. Drug-related violence has escalated dramatically since president Felipe Calderón launched the nation's military-led war on drugs in 2006. Over 90 per cent of all the weapons used in drug-related killings come from the United States. Between 1980 and 2008 the United States spent 11.3 billion USD on the war on drugs in Latin America, but during this same period the number of life-long abusers of cannabis, cocaine, and heroin has been steadily on the rise; over the past 30 years the total number of hardcore addicts across these three drugs has doubled.

María Jimena Duzán welcomes new perspectives on the topic, but does not think that either the number of murders in Latin America or the number of addicts in the United States will compel Washington to reconsider its former policy in earnest. There is, however, something she thinks will finally have an effect on Washington: the migration of the brutal phenomenon that so many of the books on her bookshelves deal with—war. "That's what has arrived in their country. War. It sounds cynical, but I think it's good that the war has reached the US. Today the entire Texas border is a war zone. People are being killed left and right. Drug violence has finally crossed the border, which has made the US wake up. The cost of this has also become evident there. That's why new ideas are beginning to take root in Washington. They're not changing their way of thinking because of the number of addicts, but because of the changed security situation. It's a good start. I'm optimistic now. Very."

MELISSA AND HER mother are standing by the statue of Simón Bolívar when Daniel Pacheco, one of the instigators of the protest and a columnist for *El Espectador*, begins to speak. The crowd draws in closer. Pigeons scatter. Cops look on. Five centuries have passed since the Spaniards were first introduced to the coca leaf, and it's been 150 years since Albert Niemann revealed the chemical formula for what would, in the 20th century, spawn the white gold that would forever affect medicine, psychology, literature, addiction, the film industry, the White House, and Latin America.

"*Hola*," says Pacheco to his listeners.

He has curly hair, and his eyes peer out through a pair of big glasses as he gazes over the urban heart of the country—where Melissa Álvarez was born in 1991, during the raging cocaine war, right between the assassination of Luis Carlos Galán in 1989 and the killing of Pablo Escobar in 1993. She is the same age as the constitution, the "secular and anti-authoritarian" document the Christian right successfully disarmed with the help of cocaine and the war on it in the 2000s. But what has played out over the last two drug-filled decades since the constitution was written has more concrete than theoretical consequences; guerrilla resources increased tenfold and, with the state as the instrument, the elite struck back with paramilitary death squads, who have now killed over 40,000 people—more than the Chilean and Argentinean dictatorships combined.

All of this has happened while the global demand for cocaine has increased, and so it will most likely continue. No one—not even the DEA, the United Nations, the European Union, or Washington—seems to think any longer that demand can be controlled; so how will it all end? Is it true, as Alfredo Rangel suggests, that legalization is the least detrimental alternative? Or is the opposite true, as Jay Bergman argues: that it is a good thing that so much has been invested in maintaining prohibition, and that, if the DEA and the other institutions fighting drugs could get just a little more funding, order could soon be restored in Colombia, Mexico, the rest of Latin America, and the world? Or is it as María Jimena Duzán says, when she claims that both the war on drugs and legalization are naïve schemes that will soon be scrapped in favor of a global policy in which selective decriminalization goes hand-in-hand with effective prevention and much better methods of crime fighting?

Perhaps it doesn't matter. At least as far as cocaine is concerned. Research into the history of drugs and addiction shows that laws play an insignificant role in how drug-related problems evolve, and that other things are far more decisive in shaping the patterns of drug use and abuse: the economy, migration, knowledge, poverty, or trends. And, not least, the invention of new drugs. Cocaine is in many important ways an outdated drug—requiring cultivation, a special climate, and expensive logistics, with a high that is appealing but in no way unique. In Misha Glenny's book *McMafia* Sandro Calvani, former director of the UN anti-drug agency in both Bolivia and Colombia, prophesizes the future of drug-related organized crime and sees cocaine playing a starring role—as the loser. Calvani ascertains that "cocaine has no future" because drug users can easily get rid of the yoke of today's traffickers thanks to chemical developments and free markets. "Wherever amphetamines and synthetic drugs have arrived onto the market, they replace everything—cocaine, heroin, the lot," Calvani states. "It works fast and doesn't involve the paraphernalia of injecting or sniffing. A much better kind of drug. More dangerous, but it works. Here, it has already started in Medellín. So the future is in the new drugs. The market will change and determine this. They don't need the narco-traffickers. The future will be completely different."

The problem for Colombia is that the white powder didn't give rise to the country's injustices and war; it just multiplied them. In other words, the end of cocaine will not solve the problems either, but only reduce them. Colombia is not dependent on cocaine, but cocaine is dependent on Colombia. The global drug industry relies on conflict, poverty, ineffectual government, police forces for sale, and criminal know-how, all of which has put Colombia on a carousel of evil: the narcotics industry is here because the armed groups are here, and the armed groups are here because the narcotics industry is here. And so it goes, round and round. Francisco Thoumi, the leading drug scholar in the country, thinks that there is only one way to put the brakes on: "What has to be legalized is Colombia, not cocaine." But that's easier said than done.

Darkness falls over the demonstrators. Even though the goal of the protest is doomed to failure, everyone is upbeat. Chaos and warfare have not caused Colombians to lose their sophisticated sense of humor. With polite irony, typical for the country, Daniel Pacheco asks the protesters to show some unreturned respect by not smoking pot right in front of the police and the Congress. They comply, but laugh. The lighted neoclassical façade on the south side of the square looks like a giant glowing grill illuminating the crowd, as Daniel Pacheco picks up a thread from one of his columns:

Do you understand why they forbid us from using mind-altering drugs? Why there are people who want to deny gays and lesbians the right to marry and adopt children? Who deny women the right to abortion? Why it is called unpatriotic to choose not to bear arms? Why people are denied the right to die with dignity? Why certain people want to forbid things that have nothing to do with them? Neither do I.

Pacheco encourages everyone to hold up a "dose of personality." It can be anything that has contributed joy and fulfillment to one's life: books, CDs, joints, mountain-climbing equipment, sex toys, Bibles, partners, guitars. In his thick glasses Pacheco resembles a young Gabriel García Márquez, and it was here exactly six decades ago that Castro, Márquez, and Gaítan all took part in the street demonstrations that ended in Gaítan's assassination, launching what remains to this day the world's longest ongoing civil conflict.

Ivonne stands eye to eye with Simón Bolívar. Her curly hair flies around in the breeze. Melissa stands by her side. What is interesting about all the talk on narcotics in one of the largest drug-producing nations in the world is that the phenomenon of abuse is rarely, if ever, mentioned. Almost never. But this is certainly not because there are no addicts in Colombia; just a stone's throw away a whole community of poor people in one of the most miserable ghettos in the city are completely hooked on *basuco*, a simplified version of crack. And in order to cope with the cold nights, the city's hordes of street kids are every evening numbing their brains by sniffing glue. Ivonne, mother of two, used harder drugs than cannabis during her student days. But her family and neighborhood smoothly prevented her from letting her life go down the drain. And that's a type of secure environment many—very many—people lack.

She looks thoughtful and her face breaks into a pensive expression momentarily as she thinks about the drug problem in relation to class and social environments. Is the reason why hardly anyone in progressive Colombia is against legalization because the educated middle and upper classes are mainly the ones committed to the debate and politically active? Are the people who raise their voices also the ones who have a social safety net? "I don't think so," she finally says. "When we think about legalization in Colombia, what we are really thinking about is getting rid of the mafia. Nothing else. The war is what matters here. I'm not thinking about misery or abuse, but about something completely different: an opportunity. Peace and liberation for this country."

NOTES ON SOURCES

I HAVE ATTEMPTED to write a book on one of the world's most complex societies that is both readable and accessible. In doing so I have chosen to work without footnotes, with all the pros and cons such an approach entails. However, this section contains additional commentary, along with a list of my sources, which will allow the reader to see which accounts and facts the analyses are based on.

To report in Colombia means acting in extremely sensitive, conflict-ridden environments, particularly in rural areas. A reporter who doesn't take the necessary precautions or is careless with information can cause fatal consequences for individuals, or even trigger social and political dynamics that may end up in massive internal displacement. Consequently, in some cases names have been changed to protect identities. In two instances I have also changed the name of the location. In the notes on the following pages, all pseudonyms are italicized. Alfonso, in the preface, goes by a different name in real life, too.

These notes are also intended as tips for further reading for those who wish to learn more about cocaine and Colombia's incredible history, which I hope this book will inspire them to do. Publishers and years of publication for the books I have used are included in the bibliography. Tips on further reading on Latin America in general, and Colombia in particular, may be found on my website: www.magnuslinton.com.

The greatest challenge with regard to sources when writing about coca and the distribution of cocaine, as well as the successes and failures of the war on drugs, is deciding which statistics to use. Two major institutions that follow these developments—the United Nations Office on Drugs and Crime, or UNODC, and the US Office of National Drug Control Policy, or ONDCP—present such drastically conflicting figures that the discrepancy between them reveals just how difficult it is to assess illegal activity. For instance, according to UNODC there were 181,600 hectares of cultivated coca in the Andes in 2007, while according to ONDCP there were 232,000 hectares. According to UNODC 99,000 of those hectares were in Colombia, while according to ONDCP Colombia had 167,000 hectares of cultivated coca—almost twice as much. UN statistics show a 25 per cent decrease in the total amount of land worldwide on which coca was grown between 1990 and 2006, while the US agency shows an increase, claiming that in 2007 more hectares were used for coca cultivation globally than ever before. If you factor cocaine *production* into the equation, the situation becomes even more confusing; according to UNODC, in 2007 a total of 902 tonnes of cocaine was produced in the world, while ONDCP, which reported 50,000 more cultivated hectares that same year, claimed that only 785 tonnes were produced—that is, nearly 15 per cent *less*.

For Colombia, the fluctuations in statistics in recent years have been extreme. In 2007 there was, according to the UN office, a dramatic increase in the number of hectares used for coca cultivation, compared with 2006 (the figure rose from 78,000 to 99,000); the following year a nearly equal reduction was reported (from 99,000 to 81,000), while the US stats showed an increase for both years. According to the latest UN figures on Colombia, the total amount of pure cocaine produced decreased from 545 tonnes in 2007 to 390 tonnes in 2008, while production in both Bolivia and Peru increased. I've chosen to use the United Nations' statistics since UNODC openly reports the methodology they use in their assessments, which includes satellite photography, whereas ONDCP doesn't.

However, I encourage the reader to take all statistics in this regard with a grain of salt. As explained by the expert Francisco Thoumi and as shown in the chapter "Green Gold," the reporting of figures is highly politicized. The majority of coca farmers I spent time with camouflage their coca plants among other crops so that the plants won't be detected in satellite images. Another problem with obtaining reliable statistics on the actual spread of coca cultivation is that much of the land that has been heavily cultivated in Colombia in recent years is in the rainforest provinces, which are nearly always cloudy, and this complicates satellite photography—so much so that, according to the UNODC research team in Colombia, it seriously affects the monitoring. However, an actual decline in production in Colombia, as reported in 2008, is plausible, given the United Nations also reports that 230,000 hectares of coca were destroyed (130,000 by herbicide spraying and 100,000 by manual elimination) in the same year, almost three times as much as the organization had reported as having been cultivated.

In light of the more than two decades of United Nations statistics, from 1990 to today, it can be concluded that the number of cultivated hectares—the total amount in Colombia, Peru, and Bolivia, after all the efforts of the war on drugs—has been reduced by 25 per cent, while production during the same time has increased by 28 per cent. More-potent plants, better processing techniques, and faster replanting following herbicide spraying are some of the reasons why the increased demand has been able to be satisfied. Dramatic fluctuations, particularly in Colombia, will most likely continue, and the statistic I report in this book, with Colombia's share of global production at around 60 per cent, is an average calculation for the most recent decade as a whole, based on the UN statistics.

1 — Cocaturismo: Medellín as Heaven

All interviews used in this chapter were conducted in Medellín in November 2008, May 2009, and November 2009, during my visits to the districts of San Javier (Comuna 13), Moravia, Barrio Pablo Escobar, El Pablado, and Barrio Antioquia; the nightclubs Karma, Tutaina, Tuturama, Blue, Kukaramakara, PH, Fase II, White, Mangos, and Carnival; and the hostels Casa Kiwi, The Pit Stop Hostel, and The Tiger Paw. I conducted interviews with the following people: *Alonso*, assassin; Antonio Jaramillo, executive manager of Corporación Región; César Álvarez, taxi driver; Deyner, resident of Comuna 13; Diana Barajas, sociologist at Instituto Popular de Capacitación; Dioselina Vasco, resident of Comuna 13, mother whose five sons were killed; *Lucy*, Irish backpacker; Felipe Palau, director of the Fuerza Joven program of Medellín; *Håkan*, Swedish backpacker; Javier, resident of Barrio Antioquia; *Lina Cuevas*, victim of violence and resident of Comuna 13; Lourdes Duarte, resident of Moravia; Maria Herlinda Arias, resident of Moravia; Max Yuri, sociologist; Olga Lucía Perez, resident of Comuna 13; Pablo Emilio Angarita, political scientist; Paul Thoreson, proprietor, Casa Kiwi; *Greg*, Canadian backpacker.

In addition to some 30 news reports from the Colombian daily newspapers *El Colombiano*, *El Espectador*, and *El Tiempo*, I used the following printed sources in those passages of the text that deal with Medellín during the first decade of the new millennium: Forrest Hylton's "Extreme Makeover—Medellín in the New Millennium" (in the anthology *Evil Paradises*), Diana Grajales' *Genealogia de las Bandas* (Universidad de Antioquia), Claudia López's "La Ruta de la Expansión Paramilitar y la Transformación Política de Antioquia" (in the anthology *Parapolítica*), and the Amnesty report *The Paramilitaries in Medellín*, as well as the following reports: Jonathan Franklin's "The World's First Cocaine Bar" (*The Guardian*, 29 August 2009), Anthony Faiola's "Sustaining the Medellín Miracle" (*The Washington Post*, 11 July 2008), Malcolm Beith's "Good Times in Medellín: a city tainted by violence is experiencing a renaissance" (*Newsweek*, 5 June 2004), Juan Gabriel Vásquez's "Cocaína y Turismo" (*El Espectador*, 4 April 2008), Alice O'Keeffe's "Colombia: progress at a price" (*New Statesman*, 23 April 2007), and Daniel Kurtz-Phelan's "Colombia's City On a Hill: Medellín goes from murder capital to model city" (*Newsweek*, 10 November 2007). I obtained official city murder statistics from Medicina Legal, the Colombian agency dealing with forensic pathology.

For the historical exposé I used David T. Courtwright's *Forces of Habit: drugs and the making of the modern world*; Richard Davenport-Hines' *The Pursuit of Oblivion: a global history of narcotics, 1500–2000*; Paul Gootenberg's *Andean Cocaine: the making of a global drug*; and Tom Feiling's *The Candy Machine: how cocaine took over the world*.

The passages on the rise and fall of the *marimba* bonanza stem predominantly from Francisco Thoumis' *Illegal Drugs in Colombia: from illegal economic boom to social crisis*, Fabio Castillo's *Riders of Cocaine*, and Virginia Vallejo's *Loving Pablo, Hating Escobar*. The quote on pp. 28–29 is also from Vallejo's book, but my translation is taken from the Spanish edition.

Sections pertaining to the time in which president Álvaro Uribe served as head of the Civil Aviation Authority and his possible collaboration with the mafia are based on information from Joseph Contreras' *Biografía No Autorizada de Álvaro Uribe Vélez* and article "Gaviria Contraataca y Uribe se va Contra Liberales" (*Semana*, April 2008). The same story is also featured in Vallejo's *Loving Pablo, Hating Escobar*, in which Álvaro Uribe and Pablo Escobar are portrayed as close friends who were mutually dependent on each other's services. The quote by Don Berna regarding the importance of keeping in step with globalization originates from Hylton's "Extreme Makeover."

2 — Green Gold: The Carousel of War

The trips essential for this story took place in May 2007 (the Pacific Coast and the inland of Chocó), June 2007 (Atrato River from

Quibdó, north to Río Arquía), December 2007 (Atrato River from Turbo, south to Riosucio), April 2008 (Tumaco, Nariño), May 2008 (San Andrés and Providencia, Caribbean), April 2009 (Buenaventura, the Pacific Coast), May 2009 (San Juan River from Bajo Calima to Istmina), June 2009 (Putumayo), and December 2009 (Golfo de Urabá and the Darien Gap, border to Panama). I interviewed the following people: *Andrea*, coca cultivator, San Juan River; Carlos Nuñez, social worker, Bogotá; *César*, coca cultivator, San Juan River; Claudia López, social scientist, Bogotá; Dora Rodríguez, internal refugee, Medellín; *Edgar*, small farmer, Putumayo; Edwaer Picón, coast-guard captain, Buenaventura; *Ester*, small farmer, Putumayo; Fabiola Rodríguez, mother of murdered son, Buenaventura; Francisco Thoumi, professor of economics, Bogotá; *Graciano*, coca cultivator, San Juan River; Gloria Zamudio, investor in the pyramid scheme DMG, Putumayo; Gustavo Guevara, prosecutor, Buenaventura; John Wayne, internal refugee, Chocó; José Mario Riascos, internal refugee, Buenaventura; *José*, small farmer, Putumayo; José-Eduard Pizo, priest, Soacha; *Iván*, fisherman, Chocó; Iván Torres, social worker, Bogotá; Jackson Chavarro, defender of the DMG pyramid scheme, Putumayo; Laura-Rosa Velez, internal refugee, Buenaventura; *Leo*, fisherman, Chocó; Leon Valencia, head of Nuevo Arco Iris, Bogotá; Leonarda Barco Riva, internal refugee, Buenaventura; Leonardo Correa, analyst, SIMCI/UNODC; Lucy Giraldo, social worker, Buenaventura; Luz-Dary Santiesteban, internal refugee, Buenaventura; Maria Cuevas, shopkeeper, Soacha; Mauricio Romero, conflict scholar, Bogotá; Melba Canga, mother of murdered son, Buenaventura; Nancy Sanchez, coordinator, Minga; *Nelcy*, small farmer, Putumayo; Rae Anne Lafrenz, Project Counselling Service coordinator, Bogotá; *Rodrigo*, son of murdered father, Buenaventura; *Solin*, coca chemist, San Juan River; Ted Legget, researcher, UNODC.

I obtained statistics on cocaine flows through Chocó from the Coast Guard and the regional public prosecutor's office, and the information dealing with general, global developments in cocaine consumption is from the most recent UNODC annual report. The historical account of Chocó is based on, among other sources, Orlando Fals Borda's (et al.) *La Violencia en Colombia*, Garry Leech's *Beyond Bogotá: diary of a drug war journalist in Colombia*, and Carlos Rosero and Tatiana Roa Avendaño's *Llenando Tanques, Vaciando Territorio*. The background on the social situation in Buenaventura incorporates information from the Roman Catholic Dioceses of Buenaventura and Misión de Apoyo al Proceso de Paz de la Organización de los Estados Americanos (MAPP/OEA). Pozón is not the village's real name.

In addition to the interviews, I based the section on Putumayo on, first and foremost, Oscar Jansson's PhD dissertation "The Cursed Leaf: an anthropology of the political economy of cocaine production in southern Colombia," Cruz Elena Flórez's *Órdenes Sociales en el Putumayo Antes y Después Del Plan Colombia*, Marco Palacios' *Plan Colombia: ¿anti-drogas o contrainsurgencia?*, and Mauricio Romero's *Paramilitares y Autodefensas*. Jansson, above all, forms the basis of the section on the guerrillas' and paramilitaries' respective economic relations with the coca cultivators, the "culture" that emerged in the province during the boom, and the Medellín Cartel's connection to armed groups in the region. The quote by William S. Burroughs also comes from Jansson. His work also helped me greatly with the passages in which I describe the hierarchy in the Colombian cocaine economy, as well as information on the fighting and massacres in El Azul and El Tigre. I extracted statistics on herbicide spraying, the number of cultivated hectares, the number of eliminated hectares, the successes and failures of Plan Colombia, the extent of support from the United States at various times, et cetera, from Cruz Elena Flórez's report and annual UNODC publications. Information and help for analysis on the guerrillas' description of the farmers as victims, and on the private armies' description of entrepreneurs as victims, also comes from *Palacios*, as does the discussion on the relative lull in conflict between La Violencia and the cocaine boom (1955–1985).

I wrote, but ended up not including in the final version, several pages on the 2008–2009 DMG pyramid scandal, a money-laundering scheme using Putumayo as its hub, which swindled hundreds of thousands of Colombians out of money and made headlines all over the world. That story is complex, but actually quite important for a more in-depth understanding of the development of the coca economy in Putumayo during the last decade. For readers wishing to learn more about this telling episode in Colombian history, I recommend Jineth Bedoya's book *La Pirámide de David Murcia* and Mauricio Baena Velázquez's *Captadores de Ilusiones: damnificados de las pirámides.*

The information on how different sums of money are distributed to different levels of the cocaine hierarchy comes from my interview with Francisco Thoumi, Colombia's foremost expert in criminal economy, as does the quote on the UN politicization of statistics.

The story of Arturo Beltrán Leyva's assassination made headlines in the Americas in December 2009, and the statistics I used here were extracted from the story as published in *The Wall Street Journal*, 28 December 2009. The spread of coca fields in the country and the role this has played in the *ecocidio* is documented in many sources, and the information I used (in terms of the spread of coca, the richness of Colombia's biodiversity, and information concerning the cost of manual elimination of coca plants versus herbicide spraying) come from the WOLA report *A Failed Strategy: the spraying of illicit crops in Colombia* (2008). I also used information on drug seizures, quality, rates, et cetera, from the 2008 and 2009 UNODC annual reports. *Andean Cocaine* by Paul Gootenberg offers a more academic in-depth explanation of the so-called balloon effect and its dynamics in the Andes.

The estimations I used about the number of remaining FARC soldiers were published in the Nuevo Arco Iris report *¿En qué está la Guerra?* The exact number of paramilitaries who were demobilized during the demobilization program, which ran between 2004 and 2006, was 31,689, according to MAPP/OEA, which oversaw the process. However, the OEA never estimated the number of soldiers organized into paramilitary groups before the process started, and in view of the number of registered weapons recovered, the number of paramilitaries bearing arms could not have exceeded 17,000. The other more than 14,000 "soldiers" were actually, according to Nuevo Arco Iris (the organization that has undertaken the most accurate examination of this process) people who never carried arms, and who joined or were recruited right before demobilization with an eye to being able to reap the benefits offered by the program. The book *Y se Refundó la Patria*, which takes an in-depth look at this problem and how, according to the Nuevo Arco Iris researchers, the paramilitary process paved the way for the mafia's takeover of governmental institutions at the local and regional level, was published in 2010. Statistics on what percentage of the paramilitary group's financial resources derived from coca production (70 per cent) are well known in Colombia and may be found, for example, in Alfredo Rangel's (et al.) *La Batalla Perdida Contra Las Drogas*. Several paramilitary leaders have also confirmed this information. Rangel's quote in the same section is from the same book.

Regional security policy concerns that arose, and still exist, throughout northern South America as a result of the Colombian attack on the FARC camps in Ecuador were too recent to have made it into print in book form when I wrote this text, but they received extensive media coverage in all the affected countries between 2008 and 2010. The quote from Hugo Chávez concerning the demands placed on UN troops in Colombia was published in the Colombian newspaper *El Tiempo* on 7 December 2009.

I wrote the section on the expansion of coca fields along the San Juan River after a trip through the region in May 2009. The name "El Caraño" is a pseudonym, as are the names of the majority of the interviewees (see the note about the use of italics at the beginning of this section). Passages and conclusions about what it's like to work as a domestic servant and its correlations to racism, serfdom, adoption, et cetera, are based on interviews and research conducted on the adoption industry in Colombia for other works of mine, not yet published. Daniel Samper's column on *falsos positivos* was published in *El Tiempo*, 17 January 2010. The story of the young boys from Soacha and the quote from the shopkeeper were published by a team of special investigative reporters under the title "Así Se Tejió la Trampa de los Falsos Positivos" in *El Tiempo*, 24 May 2009. Philip Alston's statements have been documented in a number of publications, including the UN "Declaración del Profesor Philip Alston, Relator Especial de las Naciones Unidas para las Ejecuciones Aarbitraries," 18 June 2009. See also the article "UN Expert Voices Concern Over Murders Committed by Colombian Security Forces" (*UN News Service*, 18 June 2009). A number of documentaries on this topic, such as *Falsos Positivos* by Italian journalists Simone Bruno and Dado Carillo, have also been produced.

Sections of the reportage dealing with the environmental consequences of coca production are partly based on the government campaign Shared Responsibility and criticism of it, such as Germán Andrés Quimbayo Ruiz's essay "¿Quién está Destruyendo el Ambiente? Coca, fumigación, ganadería y palma africana en Colombia» (*Razón Publica*, 4 May 2009). I also used Tom Feiling's book *The Candy Machine* for this section, as it includes interesting information on the ecological impact of cocaine.

3 — Pablo's Party: The State Gets Cancer

This part of the text, more an essay than reportage, is a chronicle based on several trips, but above all on a number of oral and written accounts. Pablo Escobar's fate is a fascinating story, but it has already been written about extensively, and thus was a topic I was initially hesitant about devoting an entire chapter to. Ultimately, however, I decided to include it, as it provides a very useful prism through which to understand the emergence of the new Colombia. Integral parts of the story, such as Escobar's life at Nápoles, his time in La Catedral, the DEA's under-the-table games, the attacks on Avianca and *El Espectador*, the assassination of Galán, the final days of Escobar's life, and so on, have already been documented in several books, such as Alonso Salazar's *La Parábola de Pablo* and Mark Bowden's *Killing Pablo*, as well as in hundreds of articles published after the murder. In the passages about Escobar's life and death I have basically just followed the accepted version of the story, as it has been told many times before. However, one book in particular—James Mollison and Rainbow Nelson's impressive *The Memory of Pablo Escobar*—has been more essential than other sources for this chapter.

In order to enhance the historical account and my analyses, and to set the scenes, I also drew from Virginia Vallejo's *Loving Pablo, Hating Escobar*, Orlando Fals Borda's (et al.) *La Violencia en Colombia*, Mauricio Aranguen Molina's *Mi Confesión: Carlos Castaño revela sus secretos*, Gerardo Reyes' *Nuestro Hombre en la DEA*, Germán Castro Caycedo's *En Secreto*, Ana Carrigan's *The Palace of Justice: a Colombian tragedy* (published in English in 1993 and translated into Spanish with a new preface in 2009), Natalia Morales and Santiago La Rotta's *Los Pepes: desde Pablo Escobar hasta Don Berna, Macaco y Don Mario*, Alfredo Rangel's (et al.) *Qué, Cómo y Cuándo Negociar con las Farc*, Arturo Alape's *El Bogotazo: memorias del olvido* and *Tirofijo*, Luis Cañón's *El Patrón: vida y muerte de Pablo Escobar*, and Nicolas Entel's documentary *Sins of My Father*.

In 2009 and 2010 I spent time in Barrio Pablo Escobar, Hacienda Nápoles (today a museum and zoo, with remnants of Escobar's empire), Escobar's grave in southern Medellín, the location of La Catedral, the Monaco building, the house where Pablo was killed in 1993, and a number of other buildings in Medellín that were damaged in explosions following the terror attacks during the cocaine war.

The following people, with whom I conducted interviews, have been integral to this work: Alonso Salazár, mayor of Medellín and Escobar's biographer; Antanas Mockus, former mayor of Bogotá and presidential candidate in the 2010 election; Carlos Lozano, editor-in-chief of *Voz*; Carlos Vidales, historian and former member of the M-19; Enrique Peñalosa, former mayor of Bogotá; Fabio Castillo, investigative reporter at *El Espectador* in the 1980s; Gloria Cuartas, former mayor of Apartadó; Jorge Parra, Barrio Escobar resident; Juan Manuel Galán, son of Luis Carlos Galán (murdered under Escobar's order in 1989); Pablo Escobar's son Juan Pablo Escobar (today Sebastián Marroquín); Maria-Etelvina Restrepo, visitor of Pablo Escobar's grave; Rodrigo Lara Restrepo, son of justice minister Rodrigo Lara Bonilla (murdered under Escobar's order in 1984); Ruben Darío Yepes, priest at the church built at La Catedral; Sandra Hincupié, visitor of Pablo Escobar's grave.

I reconstructed the scenes from Hacienda Nápoles with reference to books by Vallejo and Salazar, relics and archival material collected at present-day Nápoles, and Entel's documentary. I based my sketches of various guerrilla movements on Steven Dudley's *Walking Ghosts* (FARC), Leon Valencia's *Mis Años de Guerra* (ELN), Ana Carrigan's *El Palacio de Justicia: una tragedia colombiana* (M-19), and Alvaro Villarraga and Nelson Plaza's *Para Reconstruir los Sueños: una historia del EPL* (EPL). The latest report on the dramatic events at the Palace of Justice in November 1985—*Informe Final de la Comisión de la Verdad sobre los Hechos del Palacio de Justicia*—is available for download at www.ictj.org.

Among the works on which I based my account of the atmosphere and course of events in Bogotá in 1948 are Miguel Torres' *El Crimen del Siglo*, Arturo Alape's *El Bogotazo*, and Mark Bowden's *Killing Pablo*, while I wrote the passages on the culture and aesthetics of murder with the help of Orlando Fals Borda's (et al.) classic *La Violencia en Colombia*. The scenes, and the depiction of the various characters in the criminal brotherhood that Virginia Vallejo was introduced to at Nápoles in the early 1980s, are based on Salazar's *La Parábola de Pablo*. I based my description of Fidel Castaño's transformation to a Colombian Rambo on information in Dudley's *Walking Ghosts* and in Carlos Castaño's autobiography. Virginia Vallejo's description of the general perception of cocaine in the early 1980s as relatively harmless comes from an interview with Vallejo on the talk show *Maria Elvira Live* on 6 May 2009, broadcast by the Miami-based television station Mega TV. The quote from Guillermo Cano is from Fabio Castillo's *Riders of Cocaine*.

For the section on Isaac Guttnan and *el sicariato* I have used information from Fabio Castillo's book *Riders of Cocaine* and Diana Grajales' essay "Genealogia de las Bandas." Victor Gaviria's documentary *Rodrigo D: no futuro* offers, for those primarily interested in the "no futuro culture," a good but disturbing depiction of the phenomenon, as does his sequel *La Vendedora de Rosas* and Alonso Salazar's legendary book *No Nacimos Pa'semilla: la cultura de las bandas juveniles en Medellín*. The scene about the Galán family the day Luis Carlos Galán was assassinated was described to me by Juan Manuel Galán. I based other sections in the same passage on Maria Jimena Duzán's *Crónicas que Matan*. The section on Nadaismo is based on information from Salazar's biography on Escobar and Bowden's *Killing Pablo*.

Descriptions of the arrival of Delta Force, the actions of Los Pepes, Escobar's final birthday, connections between the Reconnaissance Commando and US elite forces, president Gaviria's juggling in order to allow foreign troops into the country, the murders of Moncada and Galeano, Pablo's contacts with his family, Joe Toft's doubts, the details of the final days of the hunt for Escobar, et cetera, all come from Cañón's *El Patrón*, Bowden's *Killing Pablo*, Salazar's *La Parábola de Pablo*, and Morales and La Rotta's *Los Pepes* (information pertaining to Gilberto Rodríguez Orejuela's agreement for payment following Escobar's death is from Bowden, as well as several details from the scene prior to the shooting). Carlos Castaño's statement, that it is essential those killings the state cannot take care of be carried out by someone else, comes from his autobiography.

The arrest of General Maza Márquez in August 2009 was a shock to the entire country and was reported by all Colombian news media.

I took the quote from former president César Gaviria, in which he states that the money for the war on drugs should be invested in other methods, from the report *Drugs and Democracy: toward a paradigm shift*. Details of the final scene with Virginia Vallejo are from her book *Loving Pablo, Hating Escobar*.

A major problem that comes from writing about Pablo Escobar in the wake of events, taking information from second- and third-hand sources, is that after so many years the myth has taken on a life of its own. Many of the people who were in the inner circles had good reasons to lie, keep quiet, exaggerate, understate, or cut down enemies in the carousel of moral corruption and defilement that continued after his death. In December 2009, when I interviewed Pablo Escobar's son Juan Pablo (today Sebastián Marroquín), he stated—without denying that his father was one of worst mass-murderers in history—that "no one who has ever written about him [Pablo Escobar] has even come close to depicting the person he really was." I drew many facts for the second half of the chapter from James Mollison and Rainbow Nelson's well-researched and visually stimulating work *The Memory of Escobar*, because it was published in 2007 and thus has a healthy distance from the events; moreover, because a great deal rests on the statements of individuals who were once involved, and they are now older and many no longer have anything to gain or lose from the truth. The quotes on p. 119 (on legalization) and p. 134 (Gustavo Gaviria) are from the same book.

4 — The War on Drugs: From Nixon to Obama

The two operations that I attended in this chapter were carried out by the Colombian anti-narcotics police and the Coast Guard in March 2009 and April 2009. That same year I also spent time in the city of Buenaventura, as well as the urban and suburban districts of La Playita, Alfonso López, Lleras, Punta Del Este, and Firme. I interviewed the following people: Aida Orobio, nun, Buenaventura Diocese; Borman García Aguilar, sergeant, anti-narcotics police; David Cifuentes, soldier, anti-narcotics police; Edwaer Picón, captain, Coast Guard; Gabriel Rojas Vallona, prosecutor; Gustavo Guevara, prosecutor; Hector Correa, colonel, anti-narcotics police; Jay Bergman, regional DEA head; John Sanchez, soldier, anti-narcotics police; Juan Carlos Rivero, sergeant, anti-narcotics police; Juan Quiroga, major, anti-narcotics police; and Óscar Naranjo, national police chief.

Most of the information about and descriptions of logistics and the running of an HCl laboratory was given to me by Jay Bergman, who I interviewed in June and December 2009, and Leo, an itinerant proletarian working in the drug trade whose fate I have followed since 2007. I took Richard Nixon's statement pertaining to the Shafer Commission, as well as calculations on how US yearly investments in the war on drugs grew from 16 million to 18 billion USD, from Tom Feiling's *The Candy Machine*. Dick Cheney's efforts in establishing the term "narcoterrorism" in US geopolitical policy, and Bill Wagner's work in Latin America during the Cold War, are covered in several books, including Jonathan Marshall and Peter Dale Scott's *Cocaine Politics: drugs, armies, and the CIA in Central America* and Mark Bowden's *Killing Pablo*. A more detailed account of how the European Union turned out to be peripheral, in comparison with the United States, during the initial phase of Plan Colombia may be found in Marco Palacio's *Plan Colombia: ¿anti-drogas o contrainsurgencia?*, from which I also took the two quotations by Andrés Pastrana.

Adriana Rossi's thesis on the impact of the contra war on production, and information on CIA involvement in cocaine smuggling during the first decade of the new millennium, were published in a special feature issue in the South American edition of *Le Monde Diplomatique* called "Crisis, Crimen Organizado y Gobernabilidad" (April 2009). In February 2007 the same newspaper published a similar dossier under the title "Narcotráfico versus Democracia," but with more focus on drugs and the war on drugs as a threat to democracy. Jay Bergman's rejection of the idea that the Colombian police force lacks a real interest in stopping drug production comes from my interview with him in June 2009. Cuchillo's power over the Colombian military in the eastern part of the country was a recurring scandal in 2008, and has been featured in publications such as *El Tiempo* (6 November 2008). The information on how the mafia in Putumayo offered payment to the military comes from Garry Leech's *Beyond Bogotá: diary of a drug war journalist in Colombia*.

I based my analyses of the people, government, racism, and development in Buenaventura on a number of interviews I conducted in the city during 2009 (see details above). An interesting documentary on the same subject is *Los Pacificadores del Pacífico*. Ever Veloza's testimony on the arrival of the AUC in Buenaventura and its funding from "state representatives" comes from "El Ventilador the HH" (*El Espectador*, 6 September 2008). The website www.verdadabierta.com features a large number of documented confessions of paramilitary leaders. A more theoretical analysis of the FARC and the paramilitaries' war over Buenaventura, and the role that conflict played in the people's loss of trust in the state, may be found in Renata Moreno and Alvaro Guzman's chapter "Autodefensas, Narcotráfico y Comportamiento Estatal en el Valle del Cauca, 1997–2005" in *Parapolítica*.

The progression pointing to increased production in Bolivia and increased trafficking through Venezuela is described in the 2009 UNODC *World Drug Report*, as well as statistics on the number of blown-up labs and sprayed hectares in the last decade. Evo Morales' quote is from Noam Chomsky's essay "Militarizing Latin America," published on his website www.chomsky.info on 30 August 2009. An interesting analysis by Greg Grandin, author of *Empire's Workshop: Latin America, the United States, and the rise of the new imperialism*, of how seven military bases contributed to increased tension in the region, was published in *The Nation* on 21 January 2010.

5 — Mañana: The Future of the Powder
The main interviews in this chapter were conducted between 2008 and 2010, a period in which I was following in detail the left and

liberals' fight against right-wing efforts to dismantle the 1991 constitution, including the symbolic paragraph on "the personal dose" (Case C-221, *de la Corte Constitucional*, 1994). Carlos Gaviria, leader of the social democratic party Polo Democrático and leftist presidential candidate in the 2006 election, was chief judge in the constitutional court in the 1990s and the intellectual architect of what became the national legislation on personal use. Audio of his defense of "the personal dose," right before the government's victory, is available under the heading "Ponencia the Carlos Gaviria I and II parte" at *Dosis de Personalidad* (www.dosisdepersonalidad.com).

I interviewed the following people: Aldo Lale-Demoz, director, UNODC Colombia; Alfredo Rangel, head of the think tank Seguridad y Democracia; Ariel Ávila, researcher, Nuevo Arco Iris; Carlos Gaviria, founder of the party Polo Democrático and former presidential candidate; Gustavo Duncan, political scientist; Ivonne Wilches, psychologist and activist for the personal dose; Jay Bergman, regional DEA head; Juan Manuel Galán, senator; Melissa Alvarez, activist for the personal dose; María Jimena Duzán, author; Piedad Córdoba, senator.

Other information, analysis, and speculations in this chapter are based primarily on María Jimena Duzán's *Crónicas que Matan*, Mike Jay's *Emperors of Dreams: drugs in the nineteenth century*, Alfredo Rangel's (et al.) books *La Batalla Perdida Contra Las Drogas* and *Narcotráfico en Colombia*, Tom Feiling's *The Candy Machine*, Misha Glenny's *McMafia*, and Gustavo Duncan's *Los Senores de la Guerra*. Some dates on how the power behind drug trafficking became concentrated to Mexico, and the number of people employed by the Mexican cartels, was taken from a study featured in *The Wall Street Journal* (28 December 2008), and statistics on the increase in cocaine prices over the years are from the UN *World Drug Report 2009*. The report of the three former presidents, *Drugs and Democracy*, can be downloaded from the website for the American Commission on Drugs and Democracies (www.drogasedemocracia.org). A complete text of the RAND report *Controlling Cocaine* may be downloaded from their website (www.rand.org). Noam Chomsky's commentary on the RAND report and his analysis of the drug war were presented at the seminar "The US War on Drugs in Latin America" at MIT on 15 December 2009. A compilation of Chomsky's ideas on cocaine production and its global contra war are available on a CD called *An American Addiction: drugs, guerrillas, counterinsurgency*. The section on "decertification" and US economic sanctions on nations that deviate from the global prohibition policy is based on information from Feiling's *The Candy Machine*. Swedish journalist Tomas Lappalainen's *'Ndrangheta: en bok om maffian i Kalabrien* deals with connections between the Italian and Colombian mafias and the role played by the former in the currently booming European market. The arrest of 320 mafiosi in different parts of the world, including the top level of the 'Ndrangheta, on 13 July 2010, was extensively covered in the international media. The consequences of this crackdown on cocaine distribution in Europe, however, are still uncertain.

The story of *Jairo Villegas* was published in the article "Así Operan Las Alas De La Mafia" (*El Tiempo*, 14 February 2010), and the quotes I have used from national police chief Óscar Naranjo were published by several news-media outlets during the dissolution of the so-called Pilot Cartel in early 2010. The data on the reduction of Colombian cocaine production comes from the UNODC *World Drug Report 2009*. The quote from Carl Bildt was published on his blog http:// bildt.blogspot.se/ on 28 May 2006.

César Gaviria's statement on the hopelessness of the war on drugs if the issue of demand continues to be ignored is from Marshall and Scott's *Cocaine Politics*. A detailed account of Colombia's tragic history with regard to how the decentralization of politics in the 1990s also paved the way for the paramilitary takeover of large parts of the countryside may be found in Mauricio Romero's *Paramilitares y Autodefensas*. The elimination of the left-wing party Unión Patriótica, touched upon in my interview with María Jimena Duzán, has been analyzed in a number of books, but nowhere with the same chilling accuracy as in Steven Dudley's *Walking Ghosts*—the best book written about the state's sordid war against dissidents and the FARC's cynical games with people's lives. Information on the 40,000 people (38,000, to be exact) killed by paramilitary groups comes from the regional public prosecutor's office and covers only the period between 1987 and 2003. This figure is constantly changing both because paramilitary leaders are always making new confessions and because new mass graves are being discovered regularly. According to some sources, the number has already surpassed 50,000 and may even be significantly more.

Mario Vargas Llosa's essay "El Otro Estado" was published in several newspapers, including the Spanish *El Pais* (10 January 2010). The commission assigned to draw up a new anti-drug policy for the United States is called the Western Hemisphere Drug Policy Commission. The mandate for its work has been published under the heading of "Text of H. R. 2134: Western Hemisphere Drug Policy Commission Act of 2009" and is available on the United States Congress website: www.govtrack.us. References to the "global framework" and "UN conventions" in the text refer to *The Single Convention on Narcotic Drugs* (1961), *The Convention on Psychotropic Substances* (1971), and *The United Nations Convention against Illicit Traffic in Narcotic Drugs and Psychotropic Substances* (1988), all ratified by the vast majority of the world's nations. The common aim of the conventions is to promote and enforce the notion that there should be no use of the listed drugs—including cannabis, cocaine, and coca leaves—other than for strictly medical or scientific purposes.

AUTHOR'S NOTE

THIS BOOK COVERS two crucial decades at the ground level of the drug trade, starting with my first trip to Colombia in 1989. After the first edition went into print in 2010, three key events of structural importance have occurred.

First, the man who was right-wing Álvaro Uribe's close ally and defense minister during the time of my research, Juan Manuel Santos, unexpectedly turned his back on Uribe's hard-line military approach to solving problems after he was elected president in 2010, with a number of consequences.

In November 2012, peace talks were initiated between the Santos government and the FARC, and in May 2013 the two parties agreed on a detailed land reform. This was truly historical, and may—if it is ever implemented—finally bring about a long-term change in the uniquely violent patterns of politics and poverty in rural Colombia that have for decades been so essential to cocaine production. Yet as I write this, in July 2013, everything is still up in the air, since "nothing is agreed until everything is agreed," and no one yet knows whether the future has in store a final and lasting peace accord, leading to the demobilization of Latin America's oldest and strongest guerrilla.

A more certain consequence of the negotiations so far is that the country's radical right, still strong thanks to enduring support for Uribe, is now mobilizing all forces in order to obstruct the peace process and its threat to the landowning elite's territorial interests. Meanwhile, the FARC—long since dependent on drugs—is putting odd topics on the negotiating table, and the guerillas' real interest in a lasting peace is very questionable. If a demobilization ever becomes a reality, a likely outcome is that the guerrilla will divide: one part transforming itself into a left-wing political party, and the rest offering its military skills to illegal businesses new and old—mainly drugs, but also gold and other minerals, the new booming sector for illegal enterprises—as happened, in much the same way, with the demobilization of the paramilitaries in the 2000s.

The second occurrence of structural importance is the death of Hugo Chávez. During the 2000s, Venezuela's socialist leader played a key role in the erratic geopolitical brew caused by the US war on drugs and its enormous military aid to Colombia, but after Santos turned his back on Uribe, relations between the two countries stabilized. Chávez, adored by the FARC and respected by Santos, even became a crucial figure in paving the way for the peace process. The paranoid political triangle built by cocaine, described in chapters four and five, was thus considerably eased during the first years of the 2010s but it is now partially back; successor Nicolas Maduro hadn't even been president for a month before accusing Santos of "backstabbing" his country, declaring he had "information" proving that Colombia, supported by the US through its anti-drug money, was plotting to overthrow him.

And thirdly, there is the balloon effect. According to the UN World Drug Report 2013, nothing has changed significantly in regard to the global production and consumption of cocaine; the world keeps snorting around 900 metric tons a year, all of which is produced in Colombia, Peru, or Bolivia. But *within* the producing regions, the trends outlined in the book have sharpened. Both Colombia and Peru have recently experienced a small increase in coca-bush cultivation; yet a wider perspective shows that the 100,000 hectares sprayed with chemicals every year in Colombia has continued to pay off: Colombia's share of the amount of cocaine manufactured globally has dropped drastically over a five-year period (some production having been pushed to Peru) and is now down to 345 tons a year, representing 40 per cent of the global total.

But for the regions described in this book—Putumayo and Chocó—the statistics show an opposite pattern: in Putumayo, the number of planted hectares of coca doubled from 2010 to 2011 (the latest year of statistics); and in Chocó, the cultivated area has increased by 40 per cent since I visited the region in 2009—despite the fact that 4,287 hectares (two times the planted area) were sprayed in Chocó in 2011. This has caused an exodus of people from all the areas that figure in chapter two, but I haven't been able to find out whether Andrea, César, Graciano, Edgar, Nelcy, and the others are now on the run or still at work, since it requires a trip to their homes.

On a more detailed level, many other things have occurred since 2010. In 2011 the national intelligence agency, Departamento Administrativo de Seguridad, was dismantled after repeated scandals revealed agents illegally wiretapping critics of the government and selling classified information to drug lords. Buenaventura saw a few years of decreasing violence, but in the end of 2012 a fourth wave of massacres shocked the inhabitants; during just two months, October and November 2012, 1,287 families had to leave their homes, and 57 people were murdered, in the tiny city while drug-trafficking organizations fought over the ports' most attractive routes. Philip Alston's final report on the *falsos positivos* was published after my manuscript was handed in, and it stated that the well-known impunity rate for extra-judicial executions in Colombia—98.5 per cent—was integral to the dynamics of the scandal, since the soldiers and officers knew that the chance of getting away with their actions was practically 100 per cent.

More positive signs have been that in August 2011 the Supreme Court sent Alberto Santofimio back to jail to serve his 24-year sentence, and that Jay Bergman was proven right in his predictions about "dead men walking." During a police raid on Christmas Day 2010, Cuchillo once again managed to escape, but got severely wounded in the gunfire and was later found drowned in a creek. In May 2012, Comba handed himself to US authorities after his lawyers negotiated the terms with the DEA, and in September 2012 the "last of the top ten Colombian kingpins," Daniel "El Loco" Barrera, was captured in an operation including both the MI6 and the CIA, which was coordinated from Washington. Yet as I discuss in the book, these types of captures are of high symbolic value but of little strategic importance to the flexible and decentralized drug-trafficking industry. Most scholars agree that, besides heavy aerial spraying, the decrease in overall Colombian production is likely due to a transformation of the country's criminal structures; parts of the ambulating day labor and criminal organizations crucial for efficient drug production have abandoned coca for better yields in illegal gold exploitation. A more lasting strategic success for the government came when another important FARC leader, Alfonso Cano, was killed by the military in November 2011, weakening the guerrilla even further.

Three years after *Cocaína* was originally published, Colombians are again breathing the rare air of a peace within reach and of possible change. A daring president and a functioning judiciary has avoided— at least temporarily—a future in which the entire state apparatus would be taken over by a radical right funded by drug money, a threat that was in the cards in the 2000s. But there is also an enormous dilemma behind the new scenes of hope. The economic integration of the poor and isolated peasantry, who are central to cocaine production, is the principal task for any peace negotiator in Colombia. The guerillas' vision is integration through a nationally protected, small-scale order that would *save* farmers from the revolutionary forces of global capitalism, while the government's vision is the exact opposite: rural integration through a large-scale agro-industrial order that would *connect* remote areas to the rest of the world by attracting global capital. It remains to be seen if a compromise between these two opposing worldviews is possible within coming years; and if this peace initiative fails, as all have before, the war between drug-driven projects—political and apolitical—will, unfortunately, continue to dictate rural life in the northern slopes of the Andes for the coming decades.

Magnus Linton
Stockholm, 2013

REFERENCES

Books

Alape, Arturo, *El Bogotazo: memorias del olvido*, Pluma, 1984.

Alape, Arturo, *Tirofijo: las vidas de Pedro Antonio Marín*, Planeta, 2004.

Aranguren Molina, Mauricio, *Mi Confesión: Carlos Castaño revela sus secretos*, Oveja Negra, 2001.

Baena Velásquez, Mauricio, *Captadores de Ilusiones: damnificados de las pirámides*, Debate, 2009.

Bedoya, Jineth, *La Pirámide de David Murcia*, Planeta, 2009.

Bowden, Mark, *Killing Pablo*, Penguin, 2002.

Braun, Herbert, *Our Guerrillas, Our Sidewalks: a journey into the violence of Colombia*, Rowman & Littlefield, 1994.

Camacho Guizado, Àlvaro (ed.), *Narcotráfico: Europa, Estados Unidos, América Latina*, Ceso, 2006.

Cañón, Luis, *El Patron: vida y muerte de Pablo Escobar*, Planeta, 2002.

Carrigan, Ana, *El Palacio de Justicia: una tragedia colombiana*, Icono, 2009 (published in English as *The Palace of Justice: a Colombian tragedy*, Thunder's Mouth, 1993).

Cepeda, Iván and Rojas, Jorge, *A Las Puertas de El Ubérrimo*, Debate, 2008.

Chant, Sylvia and Craske, Nikki, *Gender in Latin America*, Rutgers University Press, 2003.

Contreras, Joseph, *Biografía No Autorizada de Álvaro Uribe Vélez*, Oveja Negra, 2002.

Courtwright, David, *Forces of Habit: drugs and the making of the modern world*, Harvard University Press, 2002.

Davenport-Hines, Richard, *The Pursuit of Oblivion: a global history of narcotics, 1500–2000*, Weinfeld and Nicolson, 2001.

Davis, Mike and Monk, Daniel Bertrand, *Evil Paradises: dreamworlds of neoliberalism*, New Press, 2007.

Dudley, Steven, *Walking Ghosts: murder and guerrilla politics in Colombia*, Routledge, 2006.

Duncan, Gustavo, *Los Señores de la Guerra: de paramilitares, mafiosos y autodefensas en Colombia*, Planeta 2006.

Duzán, María Jimena, *Crónicas que Matan*, Tercer Mundo Editores, 1992 (published in English as *Death Beat: a Colombian journalist's life inside the cocaine wars*, HarperCollins, 1994).

Ellner, Steve and Hellinger, Daniel, *Venezuelan Politics in the Chávez Era*, Lynne Rienner, 2003.

Enkvist, Inger, *Latin American Icons: nine populist myths of the twentieth century*, Atlantis, 2010.

Fals Borda, Orlando; Guzman Campos, German; and Umaña-Luna, Eduardo, *La Violencia en Colombia*, vol. I and II, Taurus, 2005 (1962).

Feiling, Tom, *The Candy Machine: how cocaine took over the world*, Penguin, 2009.

Fonseca, Linsu, *Una Colombia que nos Queda*, Mujer y Futuro, 2007.

Gonsalves, Marc; Stansell, Keith; and Howles, Tom, *Out of Captivity: surviving 1967 days in the Colombian jungle*, William Morrow, 2009.

Grajales, Diana, *Genealogia de las Bandas*, Universidad de Antióquia, 2008.

Green, Duncan, *Silent Revolution: the rise and crisis of market economics in Latin America*, Monthly Review Press, 2003.

Hernández-Mora Zapata, Salud, *La Otra Colombia: años 1999–2007*,

Debate, 2008.

Hylton, Forrest, *Evil Hour in Colombia*, Verso, 2006.

Jansson, Oscar, *The Cursed Leaf: an anthropology of the political economy of cocaine production in southern Colombia*, Uppsala University, 2008.

Jay, Mike, *Emperors of Dreams: drugs in the nineteenth century*, Dedalus, 2000.

Kozloff, Nikolas, *Revolution!: South America and the rise of the New Left*, Palgrave Macmillan, 2008.

Lappalainen, Tomas, *Camorra: en bok om maffian i Neapel*, Fischer & Co., 2007.

Lappalainen, Tomas, *'Ndrangheta: en bok om maffian i Kalabrien*, Fischer & Co., 2010.

Leech, Garry, *Beyond Bogotá: diary of a drug war journalist in Colombia*, Beacon, 2009.

Livingstone, Grace, *Inside Colombia: drugs, democracy, and war*, LAB, 2003.

Lutteman, Markus, *El Choco: svensken i Bolivias mest ökända fängelse*, Norstedts, 2007.

Marshall, Jonathan and Dale Scott, Peter, *Cocaine Politics: drugs, armies, and the CIA in Central America*, University of California Press, 1998.

McCaughan, Michael, *The Battle of Venezuela*, LAB, 2004.

McPherson, Alan, *Anti-Americanism in Latin America and the Caribbean*, Berghan, 2006.

Molano, Alfredo, *The Dispossessed: chronicles of the desterrados of Colombia*, Haymarket, 2005.

Molano, Alfredo, *Trochas y Fusiles*, Ancora, 1994.

Mollison, James and Nelson, Rainbow, *The Memory of Pablo Escobar*, Chris Boot, 2007.

Murillo, Mario, *Colombia and the United States: war, unrest, and destabilization*, Seven Stories, 2004.

Neurwirth, Robert, *Shadow Cities: a billion squatters, a new urban world*, Routledge, 2006.

Otero, Alfonso, *Paramilitares: la modernidad que nos tocó*, Quedecor, 2008.

Palacios, Marco, *Plan Colombia: ¿anti-drogas o contrainsurgencia?*, Universidad de Los Andes, 2007.

Pardo Rueda, Rafael, *Fin del Paramilitarismo: ¿es posible su desmonte?*, Ediciones B, 2007.

Perez, Luis Eladio, *Siete Años Secuestrado por las Farc*, Aguiliar, 2008.

Pinchao, John, *Mi Fuga Hacia la Libertad*, Planeta, 2008.

Prashad, Vijary and Ballvé, Teo, *Dispatches from Latin America: on the frontlines against neoliberalism*, South End Press, 2005.

Puentes Marín, Angela María, *El Opio de los Talibán y la Coca de las Farc*, Ediciones Uniandes, 2006.

Rangel, Alfredo, *Qué, Cómo y Cuándo Negociar con las Farc*, Intermedio, 2008.

Rangel, Alfredo (ed.), *El Poder Paramilitar*, Planeta, 2005.

Rangel, Alfredo, et al., *Narcotráfico en Colombia*, Seguridad y Democracia, 2005.

Rangel, Alfredo, et al., *La Batalla Perdida Contra Las Drogas: ¿legalizar es la opción?*, Intermedio, 2008.

Reyes, Gerardo, *Nuestro Hombre en la DEA*, Planeta, 2007.

Roa Avendaño, Tatiana and Rosero, Carlos, *Llenando Tanques, Vaciendo Territorio*, PCN/Censat Agua Viva, 2008.

Romero, Mauricio, *Paramilitares y Autodefensas*, Planeta, 2003.

Rueda, Zenaida, *Confesiones de una Guerrillera*, Planeta, 2009.

Salazar, Alonso, *La Parábola de Pablo*, Planeta, 2001.

Sánchez Baute, Alonso, *Líbranos del Bien*, Alfaguara, 2008.

Schlosser, Eric, *Reefer Madness: sex, drugs, and cheap labor in the American black market*, Allen Lane, 2003.

Serrano Zabala, Alfredo, *¿Las Prepago?: revelaciones al periodista*, Orveja Negra, 2007.

Sivak, Martin, *Retrato Intimo de Evo Morales*, Debate, 2008.

Stefanoni, Pablo and Do Alto, Hervé, *La Revolución de Evo Morales: de coca al palacio*, Capital Intelectual, 2006.

Tham, Henrik, *Drug Control as a National Project: the case of Sweden*, Stockholm University, 1995.

Tops, Dolf, *A Society With or Without Drugs: continuity and change in drug policies in Sweden and the Netherlands*, Lund University, 2001.

Torres, Miguel, *El Crimen del Siglo*, Seix Barral, 2006.

Valencia, León, *Mis Años de Guerra*, Norma, 2008.

Valencia, León (ed.), *Parapolítica: la ruta de la expansión paramilitar y los acuerdos políticos*, Intermedio, 2007.

Villarraga, Alvaro and Plazas, Nelson, *Para Reconstruir los Sueños: una historia del EPL*, Progresar/Fundación Cultura Democrática, 1994.

Wearne, Phillip, *Return of the Indian: conquest and revival in the Americas*, Cassell, 1996.

Wierup, Lasse and de la Reguera, Erik, *Kokain: drogen som fick medelklassen att börja knarka och länder att falla samman*, Norstedts, 2010.

Reports

A Failed Strategy: the spraying of illicit crops in Colombia, Washington Office on Latin America, 2008.

Afectos y Efectos de la Guerra en la Mujer Desplazada, Organización Feminina Popular, 2004.

Análisis de las Elecciones Legislativas de 2010, La Misión de Observación Electoral, 2010.

Arms-R-Us: South America goes shopping, Washington Office on Latin America, 2010.

Cocaine: a European Union perspective in the global context, European Monitoring Center for Drugs and Drug Addiction, 2010.

Colombia—Monitoreo de Cultivos de Coca 2009, United Nations Office on Drugs and Crime, 2009.

Conflicto Armado y Cultivos Ilícitos: efectos sobre el desarrollo humano en el Catatumbo, Universidad de los Andes, 2009.

Controlling Cocaine, RAND Corporation, 1994.

Drugs and Democracy: toward a paradigm shift, American Commission on Drugs and Democracy, 2009.

¿En qué está la Guerra?, Nuevo Arco Iris, 2008.

Global Drug Policy: building a new framework, Senlis Council, 2003.

Hablan las Personas Desplazadas en Colombia, Internal Displacement Monitoring Center, 2007.

Huyendo de la Guerra, Codhes, 2007.

Informe Final de la Comisión de la Verdad Sobre los Hechos del Palacio de Justicia, Centro Internacional para la Justicia Transicional, 2009.

Los Límites de la Guerra, Codhes, 2008.

National Drug Control Strategy 2010, Office of National Drug Control Policy, 2010.

Órdenes Sociales en el Putumayo Antes y Después del Plan Colombia, Universidad de los Andes, 2009.

The Paramilitaries in Medellín: demobilization or legalization?, Amnesty International, 2005.

Tensión en las Fronteras, Codhes, 2009.

UN World Drug Report 2008, United Nations Office on Drugs and Crime, 2008.

UN World Drug Report 2009, United Nations Office on Drugs and Crime, 2009.

Other Sources

An American Addiction—Drugs, Guerillas, Counterinsurgency: US intervention in Colombia, collected seminars with Noam Chomsky, on CD, AK Press, 2000.

C-221 de la Corte Consitucional de Colombia 1994, judgment by the Colombian Constitution Court, 1994.

H.R. 2134: Western Hemisphere Drug Policy Commission Act of 2009, United States Congress.

Los Pacificadores del Pacífico, documentary film, Observatorio Pacífico, 2007.

Entel, Nicolas (dir.), *Sins of My Father*, documentary film, 2009.

Ungerman, Gerard and Brophy, Audrey (dir.), *Plan Colombia: cashing in on the drug war failure*, documentary film, 2005.

ACKNOWLEDGMENTS

I WOULD LIKE to extend special thanks to all the interviewees who generously gave of their time—some at great risk—and also to the following individuals, without whose assistance, encouragement, and criticism this book would not have been possible: Alfonso Jaramillo, Anna Hellgren, Anna-Karin Johansson, Anna-Maria Sörberg, Barbro Vidmer, Boris Heger, Caroline Atkins, Conor Carrigan, Daniel Campo, Diana Gamboa, Edda Manga, Guillermo Gonzalez, Hanna Hård, Iván Álvarez, Jacob Røthing, Luís Fernando Bohórquez, Manuel Nieto, Mattias Gardell, Per Cerne, Per Lindblom, Richard Herold, Romeo Langlois, Ron Schifflers, Stefan Sunnerdahl, Steven Ambrus, Tiziana Laudato, and Yamile Salinas Abdala. For this English edition, I would very much like to extend my thanks to Henry Rosenbloom at Scribe; my translator, John Eason; and Rita G. Karlsson, my agent at Kontext Agency. I would especially like to thank Julia Carlomagno, my editor at Scribe. A special thanks is also in order to my beloved Elina Grandin for her constant and insightful criticism. And finally, thanks to Sid, our son, who came into the world in the midst of final production and whose life gives us so many moments of joy.

MAGNUS LINTON is a Swedish writer whose work tackles controversial social, political, and ethical topics. He is the author of several acclaimed non-fiction books, including *The Vegans* (2000), a provocative account of the ethics of eating meat that turned then Swedish prime minister Göran Persson into a 'semi-vegetarian'; *Americanos* (2005), a pioneering masterpiece exploring the rise of neo-socialism in Latin America; and *The Hated* (2012), which examines the emergence of the new radical right in Europe. *Cocaína* was first published in Swedish in 2010 and was nominated for the August Prize, Sweden's most important literary award. Magnus lives in Stockholm and Bogotá with his family.

JOHN EASON is an American translator and educator based in Stockholm. He holds a PhD in Scandinavian Studies from the University of Wisconsin, where he has taught Scandinavian literature and Swedish. John has also been a guest lecturer at the University of Illinois at Urbana–Champaign.